No Beethoven

No Beethoven

An Autobiography & Chronicle of
Weather Report

by Peter Erskine

edited by Rick Mattingly
book design by Kio Griffith

photography by
Shigeru Uchiyama, Peter Erskine & others

Front cover photograph: Shigeru Uchiyama
Back cover photograph: Norman Seeff, courtesy of CBS Records

© 2013 Peter Erskine
FUZZ/E/BOOKS
Fuzzy Music LLC

Exclusive Worldwide Distribution by Alfred Music
All Rights Reserved.   Printed in USA.

ISBN-10: 0-9892530-1-5
ISBN-13: 978-0-9892530-1-7

"I ain't afraid of no Beethoven."

— Joe Zawinul to Peter Erskine, circa 1979

About the Author

Peter Erskine has played the drums since age four and is known for his versatility and love of working in different musical contexts. He appears on 600 albums and film scores, and has won two Grammy Awards, plus an Honorary Doctorate from the Berklee School of Music.

Thirty albums have been released under his own name or as co-leader. He has played with the Stan Kenton and Maynard Ferguson Big Bands, Weather Report, Steps Ahead, Joni Mitchell, Steely Dan, Diana Krall, Kenny Wheeler, The Brecker Brothers, The Yellowjackets, Pat Metheny and Gary Burton, John Scofield, et al, and has appeared as a soloist with the London, Los Angeles, Chicago, Frankfurt Radio, Scottish Chamber, Royal Opera House, BBC Symphony and Berlin Philharmonic Orchestras. Peter has been named 'Best Jazz Drummer of the Year' ten times by Modern Drummer magazine. Peter graduated from the Interlochen Arts Academy and studied at Indiana University under George Gaber. He is currently Professor of Practice and Director of Drumset Studies at USC. Peter is married with two children and lives in Santa Monica, California.

Table of Contents

Foreword

Why am *I* writing this?! After reading an advance draft of Mr. Erskine's latest memoirs — the book you now hold in your hands — I proffered the following advice to the author: "You should get a heavy hitter to write a foreword." Of course, I was thinking of Wayne Shorter, given that this autobiography has the drummer's years with the influential band Weather Report as one central theme. Then again, having only recently met Mr. Shorter…well, lets just say that those who really know him might describe him as a man of few words — or at least one whose words are so carefully chosen as they may tend toward brevity, even come across as cryptic at times. Good enough. Well then, what about all the other high-level and well-known musicians that Mr. Erskine has supported and collaborated with over his long and storied career? We know that some of these folks are amazing writers! Walter Becker and Donald Fagen (aka Steely Dan), Joni Mitchell, Diana Krall, John Abercrombie, Eliane Elias, Marc Johnson, Bill Frisell, Alan Pasqua, Bob Mintzer, Russell Ferrante, Jimmy Haslip, Vince Mendoza, John Williams…shall I go on? [It's an impressive and long list of the who's who in the music industry…just check out the discography and filmography by way of Peter's website, www.petererskine.com !]

It comes down to this: I like Peter Erskine's drumming…a lot! His myriad recordings have been on my "playlist" for decades (long before iPods ever existed) and, it would seem that Peter Erskine likes my writing (as evidenced by his request for and acceptance of my liner notes for his latest trio recording, *Joy Luck*). Perhaps even more obvious in his response to my suggestion to find a celebrated writer: "I would be honored if *you* would write the foreword!" Hmm, so much for *my* idea!

So, now the circle is forming: I also like Peter Erskine's writing! In fact, I found this book to be a most engaging, informative, and at times brutally honest account of a rich and, in many ways, ground-breaking musical life. One that, if read with a modicum of compassion for the realities of life as a road warrior (touring musician) and acceptance of the "rough-around-the-edges" lifestyle that goes along with it (especially in the jazz world), will entertain and inform those who know the man, the musician, the friend. This book will also "fill in the blanks" for fans who have followed the drummer's career or the many bands with whom he has been an integral part. I would also add, and of this I am most hopeful, that aspiring young musicians (even aspiring *old* musicians) will find enlightenment from the wisdom contained herein.

Peter Erskine's life story is still evolving and his musical contributions continue to define and explore the *other* side of drumming. Sure, he swings hard and continues to function as one of the premier big band drummers to carry the mantle from his early years with Stan Kenton's band through his years with Maynard Ferguson and into the present. (I heard him perform recently here in Boston with Berklee's Jazz Orchestra, as the Armand Zildjian Visiting Artist. What a treat to hear him navigate everything from more contemporary writers to the classic Sammy Nestico charts from Basie's band!) Still, the thing that separates Erskine from many of his drumming contemporaries is his willingness, actually his insistence, on getting the musical point across without unnecessary pyrotechnics — of which, he is clearly capable.

The evolution of this drumming style (sometimes referred to by Erskine as "3-D musical architecture") relies, to a large degree, on close listening, massive amounts of preparation and the surrender of one's ego — well, not completely, but certainly in deference to the music. Speaking with Erskine on the subject, one hears an obvious reverence, accompanied by a reduction of volume in his delivery. He almost brings the conversation to a whisper, as if prefacing with "this is an important thing I'm going to say now, so pay close attention." This describes Erskine's approach to drumset playing, as well. His manner of speaking and his playing are one. Rule #1: You must listen closely in order to truly hear what the music needs.

There is no way to stampede toward the kind of touch that Peter Erskine possesses on his instrument. Rule #2: do your homework! I have been teaching for a number of decades now and have witnessed the reluctance of so many young aspiring musicians to exact the discipline required to progress their craft. I've also seen the glowing results when practicing is seen as a daily routine and approached with joy rather than dread. I also understand that the grind of daily music making (for a living) can take its toll on practice time. In other words, get to it while you can…once your dream comes true and you are in demand as a player…well, practice now or keep dreaming.

How can and why should one ensure that one is "out of the way of the music"? Rule #3: this is NOT about you, it is always about the music, yet you cannot disappear completely. OK, well now I've said it and, while this could take up an entire shelf full of books on self-help, lets get to the point. Surrender is a large part of Erskine's philosophy of playing music…so what is he talking about? There is a way of listening, of really hearing and becoming fully aware of one's surroundings that is implied here. One that requires a diminishing of noise (critical commentary) and static (negative thought patterns) in order to get to the essence of "what comes next" in one's playing. This is especially true for improvisers. This process of listening can also be viewed as one of editing and focusing one's energy toward being very open. Openness to hearing others, openness to experiencing novelty, openness to sharing the space in which music exists, openness to flowing…

As you may surmise, I am sometimes blinded by a spirit of reverence for practitioners of the arts — in particular, musicians. More specifically, those players who have dedicated themselves to a lifelong pursuit of finding truth and beauty wherever and whenever, and who take the time to report back to the rest of humanity; they have long been my heroes. This past summer, I had the honor of working with Peter Erskine in the studio, recording my original compositions. This experience, especially after years of listening to his own trios, provided a culmination of many musical dreams and aspirations.

He played my music and, not only improved on my concept, but approached his own instrument in a way I've never heard before — he seems to constantly reinvent himself. He listens and adapts and plays inclusively. From my perspective, Peter Erskine is a masterful "compercussionist" (my term for a drummer who also plays melody, harmony and thinks like a composer when improvising). It makes perfect sense that he has continued the legacy we first encountered in the legendary pianist Bill Evans' approach to the trio — the art of conversational playing.

So you see, dear reader, one cannot help but be influenced by Peter Erskine's music, philosophy, or his writing; for there exists a deep commitment and long history of forging new paths that, for some, is both intriguing and inspirational. He crosses interdisciplinary boundaries with great aplomb, he expands the physical limits of the instrument with grace and economy of motion, and he consistently transcends the definition of his art form — his *oeuvre* speaks for itself.

I started writing about his book and ended up reflecting on his influence on my own path. Peter Erskine's numerous recordings have one central thing in common: regardless of genre, there is his quiet, yet solid presence and, yes, his enviable touch that makes each musical offering uniquely his own. He listens…like we all should listen. Any sensitive reader will hear it in this telling of his own musical life. This is really Volume 1 of a continuing story…find a quiet place and enjoy.

Mitch Haupers
January 14, 2013

1. Thus Spake Zawinul

"Sad motherfucker…"

Moments before, I had surrendered my headphones to Joe on Japan Airlines flight #61 as it cruised 35,000 feet above the Pacific Ocean. We were flying from LAX to Tokyo's newly opened Narita Airport. It was Saturday, June 17, 1978, and Weather Report was about to tour Japan as a quartet with me as its new drummer. A lunch of beefsteak had been served with soba noodle starter. Seated alone on this pivotal journey and wearing a new set of clothes for the trip, I already managed to stain my shirt with soy sauce.

Too excited to sleep, and it was mid-afternoon to boot, I plugged headphones into my Panasonic cassette boom box and was listening to some pleasant music by a leading keyboard artist of the day — not bebop, more like late '70s pop-smooth-jazz — and daydreaming about my girlfriend when I spotted Joe half a cabin ahead, walking aft.

Somehow, I knew he was headed straight for me, and I knew what was going to happen next. My Coltrane and Miles tapes were in the overhead baggage compartment, and there was no chance to grab one of them by the time he was upon me. He motioned for me to give up my headphones so he could hear what I was listening to. I smiled weakly and offered up my Koss headset, which he donned in brisk fashion. Zawinul stood in the aisle with a fist on each hip, similar to a football referee's indication of "offside," while looking forward and backwards and up and down the aisle with an expression I hadn't yet come to know or understand, but I could tell that he wasn't digging the music I was listening too very much.

He finally looked directly at me and yelled the way that people wearing headphones always shout, demanding I confirm the identity of the offending musician whose name he had just bellowed as a question. [Beat.] I kept smiling and nodded to convey, "Yep, that's who it is." [Another beat.] Joe took the headphones off and held them astride my ears as he simply said, "Sad motherfucker...," and then plopped the phones back onto my head and walked away.

Thus spake Zawinul.

I wondered how and if I was going to survive this macho jazz gauntlet.

Welcome to Weather Report.

photo: Shigeru Uchiyama

The road to this trans-oceanic journey begins 20 years earlier when, in my infancy, I'm playing along to my father's vinyl LP records on a makeshift drumset that he has put together for me in front of a large Klipsch monaural speaker cabinet in our family's living room. Being that young, I don't understand the concept of recordings; I think that there are little people inside this large speaker cabinet, and that putting a round piece of plastic into the machine wakes them up and they make music for me — His Majesty the Baby.

The music includes LPs by Tito Puente, Art Blakey, Martin Denny, Specs Powell, Esquivel, and Henry Mancini. The conga drum comes from Cuba and the small rivet cymbal from who-knows-where, and this setup functions not only as a thrown-together kit but also as a sort of compass. I'm four years old and I already know that I will be playing the drums for Weather Report. Well, I can't actually know that just yet, but I pretty much have already figured out that this is what I'm going to be doing for the rest of my life.

First will come private lessons and summer music camps, always to the accompaniment of parental cheering and sibling support. Next will come conservatory training, followed by my first gigs…

2. Club Harlem

It was the summer of 1972 and I was returning to my position as house drummer for the band at the legendary Club Harlem in Atlantic City. The club was 38 years old at that point in time; I had just turned 18. The year before, when I first did the gig, my mom had to drop me off and pick me up in front of the club for a couple of weeks until I got my driver's license. The Club Harlem was located on Kentucky Avenue. Atlantic City has changed a lot since 1972, and while Kentucky Avenue is still there, the Club Harlem no longer exists. But it was home in its heyday to such legendary visiting black artists and entertainers as Sammy Davis, Jr., James Brown, Sam Cooke, Ella Fitzgerald, Stevie Wonder, Sarah Vaughan, Ray Charles, Redd Foxx, and many others. Acts would usually come there for a one-week stint. The Club Harlem had a show room in the back that could seat 900 people. It also had a bar in the front where organ trios would play in-between the shows in the main room. I got to hear such jazz greats as Lonnie Smith and Jimmy McGriff during my breaks.

The really fun part about the Club Harlem was that there was a breakfast show that started at 5 A.M. on Sundays. All of the celebrities appearing in Atlantic City on any given weekend would come to the Harlem's breakfast show after the other nightclubs closed for the evening. The club served scrambled eggs, Bloody Marys or Screwdrivers, and we played a final set. And then the organ band in the front of the club would play their last set. All the while, aromas from the various soul food eateries and the "head" and incense shops on the street mingled with the perfume of the nearby Atlantic Ocean.

So, it was the beginning of summer and I greeted bandleader Johnny Lynch — a lovely old man with a wig fashioned in the style of the day, a large Afro. The band consisted of Johnny on trumpet, two saxophone players, bass (the excellent Eddie Mathias), piano, and drums. Believe it or not, for the dance routine (two women with natural Afros and one male dancer, all of them dressed in leopard-skin fur) and resident vocalist, we had a conductor who wielded a big baton. His name was John Usry, Jr., and his sister, Soundra, was the singer. John went on to have some success producing disco recordings, I believe. For fun, the pianist in the house band, Gary Gannaway, used to find Usry's baton just before show time and toss it into a hole in the wall backstage that led to a long-forgotten basement. Usry would panic and curse behind the red velvet curtain that was just to the right of the drumset. I learned some new and imaginative combinations of colorful language in 1972.

The Three Degrees was the first group I worked with that summer. I rehearsed their book with the house band on the day before they were scheduled to come to town. Some nice tunes, including one of their hits, "Everybody Gets to Go to the Moon" (the same song they sing during their cameo appearance in the 1974 film *The French Connection*), and a cool arrangement of Aretha Franklin's hit "Rock Steady."

The girls arrived for their first show, and I was informed that they had their own drummer, but I could play percussion during their set. Bummer, but okay. They also had their own conductor, a man named Richie Barrett, who discovered them, produced them, managed them, etc.

So, the first night of the Club Harlem summer season begins, and the house band plays a set for cocktails and dancing by those audience members who have gotten there too early, and then it's show time. Maestro Usry comes onstage through the thick velvet curtains on this small bandstand, takes a deep bow, and we play the book for his sister Soundra, the singer. I can't quite remember the sequence of events, but we also played music for the aforementioned dance trio as well as for a comedian. Then the Three Degrees were announced, and I moved over to my tambourine spot while their drummer sat down at my kit and played their show. He was good.

"This would be fun to do!" I thought. So, early on the second evening I went up to the Three Degrees' conductor/manager/producer, Richie Barrett, and I actually had the nerve to say, "Excuse me, may I ask you a question?" His reply: "Yeah, what?" "Well, I was just wondering if it might be possible for me to play one of the shows this week — you know, play drums on the show? After all, it's only fair, I DID play the rehearsal, and…" He interrupted me with an "Are you kidding?" and walked off. Oh well; nothing ventured, nothing gained.

It might have been later that night, or possibly the next evening, but between shows 1 and 2, the Three Degrees' traveling drummer came back from the break late and drunk. Apparently, this was not the first time that something like this had happened. And so, while we played some extra tunes out of the house-band book, I heard the following take place on the other side of that velvet curtain that was next to my drumset:

"THIS IS THE LAST TIME YOU PULL THIS SHIT!"

"AW, FUCK YOU, MAN."

"OH YEAH? FUCK ME? WELL, FUCK *YOU*! YOU'RE FIRED!"

The band stops playing. Sounds of pushing and shoving, and probably a few more F words.

Suddenly, Richie Barrett charges through the velvet curtains and strides angrily across the stage to give the downbeat for the Three Degrees' first number. Halfway there, he stops, points HIS conductor's baton right at me and says loudly enough for everyone in the club to hear:

"OKAY, YOU GOT YOUR CHANCE, MOTHERFUCKER!"

I played that show and finished out the week. Looking back now, I realize that this was all part of the training. The last night of the engagement, I got a signed photo from the girls as well as a kiss on the cheek from each of them. Barrett never offered to pay me anything extra for playing their show, and it didn't even occur to me to ask.

The Three Degrees went on to have a couple of big hits, including "When Will I See You Again" as well as "TSOP" (the theme for *Soul Train*). Shortly thereafter, I began working with the Stan Kenton Orchestra, abruptly resigning my gig at the Club Harlem. Didn't get to play too much more soul music for a while…

THE THREE DEGREES CMA Management RICHARD BARRETT

3. Weather Report is a Big Band

Pre-tour press conference in Tokyo with Weather Report, Monday, June 19, 1978. Several questions to Joe Zawinul, Wayne Shorter, and Jaco Pastorius. No one asks me anything, and I'm okay with that — still just trying to take all of this in. Finally, a journalist directs a question to the new drummer in the band. "Peter Erskine: You have played with the big bands of Stan Kenton and Maynard Ferguson. How does this qualify you to play with Weather Report?" Nice question, especially seeing how I have not yet played my first concert with the band. "Well… good music is good music…" — my first publicly spoken words as Weather Report's drummer — "and good music is…" Zawinul interrupts my brilliant answer with, "Weather Report is a small group and we are a big band, too. Next question."

To be honest, I am confident that, had Joe or Wayne heard me with either Stan or Maynard, they never would have hired me. I suspect that it was the idea that I had played with Kenton that intrigued them, and I imagine that the Kenton in their heads was the band from the '50s. They simply liked the notion or the concept that I had played with a big band.

(Joe and Wayne both enjoyed their first "big" gig as part of Maynard Ferguson's band.) Luckily for me, it was Jaco who heard me play with Maynard.

I owe the Weather Report gig to Maynard Ferguson bandmate and trumpeter Ron Tooley, who called Jaco up when the band was playing in Miami at the Airliner Motel in March of 1977. Ron was surprised that his phone call was answered because Jaco was usually in Los Angeles working with Weather Report, and he made the call intending to just leave a message. So they talked for a while, and when Ron asked Jaco if he would like to come and see the band that night, Jaco replied, "Thanks but no thanks; I heard you guys the last time." "Well," Ron said, "we got a new drummer; you might want to check him out." "Okay, I'll be there."

Even though the epochal album *Heavy Weather* was just about to be released, drummer Alex Acuña was apparently already making plans to leave the band. So I met Jaco that night and we chitchatted for a while. At first I was staring at him because he looked so different in person compared to his solo album cover photograph — that stylized black-and-white photo that made him look European. Here was this guy with stringy long hair wearing a Phillies baseball cap, horn-rimmed glasses, and a striped shirt that was buttoned all the way up to the top.

Eventually the band break was over and I had to go back to the stage to play the second set. Jaco then said something to me no one else had ever said. As I was walking towards the stage I heard, "Hey, man!" and I turned around to look. Instead of saying something like, "Play well" or "Have a good set," Jaco yelled, "HAVE FUN!" And I thought, "Wow, that's a nice **idea**." So I went up and had fun — smiling and laughing and enjoying myself, and that's how I played. Jaco was that kind of person: He truly enjoyed bringing out something in people — most often bringing out their best. Sometimes, getting any type of reaction was good enough for him (even if it meant trouble to follow). One nickname he had for himself was "catalyst."

After the Maynard gig was over that evening, Jaco and several of us sidemen stayed up all night listening over and over again to the cassette tape that Jaco had brought with him of *Heavy Weather*. I told him, "This is the version of Weather Report I have been waiting for." He told me that he would be calling me one of these days.

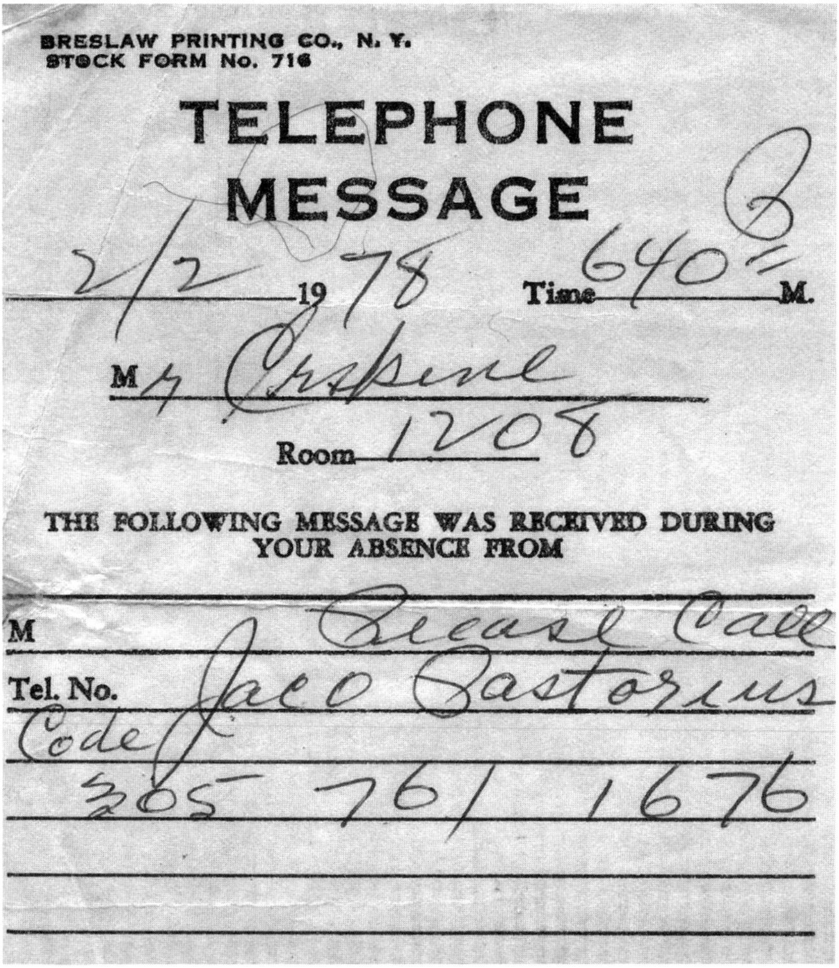

A handwritten telephone message slip reads:

BRESLAW PRINTING CO., N. Y.
STOCK FORM No. 716

TELEPHONE MESSAGE

2/2 19 78 Time 6:40 M.

M Erskine

Room 1208

THE FOLLOWING MESSAGE WAS RECEIVED DURING YOUR ABSENCE FROM

M Please Call

Tel. No. Jaco Pastorius

Code 305 761 1676

4. I Join the Band

What follows is a glorious period of spring touring with Maynard, and I'm listening to that cassette tape of *Heavy Weather* at every opportunity, knowing that there is a great musical vista around the corner. "This is the kind of music I want to play when I grow up." It isn't the first and won't be the last time that thought occurs to me. The sound, the compositions, and the playing on *Heavy Weather* mesmerize me — me and everyone else who hears the album (except for some of the trumpet players on Maynard's band who only seem to like older Maynard recordings. To be fair, the rhythm section guys are playing that tape a lot on the long bus rides between towns). It's intoxicating. And so is listening to Jaco on Joni Mitchell's *Hejira*. The two best things I'm hearing both have Pastorius all over them.

Jaco is true to his word and does indeed call me a few months later. It's the beginning of a severe winter, and Weather Report is starting work on a new album. I'm invited to come out and audition in the form of recording for a day in the studio with the band. With the combined elements of the weather being so bad (making it risky for me to fly out of and back in for a Maynard tour without possibly hanging him up) and my lack of studio experience, I turn down the offer to play with Weather Report! "Sorry, I'd love to do it, but the timing just isn't right." Without my realizing it, this apparently makes some sort of good impression. The band proceeds to work on the album that would become *Mr. Gone* with drummers Steve Gadd and Tony Williams. Eventually, a tour of Japan and Australia is planned and Weather Report needs a drummer for that. I get the call again, and this time I accept the invitation.

I'm not thrilled to be leaving the employ of Maynard Ferguson, as he has been a terrific boss, and I've had a good time traveling and playing, but music calls. Actually, Joe Zawinul calls and I'm taking an afternoon nap. The conversation is awkward and inconclusive. I'm called again a few days later by someone in Weather Report's management. Paul Bruno says, "Hi Peter. Joe Zawinul has asked me to ask you if you can play the beat to 'Nubian Sundance'." Call it the impetuousness of youth, but I reply, "You tell Joe I can play the shit out of it." "Okay," Paul says amiably, "I'll let him know." And so, I get the gig. I sit as tight as I can on this news for a couple of months, but word gets out. I ask my drum company, Slingerland, to prepare a kit for this tour, and they comply with a one-of-a-kind spruce-veneered kit, outfitted in custom flight cases and pre-shipped to Los Angeles ahead of the tour's start. I bid Maynard and the band farewell and fly out to L.A., checking into the Sunset Marquis Hotel, Jaco's hotel of choice. He's nowhere to be found that evening. I find out later that he was up the street at the Roxy, attending a CBS Records album rollout gig for Billy Cobham. Jaco later brags to me that he and Stanley Clarke were picking grapes, raisins, and nuts from a record company-supplied fruit basket on the table and throwing them at Billy during one of his drum solos.

Rehearsal is set to begin early the next afternoon, and I decide to walk from the hotel situated near La Cienega Blvd. in Hollywood to the S.I.R. rehearsal studio that's located near Highland Ave., a distance of two-and-a-half miles. I enjoy the morning trek and am pleased to see my new drums in their cases waiting for me at the studio. Several crew members are milling about, and I introduce myself to them and then begin setting up this new kit.

While I am doing this (a start-of-tour ritual I will repeat often during the ensuing years), a manager comes over and informs me that the "guys will be a little bit late" getting to rehearsal. So, the 1 P.M. rehearsal is now looking like a 3 or 4 P.M. rehearsal start — no problem. The crew guys are very helpful, and we're experimenting with the setup, working in some Chinese gongs I brought along, instruments I found in London during a tour with Stan Kenton. (I will take Jaco to this same shop during a later Weather Report tour, and it is here he will find the Chinese koto that is heard to prominent effect on his album *Word of Mouth*.) Four P.M. rolls around and we've figured out the gong setup. The same manager comes over and apologetically informs me that he has been told that the "guys will be delayed another couple of hours."

It must be 6:30 or 7 P.M. by the time Joe, Wayne, and Jaco enter the rehearsal studio together from the parking lot. I'm happy to see Jaco and walk over to greet him, but he only smiles, waves, and departs as quickly through the doorway as he had entered. Instead, I shake hands with Joe Zawinul, who has a small, dried-out marijuana roach stuck to his lower lip. He stares at me and shakes my hand, almost glumly. Wayne is far friendlier and smiles warmly and broadly. They go their way towards the stage where the band setup is waiting.

Zawinul begins noodling on his recently repaired and factory-returned Prophet 5 keyboard while keyboard tech and programmer Alan Howarth explains what work has been done during the machine's absence. Wayne is unpacking his tenor saxophone. Now, had I stayed true to my big band experience, I would have awaited instruction or invitation to play. Any band with a dozen or more musicians requires this sort of traffic control, and a good sideman knows his place. But I'm bored by all of the waiting around, and so I do something uncharacteristic for me and begin playing the drums — BAM! — throwing the gauntlet down to Joe instead of waiting for it to come from him. He turns and looks almost startled but pleased, and so he begins to play. We're just jamming at this point, and Wayne wastes no time joining in. The monitor mixer is vigilant and everything is sounding really good.

I look out into the rehearsal space and see Jaco re-entering the building, this time with a 6-pack of Heineken beer and a big smile. He quickly deposits the beer into the rehearsal studio fridge and jumps up onto the stage, turning to catch a Fender bass that's airborne as soon as he is ready to catch it. He grabs it midair with ease and fastens the strap around himself, turns a knob, and we're off to the races. What unfolds is an impromptu medley of Weather Report tunes, all sounding very familiar to me because I had done my listening homework. The experience feels as familiar as possible, and yet I know I am on new ground and that I am, in effect, playing for my very life. These guys are my heroes, and these are the musical moments to live for. An Olympic downhill skiing run where turn after turn only reinforces what we already know: that we're going to enjoy this and that we're going to win.

There is a theory I've read that states, in effect, that musicians reach their moment of readiness after they've put in about 10,000 hours of playing-time on an instrument. I added up all my hours while sitting in a bathtub one day, and my 10,000 hours pretty much coincided with the time that I joined Weather Report. I played a lot when I was young. And here I was, going for it with Joe Zawinul, Wayne Shorter, and Jaco Pastorius.

We cover a lot of musical ground and play a lot of tunes non-stop for over 40 minutes without a word being spoken. I look out into the rehearsal room space at some point during all of this and see saxophonist Tom Scott (whom Jaco had invited to come over) standing there motionless with his mouth open. By this time we are playing "Gibraltar," which has a rousing vamp for a finale, and we all seem to know that it's time to end together, Zawinul confirming this with a jubilant and vigorous nod of his head. "Bup-bup-buh, bap-bu-DAP!" The guys are high-fiving and laughing and smiling, I'm catching my breath, but of course I am smiling, too, and this all seems like a good thing. This is confirmed by rehearsal being called for the night, with a photo session hurriedly scheduled for the following day.

The night, however, has just begun, and I'm riding shotgun with Jaco as we go from one L.A. landmark to another, ending up at the former home of Stan Laurel. From a jam session with Michel Colombier to a drawn-out existential dialogue between Jaco and Steve Gadd that I overhear from the couch where I'm napping (and left to wonder how in the world these guys can stay up so late), I discover that Jaco's sound is indeed in his hands and that Tom Scott is a nice fellow, and that Jaco and Steve can really TALK.

Jaco takes me to a clothing store on Santa Monica Blvd. the next morning so I can get some hip stage clothes as well as something for the band photo. I put on my new white T-shirt and join Joe and Wayne, who have been waiting for us to get into the picture.

Feeling bold, I venture to ask Joe while we're posing:

"Hey, Joe."

"What?"

Pose. Snap.

"Can I tell my friends that I'm in the band?"

Pose. Snap.

Pose. Snap.

"You can tell your friends that you are going to Japan."

Pose. Snap. Snap.

WEATHER REPORT

at my first Weather Report soundcheck in Japan, 1978   photo: Shigeru Uchiyama

5. Mr. Gone

Zawinul: "We don't have too many rules in this band, but we got one very important rule you need to know."

Peter: "Okay. What's that?"

Zawinul: "No boogers allowed."

Peter: "Boogers? Uh, what do you mean, 'No boogers allowed'? What's a booger?"

Zawinul: BOOGERS! UGLY BITCHES, MAN! No fucking boogers allowed!"

Peter: "Um…you're joking, right?"

Zawinul: "I see you with an ugly booger, I'll fire your ass!"

In the days between my introduction to the band and our flight to Japan, I was invited to visit Devonshire Studios where Joe, Wayne, and Jaco had been hard at work on *Mr. Gone*. Devonshire Studios is in North Hollywood and was the scene of some incredible recordings by Weather Report. I was amazed to see that room for the first time. THIS is where they recorded *Heavy Weather*? The room seemed quite small, longer than it was wide, and the narrow confines of Studio A made it an unlikely place in which to create classic recordings. But thanks to the cleverness of the engineers and the musical vision of Joe, Wayne, and Jaco, a lot of great music came out of that room.

My first recording experience was to do a hi-hat overdub on Joe's tune "Young and Fine." He wanted to tinker with the feel of the fine drum track that Steve Gadd had played, and I set up a hi-hat in a small iso-booth and played along with the track from start to finish while Joe watched a World Cup soccer game on TV in the control room. When I was finished, I took off my headphones, climbed around the mic stand, and walked into the control room. Joe seemed to be concentrating on the game. I asked, "How was it?" to the room. "How was it?" Zawinul replied. "You tell me." And so I said, "I think it was good." "Okay then," he said. "Watch the game."

The next day or so I was in the studio with my full drumset. We started off with a soundcheck for the engineer that morning and someone suggested that we run Wayne Shorter's "Pinocchio." Wow! From being a drummer in a big band to all of a sudden playing "Pinocchio" in the same room with its composer, and with WEATHER REPORT. Meanwhile, we still needed to get a drum sound, so my excitement combined with my wanting to make some sort of an impression, as well as figuring I should hit as much of the drumkit as possible, well, that wound up being my world premiere on record with the band. I was a bit horrified when I realized that Joe, Jaco, and Wayne were seriously considering just using this rough run-through as the "take"; I was used to working laboriously over and over again to get a good "take" when I made recordings with the Kenton or Ferguson bands, and I wanted my first recording with Weather Report to be SO GOOD, especially on a tune where Tony Williams played so ingeniously and sublimely. But when I objected to the idea of the run-through being used, Jaco cut me off and announced, "Hey, you're going to join the band the same way I did: first take." And that, for better or worse, was that.

Meanwhile, I am actually assigned the homework of reading Nietzsche. I get a copy of *Thus Spoke Zarathustra* and dig on the *übermensch* parallels, but it is "What does not kill me, makes me stronger," from *Twilight of the Idols* that will have the most relevance for me regarding this new situation I'm in. Can't help but think, however, that I might have been better off spending that time listening to more Tony Williams.

6. Summer of '61

photo of Louis Hayes & Peter by Fred Erskine

I first met Joe Zawinul when I was seven years old, at the same summer music camp where I met Stan Kenton. Two future bosses in Bloomington, Indiana. Joe was there as part of Cannonball Adderley's Sextet, and drummer Louis Hayes taught some of the drum classes. Other students at this 1961 camp included Don Grolnick, Keith Jarrett, Lou Marini, Jr., Jim McNeeley, and David Sanborn. Gary Burton was at the 1960 camp while Randy Brecker was at the 1962 camp. And so on. A lot of musicians who went on to become musical heroes and/or colleagues of mine were at these camps because these camps provided jazz training that was not yet available in schools. "Jazz" was a dirty word back in those days. You couldn't even call your school band a "jazz ensemble" or "jazz band." There were euphemisms like "lab band" or "stage band" or "studio orchestra." But now, universities offer degrees in jazz pedagogy and performance. "Is there a doctor in the house?" You bet, and that doctor probably earned his or her degree in a jazz studies program.

Jazz education may well turn out to be the most important and long-lasting legacy of Stan Kenton.

Free Public Jazz Show
In Auditorium Friday

A free public jazz concert will be presented at 7:30 p.m. Friday in the Indiana University auditorium by the musicians attending the Stan Kenton music clinic this week on the university campus.

The 220 young musicians have been divided into eight bands, all of which will perform Friday night, together with Kenton and the 22 name musicians conducting the clinic.

Among those assisting Kenton with his clinic at Indiana University are such musicians as Donald Byrd, trumpet, Down Beat Poll winner; Sam Donahue, tenor saxophone, feature man with the Kenton band; Russ Garcia, arranger, noted for recording and picture work; Don Jacoby, trumpet, CBS staff artist, and Eddie Safranski, bass, NBC studio artist.

Friday night the bands will perform original and well known compositions.

The musicians attending this year's clinic which will close Saturday are from 25 states.

This year Kenton conducted two additional clinics — one at Southern Methodist University July 23-29 and a second at Michigan State University July 30-Aug. 5.

HE'S SENSATIONAL says the famous band leader, Stan Kenton, in commenting on the seven-year-old drummer, Peter Erskine of Linwood, N.J., who this week is attending Kenton's third annual music clinic at Indiana University. Son of Dr. and Mrs. F. A. Erskine, Peter, who was seven in June, has been playing the drums since he was five and has been making professional appearances the past year. Peter explains that he has always liked "exotic" music—never having had any use for "nursery songs."

I acquired the jazz bug quite seriously at that 1961 camp. At the same time, one of the teachers and musical personalities at the camp, a composer and arranger named Johnny Richards (who was one of the staff writers for the Stan Kenton Orchestra; some of his most famous works include the suite that he wrote for Kenton called "Cuban Fire" as well as the *West Side Story* album), encouraged me on a most important point. I remember him kneeling down and grabbing both of my shoulders, looking me in the face and saying, "Peter, you be sure to listen to every kind of music." And so my musical appetite thereafter was fed not only by jazz but by a lot of classical music, which I grew very fond of, as well as by what we now call world music: a lot of recordings from the Caribbean, including calypso, salsa, and Cuban, as well as African musics. I had diverse and interestingly rounded listening experiences as a young musician.

Johnny Richards gave me that sage advice when I was all of nine years old at the close of the Summer Jazz Camp in Storrs, Connecticut. But those first two camps I went to were located a third of the way across the country — a country that had not yet completed its interstate highway system — requiring a two- or three-day driving journey by my parents with older sister Lois in tow. These road trips cultivated my tolerance, if not taste, for long miles and hotel and motel living. I actually enjoyed the smell of the tiny bars of soap that were just placed in our recently cleaned room upon checking in, and a swimming pool in the parking lot seemed like a pretty good concept to me at the time. The road to this first camp was not all just highway or route numbers. It took a telegram from my mother to the jazz camp offices to make this happen.

My teacher, Johnny Civera, and I met at the local music store when my father took me there for my first drum lesson when I was five. I remember asking my dad, "Can I begin taking drum lessons now?" and that was that. Luck was very much on our side for Johnny to be in the store that evening; he was the most patient, loving, and instructive of teachers, and he's my drumming buddy for life. I liked everything about him: the way he dressed, the way he spoke, and the way he played, of course. Johnny was a swinger (he had worked with Patti Page and Billy May, among others).

It was Johnny who mentioned the Kenton jazz camps to my mother, whereupon she fired off a telegram telling them about this incredible kid drummer — and she signed the telegram in Johnny's name. Of course, she neglected to mention any of this to Johnny, but when he received a telephone call from the camp offices about me, he caught on quickly enough to recover and claim ownership of the contact, and I was invited to come to the camp. Only problem was that the minimum age for a student attending the camp was 14. This dot did not get connected, but by the time we had driven 700-plus miles and arrived, weary and expectant, the camp staff was divided as to how best to resolve the situation.

Enter Stan Kenton. A separate audition session is set up for that evening where I am to play for Stan personally, and he will decide whether or not it will be appropriate for me to stay. Meanwhile, he (or someone) has invited a photographer from the local newspaper to be there. My parents take me to the audition room where I meet Stan and play for him. I recall thinking that I did not play so well, but we were invited to stay at the camp for the duration — my parents would stay in the dorm room with me — and I could attend theory and drumming classes, rehearsals, and concerts.

Stan was never "Mr. Kenton" to me, only "Stan." And I grew to love him and the members of his band as well as the other instructors to the point where each summer camp's end would result in tears on my face. I didn't want the music to end.

And even though the summer camps had to run their course, I remained enthralled by the musical experience, listening to as much jazz as I could — before school, after school, even during breakfast and dinner, much to the annoyance but abiding acceptance of my two sisters and brother — and occasionally sitting-in with the Kenton band when it would play at the Steel Pier in its ballroom located a half mile out to sea.

There is an audio recording of my playing with Stan's band, circa 1963, and my drumming style is in many respects much the same now as it was then. The acorn does indeed grow to become the oak tree, and we are who we are. But I have always depended on the kindness of strangers and friends, musical and otherwise, to get to where I was going. And the music world, particularly the brother-and-sisterhood of drummers, is friendlier than most when it comes to encouragement and the sharing of wisdom, knowledge, even trade secrets. In any event, musicians love what they do, and this is reflected by the love we have for one another as human beings. And the teachers at those camps were all very generous people with their time, talent, and wisdom.

Peter w/ Paul Guerrero, NTSU One O'Clock band drummer, 1961

7. Joe

Fukuoka, Japan, in the middle of a Weather Report tour during the summer of 1980. Joe is taking me shopping so I can pick out a briefcase that the band is going to buy me for my birthday. We get to the department store just before opening time. As soon as the doors open, we begin riding the escalators up to the floor where office goods and bags are being sold. Each store employee we pass bows in reverence as they say "Irrashaimase," which simply means "Welcome." Floor after floor and person after person bowing and saying this, I'm pleasantly impressed and proud to share this moment with Joe, who is actually moved to tears by the display of hospitality. I ask "Hey, Joe, are you okay?" and he replies: "The humanity of this…the humanity…. It's unbelievable, man." He shows a side that he doesn't share often. Just as quickly, he amends: "Well, you know, they're probably all saying 'fuck you' under their breaths."

Lest anyone reading this think that Joe Zawinul's rough, gruff exterior was all that there was to the man, then I would be guilty of painting a one-dimensional portrait. He was gruff and he could be rough as well as scatological and hyperbolic in the extreme. But he was also a sweet and very funny man. Easily the most intense musician I've ever known. Joe was possessed and obsessed by the musical vision that carried him all of the way from war-torn Vienna to New York, on the road with Dinah Washington, through his travels with Cannonball Adderley and then Weather Report — not to mention the baptismal fire of *Bitches Brew*, etc. As Miles Davis said in his liner notes to Joe's 1970 Atlantic Records album, *Zawinul*:

Zawinul is extending the thoughts we've all had for years. And probably the thoughts that most so-called musicians have not yet been able to express.

MILES DAVIS

P.S. Dig the two drummers and Herbie with the Echoplex — and the clear funky black soprano sound — and the setting that Woody has to play in. All these musicians are set up. Joe sets up the musicians so they have to play like they do, in order to fit the music like they do. In order to fit this music you have to be "Cliche-Free." In order to write this type of music, you have to be free inside of yourself and be Josef Zawinul with two beige kids, a black wife, two pianos, from Vienna, a Cancer, and "Cliche-Free."

Some of the method I observed to Joe's cliché-free madness:

Number one: "Always compose when you play."

Number two: "You were playing a beat tonight, and it didn't sound right. And I turn around and look at you, man. It didn't look right, neither."

Number three: Joe would often ask for "more." What did that mean? When people ask for that, I think they want more focus, more specificity, or more energy — not volume necessarily, but more velocity or forward motion. In drumming we have to move the music along, and even if it's a ballad it still needs to have some sense of motion. As drummers we have to provide that motion while remaining completely relaxed.

Number four: Joe asked me to play a beat for him, and when I did he noticed that my left leg was bouncing up and down in rhythm even though it was not being used to play the (hi-hat) pedal. "What's going on with your leg?" he asked. "What do you mean? I'm just moving it in time…" "No," he interrupted, "Put that energy into what you are playing."

Number five: One time in concert the beat got turned around, and I did something to try and bring it back in—you know, "Okay everybody, here's *one*." Afterwards, Joe was really bugged, furious. "Why did you do that? It was great before you did that." "Well," I said, "I was trying to get beat one straight." And he said, "One? Fuck one, man! I don't give a shit about one. One's not important." Big lesson in that.

Number six: I was big fan of Billy Cobham. Mel Lewis, Elvin Jones, and Billy were my three favorite drummers around the time I joined Weather Report. But Weather Report — Joe — was really trying to get me to find my own voice.

Joe was a constant teacher and observer.

I had taken piano lessons as a child, and while never mastering the instrument, I managed to learn a few pieces, including the first of the Two-Part Inventions by Bach. Minding my own business before a Weather Report concert, I was playing this piece on a piano backstage when Jaco chanced upon me and summoned Joe and Wayne to check it out. My band cred shot up several points instantly, and I was unofficially appointed to be Weather Report's classical music authority of sorts. (I was familiar with a lot of classical music repertoire and could name that tune or excerpt more readily than they could most of the time.) Of course, Jaco had intimate musical knowledge of Stravinsky, Hindemith, Copland, Hovanhess, et al, while Wayne had already composed a symphony, and Zawinul was well steeped in the classics. I guess they dug the fact that the drummer could actually play a bit of Bach. No Beethoven, however. Next life, I suppose.

photo: Peter Erskine

8. Educating Peter

It's interesting to look back and recognize the many future colleagues plus two future bosses who were at the camps. Teachers at the camps included Paul Guerrero, Don Jacobi, Clem DeRosa, Charlie Perry, Alan Dawson, Ron Carter, Jimmy Garrison, Ray Santisi, John LaPorta, Dee Barton, Oliver Nelson, and Ed Soph. Oliver was a gentle man and a musical dynamo. Somehow I was able to play in his band for two years running (by way of audition). I was a pretty good kid drummer; I'd been listening enough to music to know or hear what I wanted to play, I was a fast and open learner, and I was fearless — all without being too pushy. Lucky again in this regard as my parents pushed the doors open for me by way of their involvement, stage-door mom-and-dad energies, plus some M.D. advice, I suspect, dispensed freely by my father to any jazz musician in need of some discrete psychotherapy. Even now, as I listen to the end-of-camp concert recordings preserved on vinyl L.P., I'm impressed by the drumming and general quality of all of the young players. These were tomorrow's jazz musicians. In any event, I was getting used to placing in the first/"top" band following the start-of-camp audition process.

But then I hit the awkward years. As adolescence began to sneak into and ooze out of me, coupled with a new interest in classical percussion, I became, in a word, a "square." The summer of 1966 was going to be the big summer camp/family-trip extravaganza for the Erskines. My father borrowed his brother Bill's Lincoln Continental — aptly named — and the six of us piled into the car for a trip that would take us from New Jersey to Bloomington, Indiana, this time for a classical music camp, and then from Indiana clear across the country to California where I would attend the Kenton Camps at Redlands University, followed by a family trip to Disneyland. After which we drove to Texas and visited my Mom's sister Marge and family, and then onto Morehead, Kentucky, where I would attend another classical music camp.

Six people are a lot in a car, Lincoln Continental or otherwise. I was 12 years old, my sister Nancy was 16 going on 17, brother Fred was 19, and Lois was 20 going on 21. Nancy and I got stuck in the middle of the seats where the car's drive shaft bumped up the floor (and always ran hot). I can't imagine how we did it but we did (although my sisters would bail out in Texas and take a Greyhound bus back to New Jersey, a trip that was not without its own adventures).

Oblivious to the discomfort of my siblings and focused only on the music and the eventuality of being able to visit Disneyland, I was having a ball as we drove cross-country. The first camp was a tremendous immersion into the world of orchestral percussion. So much so that, by the time we left Bloomington and drove the storied miles of Route 66 and arrived in California, I had effectively forgotten what a jazz drummer was supposed to do. Or so it seemed during my disastrous audition.

A bit of background: At the classical camp, I read a snare drum excerpt poorly at an audition there, and so I tried to improve my reading accuracy during that camp. I also concentrated on the xylophone, etc., so my head was not on the interpretive-jazz side of things in California.

I enter the audition room and sit down at the drums, where a piece of big band music awaits me on the music stand. A tempo is counted off and I'm expected to start swinging as if the big band is playing right along with me — a drum chart meant to be a guide at best, but an invitation at the very least to play a beat. Instead, I play the notes literally, just like a well-behaved percussionist and completely drumset-inexperienced novice. "Beat – beat – beat – beat," etc. No swing at all, not even a beat. I look up instinctively because I know this is not sounding right and that things are not going so well, confirmed by seeing drummer Dee Barton put his head in his hands in a "Good Lord, what's happened to HIM? Jesus Christ, he's lost it!" gesture. Which isn't exactly encouraging to see.

But it was still an ice-cold-water-to-the-face shock to discover early the next morning that my name was nowhere to be found in any of the top- or medium-level bands, but was instead assigned to the LOWEST band assembled at the camp. The BOTTOM. The WORST band. The band of completely inexperienced players. The "Abandon all hope ye who enter here" band at the camp. Losers.

And the Kenton band? Seemed like that was now off-limits to my sitting in. What happened?

And this is where my relationship with Stan Kenton grows deep and why I will always be grateful to him and to those instructors at the camp. They allowed a couple of days to go by, and I adapted pretty quickly to the situation, feeling wronged by fate but accepting my circumstance, as I knew as well as anyone how badly I had played. It was a Wednesday afternoon rhythm-section class for all of the drummers at the camp, and we were expecting Ed Soph and/or Dee Barton to work with us. Instead, there was Stan who, along with Ed, would sit me down at the kit and work solely with me for the entire two hours of the class, essentially taking me apart and putting me back together again. Their expert and, frankly, loving instruction put me on the correct path towards learning how to swing and encouraged me to stay in the drumming game. Even though my love for classical percussion would continue to grow, that afternoon replanted the crucial seed of my jazz kernel. I was getting some of my mojo back. And I was then allowed to sit-in with the Kenton band before the camp wrapped up.

And six years later, I would be working for Stan as the drummer in his big band.

But first I had to finish this summer marathon. Disneyland was like a dream come true, especially having grown up on the East Coast watching *Walt Disney's Wonderful World of Color* on Sunday night after Sunday night, a television show that promoted the park along with Disney-produced films and TV programs. Between the TV glimpses of Disneyland and the promise of California living as shown on *My Three Sons*, etc., I was in 12-year-old heaven. The family piled into the Lincoln for the long drive to Texas, my sisters bailed out from there because there were no more jazz camps to go to — I think they enjoyed meeting the jazz musicians at those camps — and I then found myself in Kentucky for a once-in-a-lifetime concert band camp experience, playing under the baton of composer Václav Nelhybel and having my first real lesson with Professor George Gaber.

9. Guardian Angels

photo: Nancy Erskine

A person is lucky to have a guardian angel watching over him at some point in life. I believe that I have enjoyed a surfeit of such advantage and good fortune that only a multiple of interested overseers could provide. My parents, Lois and Fred, would certainly count as the first and most important two people in my life. Nothing unusual about that, but they did indulge my every musical whim as best they could. Since my father had been a musician all during his high school, college, and medical school studies — a swinging bass player and bandleader, "Fred Erskine and his Music for Moderns" being one of his more notably named ensembles — I was the one child out of four who caught his fathering fancy to its best advantage, to the slighting of my siblings, I'm afraid. Even though we all lacked for nothing growing up, I did receive a disproportionate amount of his attention and interest. He kept an eye and ear out for my practice sessions, took me to lessons and gigs, found me drums and drum teachers all over the world. Mom grabbed the reins of finding opportunity for me as well, her telegram bringing me to the attention of the National Stage Band Camp folks, etc. In addition to my parents, my sisters and brother were always loving and supportive. Imagine them growing up in a house where the practicing of drums took place before breakfast or during dinner! If I was treated like the star athlete in the house, they were the best sports.

George Gaber would prove to be a lifelong friend — a man whose wisdom, advice, and love for music has accompanied me every day and in most every circumstance, musical or otherwise. He's always with me in word, thought, musical choice, or touch. Gaber taught his students to always strive for the best tone. Professionalism was his calling, musicality his ethos, compassion and laughter his response to life's challenges. His advice was as sharp as his wit. Gaber would say of fame: "That, plus 50 cents, will get you a ride on any subway in New York." The train costs more now, but his advice is still true. He also offered, "There'll always be that kid with the purple drumsticks." In other words, something flashy might come and go, but musical values sustain a musician forever; i.e., it's important to find lasting musical values for oneself. He also showed me perspective, and this during our first lesson at that band camp in Kentucky, my parents in attendance.

Gaber, intuiting and clearly sensing my post-jazz camp trauma and inherent insecurity, instructed me to play a snare drum etude on the practice pad — and to not play any of it correctly. To do so would result in his walking over to the pad and hitting me with a drumstick. "Excuse me?" I asked. "You heard me," he answered. "I want you to play that piece of music, but if you play any of it correctly or as written, you're going to get hit with a drumstick. Hard. Now play it." I glanced over at my mother, and she had a puzzled if not horrified look on her face, as if to say, "Who is this madman?" But I did as instructed and played the snare drum etude on the practice pad, playing the notes upside down and completely out of rhythm, etc., rendering the piece of music unrecognizable.

When I felt that I had done this long enough, I stopped. Gaber then took a satisfied puff on his cigar, said "Good," and continued: "Now, I want you to go over to that window, look outside, and tell me what you see." I followed these instructions, and he prompted me while I was at the window: "Is the sun still shining? Are there clouds up in the sky? The trees are still there, it seems like the earth is still spinning, right?" My mother was smiling now, getting the point of where Professor Gaber was going. "Now, come back to the practice pad." I did as he instructed. "You just played that snare drum piece as badly as it will ever be played. In fact, it could not be played any worse than how you played it. And yet, what happened? Absolutely nothing. NOW, let's begin…"

If THAT'S not a life lesson, I don't know what is.

Gaber saw to it at that camp that I played snare drum in the camp band, made up of an incredible faculty of first-desk wind and brass players from professional symphonies as well as top university students, all under the direction of Czech-born composer Václav Nelhybel. This was my first chance to work under the baton of a screaming, intense, it's-all-about-the-music-and-nothing-else type of conductor, and it made a lasting impression on me. Combined with Gaber's efforts to allow me to experience that it's okay to make mistakes, I was thrust into a crucible of music that matters above all else at that moment, an intensity and appreciation so fierce that the results can be as searing as the hottest fire — at least, that's the idea. I was tremendously taken by Nelhybel, his temper and his quick-turnaround kindness, his immersion into his music's detail and potential power. His music fell out of fashion for a period of time, but his compositions were quite the rage with college wind ensembles for many years. As for me, instead of just playing the triangle, bass drum, or snare drum for a few measures at a time, separated by great distances of rests with the perils of miscounting those bars of rest always present, Nelhybel's snare drum part was the next-best-thing to a jazz drummer's part, providing the rhythmic motor to the band and always present, always audible, and in my hands at that camp, always calling attention to itself.

I'll never forget the shocked look on Nelhybel's face at the end of the concert when he cut off the final chord of his composition "Trittico" and I finished the held snare drum roll with a loud vaudevillian rimshot to close the piece. "Whack!"

I was a jazzer to the core, and as Gaber promised, the world didn't stop spinning.

10. School

My good luck extended to school. Elementary schoolteachers accommodated my musical interests by allowing me to substitute reports such as "Charles Mingus" for "Arizona," or "Jazz" instead of "New Jersey." Every Christmas-break time, my mother would send me off to school with a gift-wrapped package that she cautioned me not to drop; turns out I was giving my teacher a bottle of whiskey each year. My mother was smart; she was also privy to knowing that several of my teachers were also patients of my father's. Linwood, New Jersey was a small town. By the time I reached the junior-high level, I was ambitious enough to be the class president, plus valedictorian, scenery artist, and musical director for our 8th-grade graduation. As I recall, I played piano, snare drum, and xylophone as part of the ceremony (talk about vaudeville). My parents helped me scribe the graduation address; it was somewhat politically conservative, I'm afraid — the fear of the hippie unknown entering their bloodstreams along with most everyone else's. The year was 1968, and the times they were a changin'.

The local high school offered draconian rigidity, more teachers who were patients of my father, and a marching band as the sole musical component for my next level of studies and life lessons. At some point during my 8th-grade studies, we searched for an alternative and found it in the pages of a *Life* magazine article that chronicled a magical place called Interlochen.

In fact, Professor Gaber had alerted us to the existence of the Interlochen Arts Academy, a boarding school that had grown out of the famed National Music Camp founded in that idyllic northern Michigan setting by Joseph Maddy in 1927. The Academy opened its doors in 1962. Like the best of schools, it offered an outstanding curriculum, the facilities to bring our music dreams to life (practice rooms, rehearsal studios, and so on), an excellent faculty — a relatively young faculty now that I look back upon them, but very much adults to us at the time — and, most important, the school was a magnet to some of the best and brightest teenaged talent in the world.

Side note: My parents and I knew that we had to find someplace for me to go to school other than what was available in New Jersey at the time. A large part of this had to do with my not being able to communicate or relate too deeply about what it was that made me tick or what it was that made me want to tick-tock — i.e., music. I once experienced goosebumps while listening to part of the Oliver Nelson album *Afro-American Sketches* and asked my friend, "Did you feel that?" He said, "Huh? Feel what?" and I said, "The music...here," and I picked up the tone arm of the record player and placed it just prior to the same spot, whereupon the musical passage played again. I experienced those same goosebumps all over again and said, "There! That! Did you feel it?" He looked at me like I was nuts. Later I asked my father about this, and he explained to me that not everyone responds to music the same way as I did or, indeed, the same way at all. This was a puzzling and disturbing notion at the time. But we came to trust in the knowledge that, at Interlochen, there'd be a lot of shared goosebumps and feelings.

I looked longingly at the *Life* magazine article pages about Interlochen over and over again, and literally dreamt of the place. Of course, any place this special would require an audition tape of the highest possible quality. I began to prepare this opus, mapping out a track-bouncing scheme on our stereo tape recorder so I could perform a percussion quartet, plus a xylophone solo (I had been studying xylophone with former NBC/Toscanini percussionist Billy Dorn), a snare drum piece, and a drumset play-along to a Dizzy Gillespie album that Lalo Schifrin had composed and conducted titled *The New Continent* with Mel Lewis on drums. In retrospect, the audition tape was a bit of an over-achievement, but as they say, "Who knew?" In any event, years later I heard that outgoing percussion instructor Rick Kvistad was running down the concourse hallway holding the tape high in his hand, shouting to the school's jazz band director, Dave Sporny, "Here's your next drummer! Here's your next drummer!"

11. Interlochen

photo courtesy Interlochen Center for the Arts

A special kind of wind blows in the northern woods of Michigan. This strong breeze passes through the thickets of pine needles that form a spindly canopy over the campus of the Interlochen Center for the Arts. I spent three very formative years going to school there, beginning in 1968 when I was 14. Again, my parents drove me one-third or more of the way across the country so that I could study music. This time I would be taking all of the regular high school classes as well. And I would be away from home, much like the summer camps, only this would not be a one- or two-week camp experience, but an entire school year. That did not seem at all daunting, but it did prove to be an excruciatingly lonely experience for the first few weeks.

Jazz band director Dave Sporny is on some sort of leave or sabbatical for a couple of months. I feel really young and out of place and overwhelmed, to the point where my mother makes a second trip out just to visit and reassure me, but of course between the time her trip is planned and the time she arrives I'm beginning to settle in. The only moment I remember of this visit is her laughing uncontrollably while watching our freshman physical education class, peopled by violinists afraid to hurt their fingers and brass players scared to damage their chops while playing an intramural game of basketball, which resembles nothing more than a ball being tossed around the gym floor with all intended recipients curling up into a gangly shape of agitated fear, hands up for cover while our exasperated gym teacher throws up his hands and rolls his eyes to the heavens. This gig is certainly his karma for something bad.

As the Arts Academy was a boarding school, my immediate parental figures were found in my teachers, and my classmates were like brothers and sisters. Competition and the pursuit of excellence were the credos of the place. Discovery was the magical result. Interlochen was where I discovered Mahler, Moten Swing, and Mongo Santamaria, as well as Debussy, Shostakovitch, and Blood, Sweat & Tears, not to mention getting a high school education. Come to think of it, many of my classmates turned out to be my teachers there as well. With a total population of approximately 400, all of whom were snowbound a good percent of the year there, we taught each other about music and life.

My first moment of knowing I'm "home" is when the symphony orchestra is rehearsing "Petite Suite" by Claude Debussy. I'm playing the triangle and having the time of my life. It's not just what I'm playing that's important to me: It's the larger picture, the glorious sound of all of these musicians playing this music composed so long ago and far away, and yet here we all are, rekindling the music's spirit and creating magic. I would leave rehearsals in those early autumn afternoons and inhale the scent of the pine trees and the breeze from the lake — the school campus sits between two beautiful lakes — while still glowing from the sounds of the orchestra playing that Debussy, and I felt all grown up and truly happy. And the Debussy would be only the beginning of what that orchestra would tackle that year and the following years: Ernest Bloch's "Schelomo," Shostakovich's Fifth Symphony and Ravel's "Bolero" (I played the snare drum parts in all three of those), Mahler's First and

Second Symphonies, Nielsen's Second Symphony and Clarinet Concerto (snare drum), the Barber Piano Concerto, Hindemith's "Symphonic Metamorphosis," Elgar's "Enigma Variations," and Bartók's "Concerto for Orchestra" (timpani on those last three pieces). Guest artists would include Isaac Stern, Lukas Foss, and Dave Brubeck.

Meanwhile, there was jazz band. Dave Sporny, who also taught lower brass at the school, had come back and was holding auditions for the band. My competition would be two drummers, one of them the grandson of a major trustee at the school, the other the son of Dave Brubeck! Luckily, I played really well during the audition; all of my past big band experience and my getting un-squared-away a couple of summers earlier paid off and I won the chair. Also lucky for me was the fact that Danny Brubeck turned out to be such a cool guy. He turned me on to all of the music that was coming around the corner like Janis Joplin and Jimi Hendrix and (later) Buddy Miles, while his older brother Chris turned us all onto Blood, Sweat & Tears.

The jazz band at Interlochen was known as the Studio Orchestra, in part because Sporny wanted the musicians in the band to be able to play all styles of contemporary music convincingly and with conviction. The group's repertoire included the music of the Count Basie, Duke Ellington, Woody Herman, Buddy Rich, Stan Kenton, and Thad Jones/ Mel Lewis big bands, plus music of the time as arranged by Dave, such as tunes from the Beatles' *Abbey Road* or Simon and Garfunkle's *Bridge Over Troubled Water* albums. The Studio Orchestra, or "Stud Ork" for short, used euphemism because "jazz" was still a dirty word in most educational institutions, Interlochen very much among them, and so the band ran under the radar of the place for quite a few years. That is, until the band appeared at the 1969 Notre Dame Jazz Festival on the final afternoon set where we literally stopped the show with a galvanizing performance that still ranks as one of the all-time great high school big band gigs I know of. The band was peaking and it was on fire. What started out as a guerilla-type operation that rehearsed unofficially during the school's designated "ice cream social" once a week turned into a powerhouse big band.

After that 1969 festival gig, the Studio Orchestra became one of the most popular ensembles at the school, and its alumni list is impressive by any measure, including Chris Brubeck, Bob Mintzer (Yellowjackets, Jaco

Pastorius), Anne Hills, Chris Brown (St. Paul Chamber Orchestra), Becky Root (Rochester Symphony Orchestra), Jim Olin (Baltimore Symphony), Eddie Carroll (CalArts), Woodrow English (Master Sergeant and the U.S. Army's top "Taps" player), Walter White and Byron Stripling (both incredible trumpet players), Kiku Collins, James Cathcart, Clarence Penn, et al. (We all held positions in the Academy's symphonic orchestra or concert band, too; the perils of playing piatti in Mahler's First Symphony prepared this percussionist well for the likes of Neal Hefti and Sammy Nestico.) The symphony orchestra's list of alums from the three years I attended is even longer and more impressive; suffice to say that just about every major orchestra in the USA and abroad can count Interlochen musicians in its midst. And I haven't even mentioned the alums from the theatre, dance, and visual arts departments. Not all of the kids who go to Interlochen remain performers; some become doctors, others enter the corporate world, etc. Two drumming colleagues of mine ended up doing something completely different: timpanist Kenneth Broadway is now a world-class piano soloist, while my orchestra section-mate Stan Ragsdale is a federal prosecutor for the government.

Interlochen was where I began to learn about life, within a cocoon of music that was so intense that we naturally expanded so rapidly as to explode outside the artificial behavioral and protective barriers the school elders attempted to hold. We were "gifted youth" as the school's motto boasted, and we saw the world from afar. At the same time we were dealing with geometry, Gershwin, and the growing discontent of our generation to the unraveling events in Vietnam. We were busy trying to figure out our future identities: Would we be symphonic players or jazzers, hippies or squares, part of a silent majority or vocal minority? And did that cute girl like me or not?

Meanwhile, I've got a history paper due tomorrow, but I still need to practice that Bartók "Concerto for Orchestra" timpani part. The late 1960s and early '70s were, for us, the best of times even during the worst of the Vietnam War era, because everything pointed to a hopeful beyond. The music we heard, one album after another, all indicated or promised change. It seemed like a postcard from the future that said, "Hey, this is what music can sound like. Wish you were here!"

Weather Report's first album is released during my final year at Interlochen.

Man, it was a great time to be young. It was also a great time to make friends, many of whom are still my friends for life: singer Anne Hills, director Jack Fletcher, hornist-turned-pro golfer Tom Moss, violist Pam Peeters Havenith, harpist Katie Kirkpatrick, violinist and ECM recording artist Michelle Makarski, and saxophonist, composer, and big band leader (plus USC colleague) Bob Mintzer. I loved and love these people and the place, so I'm not sure why I was in such a hurry to leave, but a hurry I was in, and so I took summer academic courses by mail while playing gigs in Atlantic City between school years, applied for and was granted a year-early graduation. I was accepted by Indiana University, where I could continue my studies with George Gaber, and it looked like I might be able to satisfy my father's dream that I become a doctor — if not in medicine then at least in music. One year and a few weeks after my three-year-term high school graduation, I would be back at Interlochen, this time as a college dropout on his first day's gig with the Stan Kenton Orchestra.

I will always think fondly of that magical place, up in the woods between two lakes, where the wind whispers the promise of the future to tomorrow's artists. But, hey, now it's time for college.

photo : Fred Erskine

12. Indiana U.

Indiana University, Bloomington. First visited here in 1961 as a 7-year-old and am now back as a 17-year-old college freshman. This is the only college I applied to and the only place I was interested in going. I left Interlochen a hotshot in both the jazz band and symphony orchestra, but Gaber has other plans for me this year. I credit him for this insightful course of studies that he began to credit me in later years.

Fast forward: In 2006 I rented a car at some gig locale in Missouri and drove eight-plus hours on a rainy Sunday to my alma mater, IU, where there would be a celebration of my professor's 90th birthday. George Gaber still meant the world to me. I spoke during dinner to the crowd of former students, ad-libbing as jazz musicians love to do.

I found myself talking about his sense of humanity and the love he taught for music, for being musical, and for being ethical. He returned the compliment during dessert by saying that I had "Gladstone hands," and he reminded me that our two-year course of study during my university years centered around my wish for him to "work on my hands." We approached the instrument — all percussion — from the point of view of TONE. It took quite a few years for his lessons to sink in and take root. My entire drumming approach was nurtured and shaped by the generous wisdom and wealth of experience of Professor George Gaber. The hands thing was his idea, by the way.

When I learned that my professor, mentor, and friend of more than 40 years had passed away at the age of 91, I was asked to sum up my feelings for the man in four short lines of text for the *New York Times*. I wrote:

> GG taught his students well.
> Professionalism, musicality,
> compassion & laughter:
> his calling, ethos & way of life.

He shall be missed.

The other teacher of note at Indiana was Professor David Baker, jazz trombonist extraordinaire, composer, arranger, and pedagogical pioneer. Our role model for what it meant to be hip, David was the outstanding leader of the jazz department at Indiana. He was always urging us to "free it up," at the same time helping me understand the way a boogaloo beat was supposed to really feel.

My housemates at Indiana included pianist Alan Pasqua. We met at a jam session during the first week of class, took an instant liking to each other, and have been musical brothers in arms ever since.

Thanks to some touring/concertizing by the IU Jazz Band, including an appearance at the Elmhurst Jazz Festival, word was getting out to another old teacher about my drumming. That old teacher was Stan Kenton, and it turns out that he was looking for a drummer…

13. Summer of 1972

By the time I finished my first year of college, I've:

gotten drunk for the first time;

gotten laid for the first time;

gotten my first speeding ticket;

gotten drunk for the second time.

Listened to a lot of Miles, Weather Report, Larry Young, Tony Williams, the Mahavishnu Orchestra, Herbie Hancock, Woody Shaw, Elvin Jones, and so on — and I have not yet turned 18. Counting on going back to school in the fall, I take a summer job at the aforementioned Club Harlem in Atlantic City. Meanwhile, my father receives a telephone call from Stan Kenton, who asks, "Fred, is Peter ready?" My father answers, "Yes, he is, Stan," and so an audition is set up. That audition will take place in Avery Fisher Hall at Lincoln Center during an afternoon rehearsal the Kenton band is going to have with singer June Christy, who will be appearing with the band as part of a reunion-themed concert that night. (Woody Herman's band will also be appearing with three of the original "Four Brothers.")

July 3, 1972. The band does not know that I am auditioning; as far as most of them are concerned, June Christy has some young, long-haired hippie drummer. Meanwhile, Stan is changing drummers in the band because long-time drummer Jerry Lestock McKenzie had made the ill-advised maneuver of giving Stan an ultimatum — something I learned you never do to bandleaders, because THEY have to lead the band; an ultimatum takes a bandleader's leadership away, in effect — so Jerry was out and someone else would be in. (This according to bassist John Worster; Stan never discussed the firing/hiring scenario with me.) In any event, only Jerry, John, conga drummer Ramon Lopez, and Stan are aware of the audition process. Poor June Christy has no idea what is going on with this other drummer sitting down to sight-read her charts and play with the band. Stan counts off the first of her six charts we'll run down, and I give it everything I've got, necessarily so because this drumset I'm sitting-in on has the biggest cymbals I've ever seen or played in my life, and this band is really loud — on top of which I'm trying to make a strong, if not good, impression!

I guess I did okay at the rehearsal/audition, because I'm advised of when the concert will begin that evening — my first gig with what will turn out to be June Christy's final appearance with Stan — and, further, I'm told that I should pack my bags and meet the band a week or so later to become the drummer for the Stan Kenton Orchestra.

Joe LaBarbera is drumming for Woody Herman that night, and he is very kind and encouraging to me. Jerry McKenzie is, understandably, not so keen to be my pal at the moment but is friendly nonetheless. I'm pretty much bewildered and start trying to figure out the logistics of everything. My parents will once again drive me one-third of the way 'cross country in order for us to meet the band, this time in Ohio in order for me to hear the band in concert a couple of times before making my debut. So, less than a week after the Newport Jazz Festival gig, I've packed up my Ludwig kit and a suitcase and I'm ready to hit the road.

After I'd finished one year at IU, the bottom heads were off of my tom-toms and I had, as one U.K. jazz critic would later comment, "rocker written all over" me. My earlier influences, which were mostly jazz-oriented, had given sway to the burgeoning "fusion" trend in music. Stan wanted someone in the band that young people in the audience could relate to, I guess. I looked and sounded the part. And what better person to have sitting in the coveted drum chair than a student who was a product of the jazz education movement and who had gone to the summer band camps? As much as I'd like to think that talent alone got me there, it's not unreasonable to assume that Stan had factored in extra-musical considerations as well. In fact, when I would cut my hair a few weeks later in order to look more like the other members of the band, Stan was upset. I let my hair grow back.

The guys in the band were accommodating in any event, and there was a general sense of excitement that seemed to follow the band around that summer. I was learning how to play a lot of this music while boldly and somewhat blindly forging ahead with my own pre- or mis-conceptions on how best to play the drums in Stan's band while dealing with new talent requirements like how to fold up clothing, pack a suitcase, deal with long-distance romances, and be frugal. Oh yeah — about one week into touring with Stan, he and I were sharing an elevator alone up to our respective hotel room floors after a gig and he turned to me and said, "You know, Peter, we haven't discussed money yet." Whereupon I replied, "Okay, how much do you want?" That was good for a hearty laugh from the man as well as, I suspect, an additional $25 per week.

14. The Stan Kenton Orchestra

Characters: The Kenton band, just like any other road band, had plenty of them. Some great musicians, too, like the legendary Willie Maiden, who had played tenor sax with Maynard Ferguson's band in the '60s and had written some of Maynard's best charts. Willie was playing one of the two baritone saxes in Stan's sax section and held sway over the back-of-the-bus dominion otherwise known as the "Deep Six." These fellows were, generally, some of the older and harder-living musicians on the band. Willie loved the color orange, hated the color green, and avoided any and all fruits and vegetables aside from tomatoes and carrots; and if it was "good for you," then it was bad for you.

photo: Peter Erskine

Incredible arranger and Stan's right-hand musical man in many respects, Willie didn't much care for the odd-time charts that Hank Levy wrote for the band, and he would rewrite his parts in 4/4 time as opposed to counting anything like five or seven beats to a bar; jazz had four beats to the bar, and that was that.

Conga drummer Ramon Lopez was another veteran and Deep Sixer, though young at heart and a terrific rhythm teammate. Stan and the "company guys" would sit up in the front of the bus, while most of the young members of the band sat somewhere in the middle. I inherited the seat in the exact middle of the bus, actually a pair of seats, the same space each musician was allotted. Stan had a new bus that was the envy of most other road bands. It even had its own destination signs with eye-grabbing destinations like BACK EAST, DOWN SOUTH, or NO WHERE (sic).

Most bands would lease a bus for a tour or series of tours, but Stan owned his bus outright. The rules were: no music allowed out loud on speakers; headphones were required for all listening. Each musician had his "area" above his seats, and heaven help the soul whose possessions strayed outside those bounds. Don't be late. And no #2 in the toilet. Aside from the occasional flight or travels overseas, the band traveled on the bus week in and week out — 51 weeks during the first year I was on the band; we got seven days home for the Christmas holidays — spending many an overnight on what was called a "hit and run" where the band got into the bus following a concert and would ride to the next city or town, often arriving just in time to roll off the bus and present an educational workshop or "clinic" to a high school or college audience, to be followed by an evening concert. I'll remind the reader: a pair of bus seats, no bunks or any sort of horizontal resting place. The same for Stan as for anyone else. We learned to sleep sitting upright, much like economy-class passengers on an airplane.

One thing for sure: I was getting to play a lot. And I was learning a lot, too, if not about music then about life and love and getting along well with others. Sometimes I tried to share where I was coming from with Stan or the other musicians, offering up my cassette-tape headphones for their enlightenment or approval, but unless it was another player of my generation, then I wouldn't enjoy the benefit of either — the one exception being tenor saxophonist Richard Torres, who would prove to be my best friend and buddy on the band. Not everyone on the band was a fan of my drumming, and I would get the occasional earful from a disgruntled player. This practical reality was a concern to my parents, and my mother expressed as much when she flew out to see the band and me a few weeks after I had joined. It was the first night of a two-week engagement at Disneyland in Anaheim, California, and she was seated at a table along with Stan and perennial Kenton friend and fan Mort Sahl. Just as she was verbalizing her concerns to Stan, one of the trumpet players came over to Stan and complained, "Stan, Peter doesn't want to move the drums from where he's got them positioned now, even though I told him if the drums are next to the trumpets then I won't be able to hear myself, and you know what he said? He said 'You're better off' to me!" Stan started laughing and turned back to my Mom and said, "I think Peter's going to be just fine…"

Meanwhile, it was a big kick to have started things off back at my alma mater, Interlochen. Dave Sporny had prepared me well for this moment: his singing of the figures to the various horn sections during rehearsals in high school always included some great sung drum fills, and we covered a lot of Kenton material as well. Dave had always wanted to play in Stan's band. And Dave, like me, had been to the summer camps.

photo courtesy Interlochen Center for the Arts

15. On the Road

photo: Peter Erskine

The road bands were the doorways to the professional music life for most of us. A lot of players would come and go, most of them settling down eventually to a life of teaching or playing somewhere. Stan didn't have much regard for those players who left his band to settle down. And, so, he was not very encouraging when it came to a sideman's love life; he'd seen enough romances and marriages go south that he was at best a cynic and at worst a protective bandleader who didn't want to lose a good player to a woman of all things.

At one point during our travels I became quite smitten with a young Italian lady, and Stan didn't like the faraway look I got in my eyes as I sat on the bus daydreaming about her. When he stated some objection about my planning to go see her or invite her out to travel with the band, and he stated that he didn't understand why I was so taken with her, the only thing I could think of to say in terms of her main attribute was, "But Stan…she's ITALIAN!" to which he replied, "Oh yeah? Well, so is Vido Musso."

In addition to getting to meet a lot of girls, I got to meet a lot of jazz heroes, too.

Elvin Jones at the Monterey Jazz Festival: Conga drummer Ramon Lopez offers up his bottle of 151 proof Bacardi Rum for Elvin to sip at, whereupon Emperor Jones puts the bottle to his lips upside down while the rum glug-glug-glugs down his open throat. We stand in our circle of admiration, impressed but horrified at the sheer amount of liquor Elvin is consuming. When he pulls the bottle from his lips, he smiles and says, "I like that!" He proceeds to go out on stage and kill it.

Charles Mingus in an elevator at the Eastgate Hotel in Chicago: I board the elevator to ride down to the ground floor and am greeted by an overly-excited Ramon Lopez, which is like saying an overly-excited bottle of carbonated jet fuel, and he says "HEY PETE! LOOK WHO'S ON THE ELEVATOR!" and I glance upward from Ramon to the majestic visage of Charles Mingus. "MR. MINGUS!" I proclaim in total sincerity and gratitude, "THANK YOU for all of the music! What are you doing here?" He smiled and answered that he was in Chicago to get his bass fixed. And the elevator car reached the lobby and we said goodbye.

Louie Bellson at various clubs and festivals: always the consummate gentleman and benevolent musician.

Mel Lewis: He gave me a hard time about my single-headed toms, and even took me to task about it in a *DownBeat* magazine interview, but was ultimately very encouraging.

Nat Pierce: played piano with the band for a while when Stan was ill. Nat was a veteran of the Woody Herman band, and he didn't much care for Stan's band or the music. Scene: late-night bus ride, we're stuck on this thing until morning, and I'm cornered by a menacingly smiling Nat Pierce, who tells me more than once, "You're a nice kid, but you can't swing for shit," and so on. This is all good training, I guess...

Buddy Rich at several double-bills and festivals: always polite, always insanely great. Buddy sat in for Stan at the last moment at this same Monterey Jazz Festival where Elvin amazed us backstage. Stan had fallen ill near the end of the Disneyland gig at the end of that summer of 1972. (We would go on touring without him until the end of the year; he rejoined the band for a New Year's gig in the Bay Area.) Anyway, Buddy comes out after we play a few numbers on our own and he sits down at my drumset with the single-headed toms and the cymbals as big as gongs, and he makes it all sound like him, as if those are his drums.

Witnessing this is one of the great drum and music lessons in my life. We are the instrument; the sound is in us. But it's also nice to have a good relationship with the instrument manufacturers, and the drum company people love Stan. And Stan loves his band. Good things come out of this, and I'm still enjoying the practical benefits and lifelong friendships of the music industry relationships cultivated by my association with the Kenton band. Let's take a minute and look at some of the company I keep...

Buddy had just played one of his all-time impossible drum solos, like he did every night, this evening in the ballroom at Idora Park in Youngstown, Ohio. I was playing with Maynard's band at the time. Buddy was seated, so I wasn't going to make the man look up to me. Since there was no chair there, I went down on bended knee; it was simply a sign of respect. He liked that, I think, and he was always very gracious to me. I'm glad that someone captured the moment.

16. Music Companies - Interlude

Fast-forwarding to Weather Report: By this point in time I am playing Yamaha Drums, and the people at Yamaha have organized a small show for some of their dealers in the Nagoya area. This happens to be in the basement of the hotel where Weather Report stayed the night in Nagoya, and we are invited to preview these Yamaha instruments — and Joe and I are asked to play on these instruments — before the small dealer show opens in the morning. Yamaha has a drumset there and one of the new, rare digital keyboards, the GS-1. This was one of the first digital FM keyboards, and the only musicians who had one were Bob James, Stevie Wonder, and Steve Porcaro. It looks as much like a beautiful piece of furniture as it does a musical instrument.

Joe obligingly agrees to venture downstairs ahead of the band's departure time in order to try out the keyboard and perform for the Yamaha staff — something he would rarely consent to. Naturally, he is expecting that Yamaha will present the keyboard to him as a gift but, as the demo session awkwardly drags on, nothing happens. Joe would play it for a while and then comment, "This is a very nice instrument." The Japanese would nod and say nothing, and then Joe would play it a bit more and then stage whisper to me, "So, when are they going to give it to me?" and I would reply, "Patience, Joe. Give it time." More playing. More "This really is a very nice instrument." More nodding. Finally Joe gives a final, "This is a beautiful instrument," and with a twinkle in his eye he begins to rub the exquisite wood top of the keyboard while saying, "Please be very careful not to scratch it when you pack it up." He then gives me a "let's get the fuck out of here" look, and we shrug and bop out of the Yamaha dealer showroom and catch the train to our next gig.

Steve Porcaro wound up loaning his GS-1 to Weather Report for a day at Village Recorders a couple of months later while we were finishing up the *Weather Report* album. Joe remarked afterwards, "That Steve Porcaro is a nice motherfucker."

17. In Praise of Zildjian

The music industry companies that design, manufacture, and market the instruments we musicians play are models of old-world craftsmanship with new-world technology. I've been endorsing instruments for over forty years.

The two longest product associations I've enjoyed are with Evans Drumheads and the Avedis Zildjian Company. I have played Zildjians since I was five years old. However, my formal relationship with both companies began in 1972 when I became the drummer for Stan Kenton. The Kenton band required the drummer to play on Stan's cymbals, all selected at the factory by Lennie DiMuzio. What was remarkable about these particular cymbals was their size: the ride cymbal was a whopping 27 inches in diameter, and the two crashes were each 24 inches. My 22-inch Swish cymbal was the smallest cymbal of the lot. Eventually I was able to work in a 19-inch crash, much to Stan's displeasure. He liked those big cymbals. Zildjian patriarch Armand Zildjian and Lennie both loved big bands, and they were frequent guests at our many concerts in the Boston area over the three-year period I worked for Stan. This was also true during the two years I played with Maynard Ferguson's band — on smaller cymbals I might add.

My relationship with Zildjian began to evolve once I started working with Weather Report. The band's popularity, musical notoriety, and importance provided an ideal opportunity for Zildjian and myself to capitalize on this career opportunity. Even though I'd already made it into the Zildjian Drummers' Setup book and appeared in several ads, my role within the company expanded to where my ideas and suggestions were sought out, listened to, and acted upon. This is the most dynamic and valuable part of a drummer's relationship with a manufacturer. A performing drummer is on the front line and in the trenches, night after night, and it's the smart company that listens to him or her.

The real years of interaction and product development began in the '80s when Zildjian began researching the way in which to make a ride cymbal that sounded, played, and felt like those few-and-far-between classic K Zildjian cymbals of old. Shapes, new and vintage, were experimented with while novel hammering schemes preoccupied the designers and workers in the factory. Drummer feedback was crucial, and Zildjian listened.

Zildjian now markets the "Left Side Ride," designed with me over an intense two-year period of experimentation. It has all of the combinations of sound that I look for in a cymbal: clarity, darkness in tone, a silky touch, and the textural quality that three rivets placed close to its edge can bring. Rivets, much like spice, are sometimes best used sparingly to add flavor. It speaks as a ride but also functions as a crash, like any good cymbal. I came up with the moniker of "Left Side Ride" to distinguish it from the main or primary ride. For drum nerds: the Left Side comes in 20- and 22-inch sizes; my main ride cymbal is a 22-inch Medium Constantinople K Ride, low-pitched yet distinct in its enunciation. I also play on a 22-inch Swish Knocker, a cymbal that is very similar to the swish cymbal that Mel Lewis played; an 18-inch K Medium Thin Dark Crash, and I like to have a smaller crash or splash cymbal for accents and highlights; I will often play this cymbal "alone," that is, without the added benefit of a simultaneous striking of the snare or bass drum. The effect is not unlike that of water splashing upon the music. I've tried switching to different models of Zildjian hi-hats over the years, often with success, but always return to a pair of 14-inch New Beat hi-hats; they can do anything and everything.

Regrettably, Armand Zildjian passed away several years ago. As I wrote in a letter to the Zildjian family, "Armand had so much love in him, love for his wife and children and love for his extended family — the Zildjian family of artisans and fellow enthusiasts... I can't so much say 'workers' or 'businesspeople' because he didn't run the company like that... Armand, whether by instinct or cleverness, virtually invented the drumming community we live in. Indeed, the entire music industry bears his stamp."

As much as we all miss him, Armand left the company and Zildjian legacy in good hands. His daughter Craigie now runs the company as its CEO, ably assisted by her sister Debbie and brother Robert, plus a dedicated team of true believers. John DeChristopher, who recently retired, was director of artist relations for many years and the primary contact for most drummers associated with Zildjian. Colin Schofield ably performed those duties before John. Other names of note include cymbal tester Leon Chiappini, and R&D specialist Paul Francis. Paul is the closest thing today to an alchemist of old; he works wonders with metal, taking Zildjian's secret formula to new places, always in search of a sound that is timeless — no small feat considering we're talking about capturing the ephemeral and casting it into metal.

One other virtue bears mentioning, and that is Zildjian's long-standing commitment to education. One of the company's more outstanding efforts in this area has been the American Drumming Achievement Awards program that honors living drumming legends and provides scholarship educational opportunities for a lucky next generation of drumming students. In 1998, I was fortunate enough to participate in the first ADAA event in Boston, paying tribute to a then very much alive Elvin Jones. Louis Bellson, Roy Haynes, and Max Roach were also honored that night (by Steve Gadd, Terri Lyne Carrington, and Marvin "Smitty" Smith).

Here is some of what I said:

While everyone else was speaking bebop "English," Elvin Jones was busy creating a new sort of drumming Esperanto..., except his language endured, and influenced the rest of the world with far greater import than that other post-War linguistic dream... His is much more of a "revolutionary" than "evolutionary" advent. The fascinating thing about Elvin's drumming is that Elvin brought drumming full-circle back to its African roots. Elvin has explained that the inspiration for his use of the 18-inch bass drum was that it was the only sized bass drum which could fit in the trunk of the car he was traveling in. (Elvin's gift for the practical was also evident when he answered the following question at a drum clinic in New York a few years back: "Mr. Jones, how can I improve my reading?" His response: "Get a light for your music stand.") Anyway, to my ears, by his use of a bass drum that was tuned more in the range of the tom-toms as opposed to the larger "boom-boom-boom" reminiscent of "swing" or marching bass drums, coupled with the use of his trademark polyrhythmic statements on the drumset, Elvin became the African drum choir incarnate. All the while, his ride cymbal playing held it all together. Einstein couldn't describe the concept of time nearly as well as Elvin has done... "relative" to all things, then, "E," which stands for Elvin, "equals" TIME, nothing "square" about it, multiplied by passion and "a love supreme." His affiliation with John Coltrane stands as one of the most important associations in musical history.

This was met with a standing ovation when Elvin came up to the stage to receive his award from the Zildjian family and emcee Bill Cosby. Of course, stating an accolade for Elvin is merely stating the obvious, but still, it felt good to be able to acknowledge the man as my hero in front of so many drumming colleagues. Elvin is a hero to all us drummers.

photos: Shigeru Uchiyama

18. In Further Praise of Elvin

I celebrate the mind, body, and soul of Elvin Jones. I declare that today and every day is "Elvin Jones Day." This makes great sense to me as a drummer. Elvin is the musician who redefined the drums. He's also the one contemporary of John Coltrane who not only helped shape that music, but could keep up with the relentless musical searching and finding that 'Trane vigorously pursued; their duets are the stuff of legend. Elvin went from being an essential sideman to an essential leader, and he commanded some mighty bands. His style of timekeeping was its own language; his world of soloing was its own universe. His warmth and wit rank with other great humanists who love life and love what they do.

Going back to my analysis, I should add that the influence of marching or military types of drumming is clearly as evident in Elvin's playing as are his influences and incorporations of African and Caribbean rhythmic styles. He quotes from a lexicon of field and snare drum cadences both in his soloing and timekeeping. (Elvin did spend three years in the military.) Then, there are bits of Philly Joe Jones discernible here, a touch of Shadow Wilson there, and the assorted assertiveness as practiced by Art Blakey everywhere. (Elvin on first hearing Shadow Wilson: "I loved the way he played, he was flawless, and such a gentleman. He had perfect time. He understood percussive dynamics… He was so in tune with the composition.") But no other drummer sounds as original to my ears as Elvin does when playing time or soloing, and I am hard pressed to accurately pinpoint his stylistic antecedents. On the other hand, there sure are plenty of us playing today who incorporate his timekeeping vocabulary into our own style of playing. As a press release from the Berklee College of Music stated (announcing the conferring of an Honorary Doctor of Music degree upon Mr. Jones): "Jones remains one of the preeminent jazz percussionists performing today. His influence has extended beyond jazz to rock and other styles of music. His contributions to the development of free improvisation, which underplays or ignores a regular pulse altogether, were adopted by numerous avant-garde players… Jones developed a new role for jazz drummers, diverging from simply keeping the beat, to becoming an equal, collaborative improviser. His simultaneous use of several metrically contrasting rhythms, irregularly shifting accents, and interjections of counter-rhythmic motives against the prevailing pulse became hallmarks of his style."

As I write in *Drumset Essentials*, "All my life, I've tended to be an idealist, and whenever I've thought of drum solos, I've thought of Elvin Jones. I've thought of being the listener and hearing an Elvin Jones drum solo, which had nothing to do with playing for effect. This, to me, had everything to do with pure emotional expression and velocity, and being in tune or somehow plugged into a higher awareness of things."

Elvin Jones to Loren Schoenberg, Jazz UK: "Whenever I've heard people sounding like me — well, it's often when I'm there, they see me walk in and play some of my licks. I take it as a compliment. And it's part of the continuity of all music."

LS: Please talk about the significance of playing the bass drum in all styles of jazz.
EJ: Well, other than the cymbal and the snare, it's the most important part of the kit. When I first started, everybody went boom-boom-boom. But when I did that, I found I couldn't hear the piano or the bass. I thought I needed to hear it, so I stopped doing it, or played it very light, just touch the head. Anybody can play soft for 30 seconds, but do it for an hour, then you learn.

And from an article in *The Philadelphia City Paper* dated October 16–23, 1997, Nate Chinen interviews Elvin and describes how, "During his tenure with Trane, a number of jazz critics alluded to the African flavor of their music, due largely to Elvin's polyrhythmic drumming, the use of rhythmic groupings that suggested a pulse of three beats where there would usually be four. '[The African influence] was subconscious. You know, I'm an African American,' Jones laughs. 'I heard rhythms that are all related. I think American Indians have the same kind, people in the South Pacific. You can hear it in these various places, not always related to Africa particularly. I listened to the real authentic African music from the United Nations record store — you can buy ethnic recordings there — and I heard some of the more tribal gatherings, festivals, and things like that. They weren't individual drummers, they were a whole group, maybe three or four hundred people, all using the same tempo, but their rhythms were varied. That contributed to the complexity of what you hear. So I would listen to it as a whole and I would imagine: What if I could do that? But you know, it's just something that you feel; it's feeling-based more than anything else, more than an intellectual concept. It's extremely spiritual and extremely emotional.'"

So there it is: Elvin sounds like Elvin because he was trying to sound like "three or four hundred people." Makes perfect sense! And so I celebrate Elvin Jones every day, precisely because his drumming is the most universal of musical sounds I have ever heard. He passed away on May 18, 2004. When I was asked to contribute some words of condolence by the good people at the Zildjian cymbal company, I sent them the following: "There will never be a more pure or powerful drumming force, or a higher level of drumming intelligence and passion, than that of Mr. Elvin Jones. Elvin represented everything that was good and great about jazz and life: the swingin'est beat, the brightest smile, the warmest (and most sweat-stoked!) embrace... Elvin was the life force of our music. And as hard as it is to imagine life and jazz without his bodily presence, he lives on in the tremendous body of recorded work he left us, and in the memories of those who were lucky enough to know him or see him in person. Elvin Jones left the world a much better place."

Elvin came to visit Weather Report when we were soundchecking in Japan on my second tour there with the band. He picked up Zawinul in one arm and Wayne with the other and lifted them both up off the ground at the same time for a real Elvin hug.

Despite the adversities he faced in life — as a black man in America, as one-half of a racially-mixed couple (his wife and now widow, Keiko, is Japanese), for being imprisoned unjustly — he seemed to meet life and all who admired him (and who didn't?) with a warm smile and an open heart. Keiko was not so quick to forgive or forget an insult. She complained to me and my wife Mutsuko that no publisher in this country would put out the book she wrote that chronicled, catalogued, and detailed many of these hardships and inequities. Keiko went on and on about this, so I thought I would change the direction of the conversation a bit by asking her, "Keiko-san, what was the name of your book?" "Name of book?" she replied. "Name of book, *America, Fuck You*, THAT name of book!"

19. Yamaha

Back when I was playing in Kenton's band (circa 1974), one horn player after another began playing Yamaha instruments. Pretty soon, Stan's entire saxophone section and half of the brass players were all using Yamaha horns; the bass player had a Yamaha amp. When the Kenton band was touring Japan, a couple of the Yamaha horn designers came to meet with Stan's Yamaha-playing musicians to ask their opinions and get their feedback. Most of the guys were simply polite and thanked Yamaha for making such a fine instrument, but one of the saxophonists insisted on demonstrating something or other to these two hapless Yamaha designers stuck in a backstage dressing room with him, and he was honking away on this baritone saxophone HONK! HONK! BLAT! BLEAT!, relentlessly trying to get some unreachable note out of the horn, and we're all wondering what in the world is going on, but we know that the Yamaha guys are here and so no one says anything in protest. But finally Stan bellows from his dressing room: "SOMEBODY KILL IT AND PUT IT OUT OF ITS MISERY!"

Although I was very happy with my Slingerland drums at the time, I must admit that I was feeling a bit left out of the Yamaha party. But when I asked their U.S. rep, "Hey, what about the drums? How are they?" he replied, "You might want to wait a few years." As suggested, I did wait. Four years later, while doing my first Weather Report tour in Japan, the band was invited to visit the Yamaha factory and R&D center. Joe Zawinul, Jaco Pastorius, and I got on a Bullet Train early one morning in Osaka and rode to Hamamatsu where the now legendary Takashi Hagiwara, or "Hagi," met us. After receiving a tour of the piano factory (amazing), we were led to a small studio where there was a Yamaha synthesizer, a drumset, and an electric bass that was made fretless thanks to the all-night filing efforts of a dedicated craftsman. So the three of us jammed for a while, and then looked at some catalogs with Hagi while sipping green tea and jockeying for swag (free T-shirts and the like). Since I had come to Japan with a brand-new Slingerland kit, I was not tempted to change drum brands, yet was impressed by what I heard and saw that day.

photo : Shigeru Uchiyama

Two years later, for one of my then-frequent trips to Japan, I was informed that this particular jazz festival would not provide for the transport of my drums to Japan, and that Yamaha would be supplying all of the drumkits for the concerts. "Okay," I thought, "Here's a chance to really check out Yamaha drums." I should mention that, by this point, I was not so happy with several aspects regarding my Slingerland kit, especially the hardware. Almost all of the hardware designed and made in the USA during those years suffered from poor engineering and manufacturing standards; I was having one problem after another with ever-bulkier cymbal stands, hi-hats, and bass drum pedals. And so I arrived in Japan during the summer of 1980, was greeted once again by Hagi, got a nice Yamaha T-shirt — and then I saw the drums: Beautiful. British racing-green finish on birch with hardware that was sharp, intelligent, and elegant. A cymbal stand that did anything yet only required a finger's strength to tighten. The choir of angels' voices began going "Aaaaahhhh" at that moment and I soon became a Yamaha artist.

A few weeks after that festival experience in Japan, a truck pulled up in front of the house I was renting in Los Angeles and the driver asked, "Are you expecting some drums?" And I replied, "I guess so. Er, well, I wasn't expecting them so soo…." My words were cut off as the driver said "Here!" and began handing me box after cardboard box, each of them with the name YAMAHA printed in large red letters. Two drumsets' worth of drums. My first Yamaha kits were yellow-lacquered birch, and they looked and sounded great.

After that, I played Yamaha drums with the likes of Weather Report, Steps Ahead, Freddie Hubbard, Kenny Wheeler, Steely Dan, Joni Mitchell, Boz Scaggs, Kate Bush, Gary Burton and Pat Metheny, the Yellowjackets, Michael Brecker, Diana Krall, my own groups, on movie dates, even with the BBC, Berlin, and London Symphony Orchestras. I felt a kinship with their instruments. A drumset is much like a car, and whether you prefer a BMW or Porsche, Mercedes or a Lexus, when it's your car it makes you proud, and you can spot one on a busy highway in seconds.

Yamaha pioneered the wave of signature snare drums in the industry (my Limited Edition 4x14 Birch signature snare was the first of these that Yamaha produced), and dreamt up some clever alternative drumsets like the HipGig (portable) and Club Jordan (cocktail) kits with the assistance of drummers like Rick Marotta and Steve Jordan. Other innovators like Dave Weckl, Steve Gadd, Al Foster, Roy Haynes, Manu Katché, Russ Miller, et al, contributed to the collective design inspiration. Yamaha eventually offered several signature products with my name and design imprint: the FreeStanding StickBag, the 4x10 Sopranino Snare Drum, and 4x12 Soprano Snare Drum.

However, it was during a botched music industry trade show introduction of a new version of this add-on snare that my drum company switch got set into motion. The big annual music industry tradeshow known as NAMM is often a "perfect storm" where such upheavals can occur — often regrettable, but inevitably for the better, I suppose.

Yamaha, unlike the Zildjian Company, had no single patriarch in the traditional sense, but if one man could be said to have been the heart and soul of Yamaha Drums it was the now-retired Hagi. He lived and breathed Yamaha. While it may never be apropos to use the cliché "those Japanese are clever people," it can be said that Hagi was one of the cleverest people in the biz. He's the reason several generations of drummers played Yamaha. To be honest, once Hagi was no longer in the picture, things seemed to change at Yamaha, and my needs and expectations were changing as well. Interestingly, it would be a cymbal stand that would once again speak out to me with enough import to force me to rethink things and switch loyalties and brands, this time to the American-made Drum Workshop drumset, manufactured just one hour up the road from our home. And just like anything else in life, the success or failure of an association can depend on location, and/or the relationship to the people behind the product...

20. Drum Workshop

photo : Rob Shanahan, courtesy of DW

While my saying goodbye to a drum association of twenty-five years, Yamaha, and saying hello to Drum Workshop caused a bit of a stir in some quarters, I tried to remind people that with everything else going on in the world my changing drum brands was not of such cosmic importance. Still, this was a big change for me. I became enthralled with DW and their beautiful instruments and hardware. There is a tremendous amount of passion and expertise at DW, and a total willingness to try new things, combined with the ability to make any possible improvements or modifications to the instruments in short order. I feel extremely lucky to be in such inspiring company. This instrument has allowed or even forced me to make new choices when I play, and I'm liking the way I'm sounding more than ever before. A musical instrument is, ultimately, about the final result in sound. I feel more creative, more focused, more "free" as a musician. I can't think of a much better thing to say about an instrument beyond "it makes me play better."

My move did not involve money. The only "business" was the opportunity to work with a company that was interested in responding to my requests in terms of drum and hardware design. DW is a fantastic company in that respect, too.

It was the DW flush-base cymbal stand, specifically reminiscent of the type of hardware jazz drummers were using in the early 1960s, that lured me to DW's door (or, more accurately, to their NAMM display booth). I had played on a drumset "du jour" while on tour a few months earlier, a kit that had three of these cymbal stands as part of the setup, and I enjoyed playing on them so much that I sent an email to my wife after the gig about those cymbal stands. Ah, sweet nothings. At the same time, the good people at Yamaha had turned a deaf ear to me when it came to my asking, then begging, then hollering for them to make such a cymbal stand (light in weight, better-sounding in my opinion because it allows everything to vibrate freely versus the perfect/non-vibrating quality endpoint that had become the holy grail in most drum hardware design ever since the 1980s), to the point where I offered up an old Ludwig stand from the '60s for the Yamaha engineers to copy and replicate. Of course, that was ill-mannered on my part and didn't help matters any. In any event, while leaving the NAMM show for the day and the year, feeling dispirited by our morning meeting at Yamaha that went poorly, my wife and I walked right by the DW display where I saw MY holy grail in drumset design, that flush-based cymbal stand, whereupon founder Don Lombardi proceeded to nearly tear his booth partway down just so he could pull the stand off the wall and show it to us; and as Don was enthusiastically demonstrating this and that, my wife turned to me and said, "THIS is how it's supposed to be." Don offered that he had always respected my relationship with Yamaha, but would I ever "want to come visit the factory in Oxnard?" I replied, "Sure. How about next week?"

My switch occurred around the same time I was doing an unusual amount of film recording (for me), working on the films *Mission Impossible 3* and *Spiderman 3*. Hollywood loves a good sequel, and so do I. It might be fair to say, then, that with my having professionally started off on Slingerland drums when I was 18, switching to Yamaha when I was 25, and then playing DW, this was an appropriate debut for "Peter 3" in the studios.

My first public appearance playing my own DW drumset occurs in Rome, Italy at the Casa del Jazz where I am appearing in concert with the Lounge Art Ensemble, a trio I shared with saxophonist Bob Sheppard and the late bassist Dave Carpenter. The drums take some getting-used to. I write an email to my wife after the concert, confessing that, with all of the Italian drumming fans in the audience — all of whom had seen and heard me play Yamaha drums for the past 20 years — I felt like I had gone to a party with another woman, and everyone there saw me not with my wife but with this other woman, my girlfriend. And she wrote back right away: "Your DW drums are not your girlfriend, they are your daughter."

That aside, it's hard not to think of DW and "passion" in the same thought. Beautiful, beautiful, beautiful wood. For all that is said about different drum and cymbal brands, however, when I expected DW drums to sound a certain way, they would meet that expectation. Now that I have different expectations, I imagine a different sound, and it seems I'm able to get that without a problem. So I got on the other side of my prior experience or prior expectations that I put on the instrument. In other words: as long as a drum or cymbal is round, the chances are pretty good that it can be made to sound good, especially if the musician has that sound in his or her head. The aesthetics complete the picture. Life is too short not to feel good about what we do, how we do it, and whom we do it with.

Other important music-industry relationships include Evans Drumheads (my first official endorsement deal and ad). Evans heads were the Kenton band heads, so that was how I discovered them. I flirted with a rival company's products for a few years but returned to Evans. Originally run by Mr. Bob Beals out of his Dodge City, Kansas factory, the heads are now designed and made at the impressive D'Addario & Sons manufacturing compound in Long Island, New York. Everything about these guys and their products will appear in any dictionary if you look up the phrase "state of the art."

My drumsticks, brushes, and mallets are made by Vic Firth and company. Vic was the timpanist for the Boston Symphony Orchestra for many years and is the consummate musician, businessman, innovator, and friend. He markets several models of drumsticks bearing my name, two of them bearing the results of a lot of thought, testing, and morphing over time — my signature "Ride Stick" in particular being a very popular model.

It was Bob Beals who told me back when I started my family: "You've got to find a way to make money while you sleep." The signature musical instrument is a fitting way to participate in the success of a design concept along with your name. "Win-win" solutions are my favorite.

Now let's go back to those Slingerland days.

photo : Fred Erskine

21. Slingerland Drums

The Kenton band played all sorts of venues, from concert halls to shopping malls, jazz clubs to Elks Lodges. It was at an outdoor shopping center gig in Illinois that one of the reps from the Slingerland Drum Company, Brad Morey, came to see and hear Stan's band. The drummer before me, Jerry McKenzie, was a Slingerland-sponsored artist. I was brand new on the scene and only had my Ludwig kit that was, admittedly, not quite up to the task of driving that band due to the sizes of the drums. But I literally pushed the pedal to the metal with that drumset. Stan was not hesitant to recommend me to Brad, saying within earshot, "You'd better grab this kid before another company does." In fact, the Ludwig company was making a mild overture, but I recall that I may have asked for too much too soon during my lunch meeting with them following my touring the factory in Chicago. Soon afterwards I enjoyed another tour of a drum factory, this time in the Chicago suburb of Niles where Slingerland drums were made. Brad dazzled me on the tour; everything seemed friendlier and more promising in that well-lit, humming, and buzzing factory. The combination of tradition and innovation appealed to me, and Brad outlined what the company would like to do for me in terms of promotional consideration (advertising) and, of course, drums.

My mother reminded me some years later that I had expressed the wish that I could one day have enough drums to stretch all of the way from Atlantic Avenue to the Boardwalk (a long two blocks), and that wish has come true and then some, I would guess.

But it was time for me to get my first Slingerland drumset, with an appropriately-sized bass drum (22-inch, with two heads, of course), a 13-inch rack tom with 16- and 18-inch floor toms, new hardware, in the color I had always wanted my Ludwig kit to be (but the local music store in Atlantic City only had the natural maple), dark mahogany!

The kit was ordered, and when the Kenton band made its way back to the Chicago area, there was a brand-new set of Slingerland drums set up and waiting for me at the gig (in a hotel ballroom). Man, they were beautiful! I sat behind them and adjusted the individual pieces as best I could — this was a new car I would be driving — and meanwhile the audience entered and the Slingerland people sat down at a table front row center to see what this new kid drummer was about. Brad Morey had been the only Slingerland person to have actually seen or heard me play, and it was on the strength of his word combined with Stan's admonition that I got the deal. It was proof-in-the-pudding time for the President, Don Osborne, Sr. (whose son, Donny Osborne, Jr., was and is an excellent drummer in more of the Buddy Rich style than could be said for me). Oh yeah, Buddy played Slingerland Drums at the time, too. So, there's Don Osborne, Sr. seated right in front of me with his arms folded across his chest, and we begin to play — and his face is getting a more sour look every four bars or so.

The kid holds the sticks matched grip!

I wasn't sure what was wrong, but I decided just to concentrate on the music (and the new drums) and not worry about the expression or body language of this guy, and then all of a sudden everything was okay. That's because the tune changed from a "Latin" beat where I held the left stick in a "matched" or similar manner to the right hand, and instead began playing in the "traditional" grip manner, much like the way marching snare drummers used to hold their sticks. Well, after that, everything was fine. Drum industry folks loved the Kenton band. It was a good night out for them and a great feature for their instrument: We toured constantly, played a lot in schools, and were still deemed musically relevant at that point in time, so why not?

Thus began my Kenton, Maynard, and Weather Report eras' association with Slingerland.

22. I Leave Kenton

After three years and five albums with the Kenton band — and several love affairs — it was time to get off the road. My parents' marriage had been falling apart, and it was all becoming too distracting to travel and play concerts and see one or both of them whenever the band would return back east and endure their incessant hostility and arguing — too long of a story to go into, even for a book of this size — and so I landed back home in New Jersey, not sure of where to go or what to do next. Another big band? That seemed to be my entire identity at the moment. What else was I but a big band drummer? A sideman? A person who had gotten so used to writing the word "drums" after signing his name that it became habit even when I signed a poster in Weather Report. I needed a change of perspective. I got that by visiting my sister Lois, who was by then living in Caracas, Venezuela. A month there, followed by a couple of weeks in Las Vegas, and then a month back in New Jersey, I knew what I wanted to do: go back to school.

Professor Gaber welcomed me with open arms and made my re-admittance into the university system as smooth as possible; he even loaned me some of his furniture. Before I knew it, I was back in Bloomington, this time with my Slingerland drums and a bunch of Kenton posters to hang on the wall of my small rented house, and an armful of bad drumming habits engendered by three years of hitting the drums as hard as I could. But here I was, back in school, the one professional in the bunch who had left a gig to return to his studies while everyone else seemed to be chomping at the bit to get out of the place. All of which made for some interesting bedfellows and classmates.

Most of all, the year centers around my trying to figure out my identity as a musician and person while my professor concerns himself with these issues as well as the pure mechanics of my playing (which have become quite un-pure), and so we go back to the drawing board where I might relearn how to strike an instrument and maybe even reacquaint myself with practicing.

Gaber assigns me to the Philharmonic orchestra, where future rock drumming avatar and star Kenny Aronoff is playing timpani. I'm playing the Chinese temple blocks. Gaber comes up on stage after the performance and goes 'round the percussion section, saying things like "Bravo" to one player, "Terrific job" to another, and so on, while I patiently await my own accolade. When he finally reaches me, he only says, "I wanna see you in my office first thing tomorrow morning," and strides away. "Now what?" I think to myself, in addition to, "That was nice…" And so I drive into school early the next morning and knock on Gaber's office door. He answers after a moment and beckons me inside, and starts, "Why were you hitting those things so hard last night?" I had no good answer for him.

I spend the remainder of the year at Indiana working on the practice pad while enjoying being in one place for a while. I make good friends at school and also benefit from the opportunity to take a Japanese culture class. My first visit to Japan with the Kenton band made a tremendous impression upon me, and I'm curious to learn more about the place. It might seem strange for one to learn about *bunraku* in Bloomington (*ikebana* in Indiana), but that's what I do. I'm digging on being back in school and have every intention of studying and finishing my degree this time around. The road to the road is paved with good intentions, I suppose.

Near the end of the academic year, Maynard Ferguson's management called and asked if I would like to join the band. As I was back at school after three grueling years on the road, I politely declined the invitation — three times. I finally agreed to join the band for only a summer tour so I could return to school in late August, and so I flew to Chicago with my drums to meet Maynard and the band. With one rehearsal under our belts we played in concert at a jazz club in Chicago, and the audience included many friends and members of the music industry who were in town for the summer NAMM convention. It was all too much fun, being in the drumming/driver's seat once again, and I would remain with Maynard for two years of touring and recording.

23. Maynard Ferguson

The first time I heard Maynard Ferguson, I was sitting in front of the family phonograph player. The year was 1963 and I was nine years old. My older sister, who was dating a jazz musician at the time, brought home an album titled *Color Him Wild*, and I sat in awe and wonder at the stratospheric melodies and bravura cadenzas that soared above a relentlessly hot band with a hip and burning rhythm section. Maynard was wild! His big band was more like a big small group, driven on this and other recordings by drummer Tony Inzalaco. Great players like Willie Maiden, Slide Hampton, Jaki Byard, Rufus "Speedy" Jones, even Joe Zawinul and Wayne Shorter, were all sidemen on Maynard's bands. But, as great as those players were, or as hip as the arrangements sounded, it was Maynard who astounded the ears of anyone who listened.

By the time I got to high school, Maynard had left the USA and traveled to India and then to the United Kingdom, where he put together a terrific band of British musicians. The music was a reflection of the times, when jazz met rock, and his U.K. band could swing and rock most convincingly. During my first year on the road with Stan Kenton, at the tender age of 18, I got to hear Maynard's band live when we split a concert appearance at a jazz festival in Wichita, Kansas.

The great drummer Randy Jones was working with Maynard at the time, and I was already a fan of his playing from the *MF Horn* album series. After I greeted him with effusive compliments, he graciously thanked me and then proceeded to inform me that he and his mates were now going to get "pissed." USA vernacular or usage of that term had always meant "to become angered," and so I asked him, "Randy, why in the world would you want to do that?" Now, if I had known the true meaning of his mission, i.e., to get drunk, I might have asked the same question with an even bigger question mark! He just looked at me as if I were some sort of moron and took off to find a drink. Maynard's band played great later that night in spite of those pre-concert libations. Color me naïve!

Maynard was a completely generous bandleader, always featuring his sidemen with great fanfare and pride for each show. Maynard had fun and made sure that his band and audience had fun, too. His trumpet prowess was as much natural talent as it was his study and practice of Yogic breathing techniques, enabling him to do the otherwise impossible on his instrument. Maynard was like Paganini, Horowitz, Enrico Caruso, Art Tatum, Buddy Rich, and the angel Gabriel all rolled into one — with the showbiz touch of Louie Armstrong (or Liberace) to boot! Despite his prowess and his hard work on stage, Maynard always found the time to be the complete gentleman. "Gracious" is the word that comes to mind; Maynard Ferguson was one very gracious human being.

As mentioned, it was on Maynard's band that I met Jaco Pastorius, which led to my being invited to join Weather Report. Ironically, Maynard recorded an arrangement of the Weather Report hit tune "Birdland" shortly before my departure. On that same recording (*Carnival*), we did a cover version of the Earth, Wind & Fire tune "Fantasy," and I came up with a beat during the chorus of the tune that I would soon use to good effect with WR on the tune "Black Market" (one of the few signature beats I can lay claim to after all of these years). It was with Maynard where I first encountered and began to learn the how and why of playing to a click track; many thanks to guest studio musician Steve Khan who taught me that the "click track is your friend." It was also with Maynard where I saw the wondrous effect of a great artist and bandleader in action, where audiences sat with that same look of awe and disbelief on their faces that I felt when I stared at our family's stereo, listening to the greatest trumpet player this world has ever seen or heard.

During the two years that I worked for Maynard, he was always kind and welcoming to my parents and friends. Maynard treated every player's family or girlfriend like honored guests whenever they were brought 'round to meet him. Maynard was also, as stated above, incredibly generous to his sidemen in terms of sharing and shining the spotlight on them. Contrary to some other bandleaders of the time, Maynard always made sure that the guys in his band got their due. Upon hearing the tragic news of Maynard's passing, I dug out an old videotape of a television appearance the band made in early 1978. After one of the songs we played, Maynard was being interviewed by host Mike Douglas, and he steered one of the questions to provide the opportunity for him to heap praise upon his trumpet section, and use his few seconds of TV bully-pulpit time to promote music education in schools.

One funny story took place during the midst of the making of his studio album *Conquistador*. Maynard's popularity was growing by leaps and bounds, due not only to all of the hard work and time he and the band put in on the road, but by the success of these increasingly "studio" studio albums. In other words, experienced studio musicians were primarily making these records. Naturally this caused some disgruntlement in the band; being on the record was the "cookie" or reward for all of those hours spent on the bus! And some guys were grumbling louder than others. Now, this was all occurring just as I joined the band in mid-1976. But it didn't help matters when I had coffee one morning in New York City with my old boss Stan Kenton; when he asked me what I was doing in New York, I answered that I had some time off because Maynard was busy in the studio making an album. Stan realized that Maynard's guys were not making the album, and so he called Maynard up and gave him a hard time about it. So, Maynard is starting to get sick and tired of hearing from his band, and hearing from his old boss, about the fact that studio musicians are making the album.

Now, a week or two outside of New York, we finish playing this concert at a small university, and while I'm packing up my drums some fan walks up to me and asks me about the new album: "Hey, is the new record going to be you guys or some studio musicians?" And I answered him honestly (but without rancor), "Oh, it's mostly studio musicians…" and carried on packing away my drums. Apparently, this guy then found Maynard outside the bus and gave him a hard time about it. Maynard had finally had it with all of the grumbling about studio musicians, but he did not suspect it was me (the new guy) who had caused this latest ruckus; he thought it was one of the brass players. As the bus pulled away from the concert hall and headed towards a music fraternity reception, he got on the bus P.A. and asked, "Hey, who told someone that the new album is being made by studio musicians?" Innocently, I immediately raised my hand and said, "Oh, that was me, Maynar…." And before I could finish pronouncing his name he lit into me, the language and emotional tenor almost rivaling that heard on the infamous Buddy Rich cassette tapes. Wow, it was intense. But he eventually started backing off, probably realizing that it was me he was yelling at and not someone else. The tirade wound down meekly, and he signed off on the intercom. This was followed by total silence on the bus for the remainder of the ride to the reception. Needless to say, the party was not much fun, and I began to question whether I was in the right place; maybe I should go back yet again to college!

A sleepless night followed, and I wondered what I should do. The next morning was going to be a day off and Maynard would sleep in until noon or so. Imagine my surprise to hear a knocking at my door at 7:30 A.M. and to see a well-dressed Maynard standing there. He began by mocking himself in a jazz-musician-caricature way, alluding to his confused state of mind, etc., when all of a sudden he got deadly earnest and looked me right in the eye and said, "Did I yell at you last night?" I answered, "Uh, yeah." And he stuck out his hand, saying "I deeply apologize, and I hope that you will forgive me." MAYNARD FERGUSON got up at 7 o'clock in the morning on a sleep-in day so he could begin MY day with an apology. I knew then that this was a good man, a great man, to work for and learn from. And I enjoyed the remainder of my two-year stay with him, always revering his talent, wit, and graciousness.

The album *Conquistador* went on to become a number-one hit for Maynard, thanks to the success of the cover arrangement of the theme from the movie *Rocky*, "Gonna Fly Now." Studio drummer Allan Schwartzberg supplied the disco beat for that, but the band enjoyed the ripple effect of the recording's popularity, playing to packed concert houses and school auditoriums for many years to come.

The world lost its most astounding trumpeter at 8:00 P.M. on August 23, 2006, when Maynard Ferguson passed away in a Santa Barbara hospital, surrounded by his daughters. The news of Maynard's death traveled swiftly, reaching the backstage area of the Hollywood Bowl where several Maynard band alumni, myself included, had just concluded a concert in tribute to Maynard's old boss, Stan Kenton. When my wife came backstage to congratulate me on the success of the concert, she knew right away that something terrible had happened. With tears in my eyes, I relayed the sad news that had reached me only minutes earlier. His passing marks the end of an era: there are no more big band leaders of his generation or stature. We all lost a great artist, and I lost a friend. Maynard was probably the best boss I ever had.

Quotables

Elvin Praises Peter

Citing three cymbal players he admires: (Philly Joe Jones, Roy Haynes, and...) "Peter Erskine, I think, has a real deep, fine quality of touch with the cymbals that I admire, I enjoy... He brings you, makes you highly conscious of the kind of instrument, of the respect that he has for that instrument."

Jaco Praises Peter

On a British radio program he proclaimed: "Unbelievable. This cat can play no more drums than nobody."

Joe Zawinul Praises...

"Peter had the goods. He was a wild, crazy kid, but he had the goods! Peter was great!"

"Peter plays like an octopus. Peter didn't have to be broken in. He did like we did. When Wayne joined Miles he never had a rehearsal. When I joined Cannon, the record company just sent all of his albums over and I learned the music."

"Peter can really play very loose and relaxed, and being a big band drummer helped us a lot. He had some big band chops. It was one of the best periods. Erskine is a hell of a musician, man."

"Jaco was a fantastic player! And Peter was coming out fresh, paint still on him, fresh and exploring. It was a great, great group! For four people to play 'live' like that, I don't think there is too much around today to compare to it. I can say in retrospect — 'cause you never know when you're doing it — that was the height."

"*8:30* was one of my favorite records that we ever made! I love this record! I think at that point we had reached the height...that 'live' tour...every night was an event."

"We had finally reached a level of performing that surpassed most bands I've ever heard. Over the years we had always had great bands, but sometimes on stage we had a tendency to play a little bit too long. There was a period in jazz where everybody played real long; I think it was almost an illness. There was a lot of swimming going on. We tried to reduce the swimming somewhat and get more to the point. What we ripped off on the *8:30* album as a quartet, I think, was incredible! The *8:30* tour was actually the best tour Weather Report has ever done."

More Joe — no more Mr. Nice Guy

Manchester, England, November 11, 1980

Zawinul: "I'm really sorry, man. I apologize if I kept you up last night."

Peter: "No, Joe, you didn't keep me up."

Zawinul: "Are you sure, man? My room being right next to yours, and I was laughing so hard and making so much fucking noise and all…"

Peter: "No, didn't hear a thing. What was so funny?"

Zawinul: "Well, this band, ___ _____, was on the television last night, and these motherfuckers just sounded so bad. And ____ _____ ? (Joe mentions the keyboard player by name.) He should be arrested for being black and playing like that."

And even more Zawinul quotables

"I can play more than both those motherfuckers with one hand tied behind my back."

"I have the greatest ears in the history of music — greater than Mozart's."

"If you ever play like that motherfucker again, we'll kill you."

"If I hear you play that beat again I will have to kill myself."

"I don't give a fuck if he's 'nice'; I asked how does the motherfucker play?"

photo : Mutsy Erskine

24. Tokyo, Japan, 1978

Scene: a record store. Jaco and I have been visiting music stores and album shops with our tour interpreter, Mutsy, who we have stolen from the crew. (Her job was to translate for the crew members, but the band liked her so much we would always ask for her to accompany us whenever we wanted to stray outside of the hotel or concert hall.)

I notice that the record store has a copy of an album I recorded with Maynard a year before. There's a fusion production-tune extravaganza that has a lot of drumming on it, and I'm curious to hear it again and excited to play it for Jaco, and so Mutsy is put to the task of "sumimasen"-ing the store personnel and asking them to please play this album on the stereo system in the shop, and to play this specific song. They do this for us, and the music starts over the loudspeakers. All of a sudden, this tune I had been proud of is not sounding so good to me, and the musical seconds tick by like minutes. It doesn't take too long for Jaco to turn to me impatiently and proclaim, "This has got to be the dumbest fucking thing I've ever heard. Come on, let's get outta here," and that was that. Man, these guys didn't seem to like anything I played for them.

The only good thing about the excursion that day was that we were in Mutsy's company. I was getting a crush on her, but had already told her all about my girlfriend back in America, so...no dice, there. But I could not resist her and found myself snapping photos of her when she was working around the band.

Remarkably, this is the woman who would eventually become my wife, the mother of our two children, partner in all things, and best friend I could ever hope for.

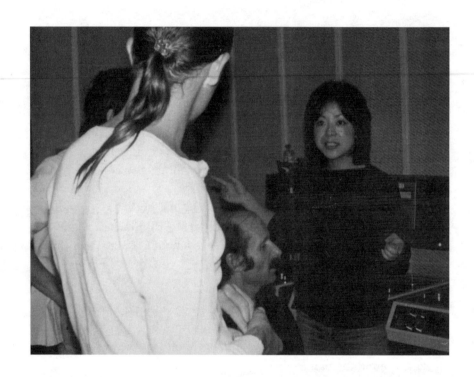

Here's Mutsy!

photo : Peter Erskine

25. Jaco

photo: Shigeru Uchiyama

Weather Report would tour Japan two more times while I was in the band, tours #2 and #3 with Bobby Thomas, Jr. added on percussion, or "hand drums," as he preferred to call his instrument. Bobby added a tremendous amount of excitement and rhythmic flow to the music.

By this point in time, Jaco, Joe, and I are hanging out like the Three Musketeers whenever the occasion presents itself, whether in the sauna of the Keio Plaza Hotel, the Chinese restaurant there that featured a terrific noodle soup with chicken ("You see that broth?" Joe pointed out. "It's clear; that's the sign of a great fucking soup"), or the "Let's Bar" after gigs in Tokyo. The three of us generally hung out quite a bit on tour, whereas Bobby and Wayne preferred the privacy of their hotel rooms or going out on their own. Every once in a while we'd all go out for a celebratory dinner after a show (or pair of double shows).

After a while, we stopped accepting invitations to after-concert receptions or parties at people's homes because those usually involved a long drive and, once we got there, it would be the three of us standing in a small circle talking about the music, and we figured we could just as easily do that back at the hotel.

Not that we were anti-social. Jaco used to get up at first light in Japan so he could sit in on one of the baseball games taking place at dawn across the street from the hotel in Tokyo.

Jaco could make friends (or enemies) anywhere he went.

Jaco and I were each half the age of Joe Zawinul and Wayne Shorter when we played together in Weather Report. Joe and Wayne were our elders and mentors, but Jaco had the genius, talent, bravado, and drive to compete with our jazz father figures — especially Joe — as an equal brother. We were family, albeit one with a scorecard. Touring, playing live or in the studio, eating, meeting people — the band ethos was to reign supreme in all matters large and small. Jaco's flame burned bright during those days that I knew him. And like any kind of fire, it consumed much of the oxygen surrounding it.

It's hard to believe that he's been gone now for twenty-five years. What music he might have created had he lived a longer life! His musical legacy has been served both ill and well since his death, with various albums — many of them bootlegs — being released, the bulk of them following his death consisting of poorly-recorded live gigs at a time when he was sick and not playing anywhere near his best. His ascendency in Weather Report and the time periods before and immediately after the band were when he galvanized the world of music with his talent and his ideas and his audacity.

One of the more common questions I'm asked during my travels is, "What was it like to play with Jaco?" In a word, it was thrilling. A general rule of thumb in music is that the company we keep on the bandstand or in the recording studio can help propel us to ever-higher heights of musical excellence and understanding. And the experience of being lucky enough to work alongside Jaco provided all of that plus more. Still, as outstanding and important as that association was and remains for me, a quarter century now since his untimely death, I count myself as being blessed to have been able to work with a number of great musicians.

Jaco Pastorius was certainly the brightest shining star in the constellation of musical personalities that I've encountered, bass or otherwise, and he made certain that our collaboration was always fun and challenging. He was a good friend. And his innate and studied sense of time, as well as his rhythmic execution, was the clearest and best articulated imaginable. The fact that Jaco started off as a drummer when he was young, and was an avid and astute listener, gave him an understanding of the beat that few bass players will ever match. The reference to "listening" is an important one. Jaco counted Frank Sinatra as well as Bernard Purdie as his influences; Johann Sebastian Bach and Igor Stravinsky were every bit as important to his education as were bassists Jerry Jemmott, Chuck Rainey, Ron Carter, and James Jamerson. Jaco was well educated, and he was completely instinctive. He was serious, and he was fun. He could play rock-solid rhythms, and he could lyrically "sing" on the bass. Meanwhile, his sixteenth-note execution was unparalleled. He could play in the style of many of his heroes, and yet he conceived, created, and composed a language on his instrument that was as revolutionary as it was evolutionary. His "Caribbean beat" on the bass consisted of conga drum patterns played on the bass, interjected with lyrical melody lines that somehow never interrupted the groove.

What was it like to play with Jaco? It was, like, one lucky four-year-plus moment for me. I'm sorry that we cannot enjoy the mighty musical magic that he would have provided had he lived a longer life. Ultimately, the question of "what was it like…?" only makes me miss him all the more — nobody like him before or since.

I got to do a fair amount of recording with Jaco in addition to the Weather Report albums, most notably in the living room of Jaco's home in Deerfield Beach, Florida. It was there that we recorded "John and Mary" from his masterpiece album *Word of Mouth*. With a remote truck parked in the driveway, and steel drum players and percussionists positioned throughout the house, we tracked that song in one take, as I recall. The toughest part of the session was getting everyone indoors — we all wanted to go swimming! A lot of other music was recorded during a memorable few days there; every morning began with a run down to the beach, followed by some fresh grapefruit juice back at his house, and then we would begin to play. Jaco had a strong vision for this album. But his dedication to it would not prevent us from shutting down work each night in time for him to jump into bed next to his wife, Ingrid, and catch Johnny Carson on *The Tonight Show*. The rest of us kind of peered into the room to watch the opening monologue before going to bed, ready for the next morning's "WHO LOVES YA, BABE? Come on, we're going to the beach!" at sunrise. Finishing up the album in Los Angeles, it was interesting to see Jaco's creativity at work, as manifested in such things as his conducting an orchestra, or setting off firecrackers in the studio's echo chamber, or overdubbing voice and Chinese koto parts!

Of course, Jaco's influence continues to extend far and wide, and any number of bassists I've worked with since those halcyon days of Weather Report bear his musical mark. For a while, it was difficult for me to listen to most anyone else play the electric bass, especially the fretless form of the instrument, without mentally comparing them to him. But several bassists' personality and sound were so individual as to command my immediate enthusiasm and respect. Among them I would certainly count Will Lee. Will is one of those musicians who always makes the other musicians sound AND feel good; he positively has always made my drum tracks sound better than they might otherwise have turned out. How does he do this? Well, his rhythmic sense is so commanding that he seems to be able to "visualize" the entire arc of a song's velocity and feel. He listens like nobody else, and his knowledge of the popular musical vocabulary of the last fifty years or more is as deep as anyone else's I can think of. Instinct, knowledge, skill, and feel, all wrapped up in someone with a great sense of humor. I'm beginning to sense a trend here.

In any event: what was it like to play with Jaco? It was, like, a real groove.

And now the circle makes another round: my nephew Damian Erskine, son of my sister Nancy and bassist John Worster (who was playing with the Kenton band when I joined), is a tremendous electric bassist who is making a lot of (good) noise in the music world. We just toured South America and made an album with pianist Vardan Ovsepian. I'm only sorry that Damian's grandfather Fred is not still with us to enjoy this family and collaborative moment. Let's hear it for the bass!

Recent revelation: I was listening to a rare live recording of Jaco with Wayne Cochran and the C.C. Riders on the Internet, and the drummer in that band was Allyn Robinson (he's still playing in New Orleans; he was a young guy at the time, maybe a couple years older than me), and when I was listening to this I realized that Jaco must have felt a comfort factor hearing me play because I used to listen to Allyn in college on the album *Cochran*. Allyn was an influence on me, and so we played some things similarly. But I also did the bebop thing, and Jaco must have thought that this would be cool to have a guy who plays R&B the way Allyn does but also does the jazz thing. I'm just speculating.

Jaco's band Word of Mouth was going to become famous just like that, by word of mouth, according to Jaco's master plan. Had Jaco's mental illness not manifested itself so destructively, he would have enjoyed a very popular band indeed. One can only despair at the thought of the lost music and comradeship that his death is responsible for. Be that as it may, I tend to remember Jaco with a smile because he was one funny man, and his life force was incredible. Jaco was an artist on the bass, on the drums, at the piano, composing as well as on the sketchpad. He drew this portrait of me in no time at all.

One time the band was playing in Tempe, Arizona at a place called Chuy's Night Club, and the emcee there announced the group as "Jaco Pastorio's World of Mouth Band." We all agreed that the guy had at least gotten part of that announcement right.

Jaco was the kind of guy who, when playing a friendly game of softball, would time an easy outfield fly ball catch so that it would become an all-out onslaught of a diving, sliding through the mud and grass with his gloved hand outstretched all of the way catch. Jaco loved drama and he liked to make people laugh. During an after-concert dinner in Oslo with a bunch of CBS reps, Jaco quietly excused himself from the table and went into the restaurant bathroom with a container of dental floss. He came out and sat down without saying a word, his face wrapped super-tight in the invisible string that caused all sorts of ridges and lines and bumps so that he appeared completely disfigured but in a hard-to-put-your-finger-on-it kind of way. He used to call it "String Face," and it was pretty funny. Or shocking. Jaco was Jaco, that's for sure.

Jaco, according to Jaco, was never too loud. Whenever Joe would complain about the volume of his bass, Jaco would protest by pointing to the knobs on his acoustic 360 amps and say, "Do you see that? It's set at exactly the same volume I played behind Phyllis Diller and Bob Hope at the Sunrise Theater in Florida. I'm not too loud."

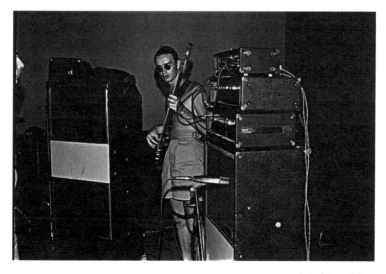

photo: Shigeru Uchiyama

26. Weather Report Attitude

photo: Shigeru Uchiyama

Weather Report was as much about attitude as most anything else. Of course, it was all about the music first and foremost, but the band saw itself as symbolic of what was truly hip and good in music and in life. Neither Joe nor Jaco were shy to proclaim themselves, their work, or their colleagues as being "the greatest" in the world or "in the history" to anyone. You spend enough time around that and it begins to sound fairly normal.

When we were "on," we were untouchable. I remember standing in the departures/immigration line at Japan's Narita airport after one of our very strong tours there, and there was the great composer, arranger, and keyboard player Dave Grusin. While the band was usually quite polite to most colleagues (and Jaco and I were both big fans of Grusin's writing), because Dave had apparently been in Japan as part of some other band's tour — playing some form of West Coast soft-jazz-fusion (probably with guitarist Lee Ritenour) or producing some Japanese artist (possibly Sadao Watanabe), then he would get the cold-shoulder treatment from the guys. Maybe all of this was merely going on inside of my head and I was the only jerk to have recognized Dave in line and chosen not to acknowledge him, still, none of us said hello. We could be a full-of-ourselves if not prickly lot. Modesty, for the most part, was not the band's credo.

Scene: a popular nightclub in Australia we've been told about where a good local band is playing. Jaco and I get out of the taxi and I begin to head to the back of the line waiting to gain entry. Jaco says, "Hey! Where you going?" and he motions me to join him as he walks up to the door of the club where a bouncer stands guard. Jaco tells him, "My name is Jaco Pastorius and I'm the greatest bass player in the world, and this is Peter Erskine who is going to be the greatest drummer, and we're with Weather Report and we want to come in," and just like that the velvet rope slides out of the way and we are admitted into the club — no fee and no wait. Jaco was not shy.

All the same, Joe would show great deference to any older musicians, especially jazz legends, some of whom were jealous about the band's success or bitter that their music and musical ways appeared to be going the way of the dinosaur (only to be reborn to some great extent during jazz's neo-classical period that began in the mid 1980s). Zawinul would get visibly excited at the mere sight of Woody Herman across an airport lobby. "WOODY HERMAN!" he yelled to the distant bandleader, who heard him and, taking one hand off his by-then-necessary walker, weakly waved in return. Joe proudly looked back at us and thumped his own chest vigorously with a clenched fist, saying, "Survivor! Woody Herman is a SURVIVOR."

I caught Joe in plenty of simmering or heated discussions with older jazz gents. Joe never showed disrespect to them and would patiently try to explain what it was that he and Wayne were trying to do with the band. One of them was the legend Milt Jackson, who was speaking with Joe in good animated humor, standing in a crowded bar located in the lobby of Copenhagen's Plaza Hotel. The band was scheduled to have its one formal dress-up dinner of the tour in the hotel's fine restaurant, an event we had been looking forward to for weeks. Our dinner reservation time was a few minutes away. The rule was to dress up for events like this, and I had on my favorite suit as I chanced upon Joe and Milt in the midst of their discussion. I politely nodded to Milt and tried to show my respect, pretty much just by keeping my mouth shut. Well, along comes Jaco, and now it's the four of us standing there while Milt replies to something Joe said, and Jaco decides to disabuse Milt Jackson of a dearly-held assumption or conviction, which is bad enough, but then Jaco notices that Milt's eyes are not focused on him — I suspect that Milt Jackson suffered from the eye condition known as strabismus — and so Jaco slaps Milt's torso with the back of his hand while saying, "Hey, man, why don't you look at me when I'm talking to you?" Jaco then shrugs to no one in particular and walks off towards the restaurant door. I can't believe what I've just seen and walk off after Jaco, too embarrassed to stick around. We join the rest of the band and crew for dinner and proceed to order and dine — all of us except for Joe, who is stuck out in the lobby, buying drinks for Milt Jackson, all the while trying to calm him down after Jaco's insulting behavior. Joe often had to clean up after our messes; as for this dinner, Joe was lucky enough to finally be able to join us just in time for dessert.

Another time, it was our excellent tour manager Brian Condliffe who unintentionally caused a terrific stir, all of which added to the macho/strutting image of the band. The band was playing a late afternoon set at the JVC Jazz Festival in Saratoga Springs, New York in the large shed indoor/outdoor venue, a somewhat rare appearance for us as we did not normally share the stage with other bands due in large part to the magnitude and complexity of the setup. Notable exceptions were festival appearances in Havana, Rio de Janeiro, and Montreux — all of them problematic for one reason or another — but the band liked to have a full day for set-up and soundchecking prior to a concert. So, in order to make this gig do-able as well as for safety concerns, a solution was worked out in advance where the stage-side areas would be kept clear of anyone not directly associated with the band's crew — in other words, no casual glimpsing or listening was to occur by other musicians or their friends, et al, on the bill.

The band plays a killer set, and we depart the festival grounds in fairly short order to ride the tour bus back to Manhattan while the crew packs up all of our gear. In a celebratory mood, we congratulate each other on a successful summer tour of Japan and the USA, on a successful gig, and toast to a successful few upcoming days in the recording studio. As we drink, say *salud*, and smile in the front lounge of the bus, Brian Condliffe (who had extensive touring experience with Led Zeppelin prior to working with Weather Report) wants to join in on the discussion, climbing back from his usual seated position of shotgun.

"So, guess what happened while you guys were playing."

Zawinul says with gusto, "Tell us, Brian!" and takes another sip of whatever we're drinking.

Brian, "Well, you remember we had to close off the side of the stage to everyone but the crew," and this, of course, was not hard to remember since the concert was just a couple of hours prior. "So a security guard comes up to me and says, 'Hey, I'm having a problem with some guy who refuses to leave the backstage area,' and so he takes me to where this guy is standing, and I go up to him and politely offer, 'Excuse me, sir, but I'm certain that you'll enjoy the show much more from out front,' and this guy says, 'I want to listen to Joe and Peter from right here.' So I say, 'Well, I'm sorry, but no one is allowed to stand here, and so I'll ask you again if you would please leave this backstage area and find yourself a seat out front.'" Zawinul is loving this; the band's road manager is kicking the ass of some jerk while the band is kicking the audience's ass. All of this seems perfectly right to Joe, and so with the blessing and encouragement of his "Go on, Brian!" and smile, our road manager continues: "And so this guy says, 'Do you know who I am?'" This is met by guffaws from Joe and the band, as we love the pomposity of this apparent idiot meeting the irresistible force of our ass-kicking road manager (who was, for visual clarity's sake, a fairly short fellow). Brian goes on, "No, I DON'T know WHO YOU ARE,' and this guy says, 'I'm Mel Lewis,' and so *I* say...." At this point I look over at Joe in a panic, and he looks stricken as though someone has just poisoned his drink, but Brian doesn't notice and he merrily goes on: "Oh yeah? Well, WHO'S Mel LEWIS? Ha ha ha, ha, and...."

Joe looks really sick, but there's no stopping Brian. "And so he says, 'If I can't stand here and listen to Joe and Peter, then my band is not going to go on,' and I say, 'Sir, I really don't give a good goddamn whether your band goes on or not'...." By now it's REALLY apparent how much damage has been done. Brian laughs at the end of his story and the bus lounge gets really quiet. He looks around with a kind of, "Uh, what happened?" look, and no one says much else for the rest of the trip, except for maybe a softly-muttered "God damn" from Joe as he shakes his head in disbelief.

This was on a Sunday. Joe spent all of the next night at the Village Vanguard where Mel's band was playing, apologizing to Mel and staying out of respect to hear the music instead of doing whatever Zawinul might have normally done on a night off in New York City.

More Attitude & WR World-View

Zawinul: "Always be good to the people who handle your bags and your food."

Jaco, walking into my hotel room and seeing my girlfriend's photo propped up by the bedside: "Man, you are pussy-whipped."

Zawinul, commenting upon Keith Jarrett's audible moaning when Keith shows overwhelming appreciation of the first chord he's played in a televised piano improvisation: "Let me tell you something: I've been playing the piano for a long time, and there's no one single chord that's that fucking hip."

Jaco, upon my requesting that gin and tonic be added to the band's dressing room rider: "Gin and tonic? What do you think this is, a rhythm and blues band? Forget it!"

Zawinul, after news of the Jonestown massacre hit the newspapers: "You know what? I can't wait until next week. Why? Because that's when *Time* and *Newsweek* magazines will come out with color pictures of this shit."

Zawinul on the bus while trying to get me to take a lit hash pipe from him for a hit on our way to a concert in Berlin: "Here man... Here man... I said, HERE MAN, goddammit!"

Wayne, as Boris Karloff bowling (elaborately imitating Karloff in a scene from Howard Hawks' *Scarface*, but in a Karloff-ian voice more reminiscent of the actor's later years): "Wu-atch this one…"

Zawinul dismissing an invitation to go to a museum: "Culture? I AM culture!"

When the guys wanted to really emphasize how good something was, they would add "in the history" to the accolade; e.g., "This is the greatest bowl of soup in the history." I like that.

27. Weather Report's Contentious Ways

...certainly extended to its relationship with the press. The infamous *DownBeat* magazine cover story from 1979, where the band took issue with that magazine's one-star review of *Mr. Gone*, was no exception. For those who don't remember that review, interview, and the incredible number of readers' letters that followed, some context may be helpful. The band had completed its tours of Japan, Australia, and Europe as a quartet and was halfway through a U.S. tour, on its way towards making a live recording at the end of the tour on the West Coast and, all in all, feeling its collective oats. Because of the high ticket demand, second shows were being added to concert dates. (The band didn't pay me any additional money for these tacked-on concerts; I don't know if Jaco got any extra dough or not.) We were working hard, playing most every day, and getting the best feedback from audiences, fans, record company executives, and Joe and Wayne's peers (the most important ears to us).

We were invited to meet with a writer from *DownBeat* for a cover story interview and a lunch on the second of a three-day engagement at Chicago's Park West club. I remember Joe being quite enthused about this opportunity for the band; he loved *DownBeat* and was all but certain that we would be treated as conquering heroes by virtue of this new band's touring successes, the release of the new album, etc.

So we met the writer for lunch at a Mexican restaurant that's located not too far from the band's hotel, and after shaking hands and as we began to seat ourselves at this large round table, writer Larry Birnbaum said, "Um, your new album, *Mr. Gone*, is getting a one-star review in the magazine," and he turned on his Sony tape recorder. We were dumbfounded and felt blindsided by this; we totally did not expect this bit of news, and so the guys really let this poor writer have it. I was the new guy in the band, so I stayed quiet throughout most of the interview — besides, Joe, Jaco, and even Wayne were not so eager to let this matter rest. So the lunch was not so great, and the interview was not so great, but the resulting magazine sales, according to what former publisher Chuck Suber told me a year later, were the best in the magazine's history. People couldn't get enough of us not getting enough stars in that poorly reasoned and written review.

As macho as the band was, its feelings got hurt pretty easily, and not just by *DownBeat*. An African-American woman fell asleep in the front row of a concert we were giving in Houston, Texas, and Joe was obsessed with our playing "hip" enough to rouse her from her slumbers. (He was the only one in the band aware of this woman's being in the Land of Nod, but he kept the concert going for an extra 30 minutes or more by extending every song so it could reach some sort of unobtainable climax. He was not happy, and neither were we.) She'd probably had too much to eat or drink before the concert — who knows or who cares? But the band did take its music and itself quite seriously while, at the same time, being the first to laugh at itself when it could. A one-star review in *DownBeat* was no laughing matter, however.

But a funny thing happened on the way to the forum. While promoting the *Night Passage* album, we are informed in Rome that the Italian press would like to meet with the band for a press conference just prior to the concert on October 24th, 1980 in Rome's Palasport venue. The press conference may have been planned for some time, but the band is informed of it on short notice. There's some going back and forth whether we want to do it, but our road manager urges the band to go ahead and meet the press. "On one condition," Joe states. "No questions about Miles. We are not Miles' children, and fuck Miles — we are doing our own thing now. We're fine as long as there are no questions about Miles, okay? First Miles question and we're out of there." The promoter agrees.

So we file into this large-sized room that is filled with journalists and photographers. Seems like a good opportunity to promote things, but, of course, the first question from an Italian journalist in Italian has "Miles" in it all over the place. A fluke or a challenge? Who knows, but the other three guys look at each other like "should we or shouldn't we?" and then Jaco takes the lead, as I recall, and initiates the band walking out of the press conference. Seemed premature to me at the time, but I now realize that this was, on some level, exactly what everyone wanted — press and band alike.

One year before this, I'm reading the contents of a five-page article that has just hit the newsstands; *Musician* magazine has printed a diatribe against the band, mere months after it was proclaimed in those same pages that we were the "best live band around." But the writer covering 1979's Montreux Jazz Festival has a bone to pick with the band and he airs it with extreme prejudice. I'm shocked and amazed to read this piece, as the writer avers things that are simply not true: misrepresentations about the band and crew and our concert performance there — saying, in essence, that while Montreux is an iconic locale for nature and jazz to commingle each idyllic summer, these arrogant bastards blew into town and spoiled the entire experience for everyone.

I remember this writer because he was scheduled to interview Wayne at Montreux, and that was set up and ready to go, but for some reason he kept calling Wayne at various hotels, awakening him during the touring leading up to Montreux, and Wayne kept complaining about the incessant phone calls to our road manager. That would be Mr. Condliffe of Led Zeppelin (and Mel Lewis) fame. So when this writer appeared backstage at Montreux and Wayne realized who he was and said, "Hey, this is the same guy who's been calling me up for the last two weeks," it didn't take long for said writer to be unceremoniously hustled out of the backstage area and treated as *persona non grata* for the rest of the night.

Meanwhile, Joe did not want the Festival to videotape that evening's performance because he had been having so much bad luck with his synthesizers and the electricity in France. (It turns out the electricity in Switzerland was just fine, but Joe didn't want to chance it.) So there was a big to-do about the band being able to use the Festival's lighting system if we were not going to allow the Festival to videotape us. Too bad, because it was a terrific set and it should have been documented. In any event, our crew created a clever work-around, but that got represented in the article that we had somehow sabotaged the Festival's lighting, damaging equipment that did not belong to us, etc. Simply not true. The writer also claimed that, yes the band played brilliantly, but people didn't know what to make of it, and as proof he mentioned that when he asked trumpeter Randy Brecker what he thought of the WR concert, Brecker had merely shrugged. I knew that Randy had shrugged because he missed all but part of the encore; I saw him later that night, and he complained to me that he had gotten the start time of the show wrong. And so on.

I'm reading this to Joe over the telephone, all five pages, and he occasionally interjects something like, "Wow, did he really say that?" or, "Wow, he really said that, huh? Go on." When I finish reading the article I expect him to explode in rage at the other end of the phone line. Nothing. So I ask, "Well, what do you think of that?" "What do I think of that?" he roared back. "I think that is one of the greatest write-ups this band has ever gotten!"

"Huh?"

"Let me ask you something: how many pages in that article?"

I answer, "Five."

"And how many musicians were at Montreux?"

"Uh, let's see, the article mentions around five hundred…"

"And who is he talking about for four of those five pages?"

"Weather Report."

"That's right. You're too young to understand this yet, but we just got a Marlon Brando review, man. Marlon Brando don't ever get no good reviews, and he's a bad motherfucker."

28. Living in California

Weather Report was definitely a door opener. Shortly after joining the band, I moved to Los Angeles from my temporary digs in Wewoka, Oklahoma (where my just-divorced Mom had moved in order to live close to her sister and niece. My parents wound up remarrying each other again a few years later!). By that time, I had already appeared on three recordings, thanks to Jaco and/or Wayne. When Joni Mitchell called Jaco to collaborate on the Charles Mingus project she had been working on and wrestling with, having recorded and re-recorded the same tunes with a number of different bands, Jaco insisted that I be the drummer. His insistence was good enough to get me on the album. I also played on Michel Colombier's eponymous album as well as on a Jon Lucien recording (my drum tracks did not make it to album release). With my relocating to L.A., renting a small house in Encino, I was all set to begin life as both a member of Weather Report and life apart from the band as a free-lance musician.

Joni Mitchell's *Mingus* album is memorable for many reasons, first and foremost because of Joni. She recounts our first meeting in a book, describing how Joe and Jaco were athletically tossing a Frisbee inside the confines of an S.I.R. rehearsal studio and that, when the high-velocity Frisbee would be directed at me, I would shrink away in fear so as not to possibly jam a finger (much like my basketball/gym class in high school) — *mea culpa* for being a wuss, but now might be a good opportunity to explain that during my Little League tryout I got hit in the forehead by a line drive and have forever since been ball-shy. But Frisbee-shy though I was, Joni took a chance on me drumming-wise. And I was, of course, a huge fan not only of *Hejira* but also of her earliest works, notably *Blue*, and feeling grateful for all of the lonely nights that music got me through.

Longtime producer and engineer Henry Lewy was at the helm in A&M Studio D. Add Jaco to this and I was in heaven. Wayne came in on the second day to play with us and to overdub on what we did on day one. We recorded everything in two afternoons. The pianist at the first day's session was British arranger Jeremy Lubbock. After we cut the first tune, "Goodbye, Pork Pie Hat," Jaco came over to me and said, "Who is this guy? I'm going to call Herbie and see if he's in town." So Jaco ran off to the telephone and called Herbie Hancock and essentially invited him to the session to take over. I seem to recall that Jaco got Joni's blessings before or during this whole process; it all happened very quickly. The take with Jeremy was good, and of course it was awkward when he found out that Herbie was on his way, but by then it was too late. So he left and Herbie entered and promptly replaced the piano on "Pork Pie" with Jaco smiling like crazy in the control room. We were all smiling and now all in on the conspiracy — no regrets and full steam ahead. We cut the rest of the album in fairly short order, a considerable achievement if not hasty, as the *Mingus* compositions are not the easiest songs to wrap one's head around — these were the longest song forms I'd ever encountered, and I'm still not sure that I was up to the task. My contribution, if any, was to be a good anchor for Jaco.

I also came up, unwittingly, with the rhythmic solution for the blues tune "Dry Cleaner From Des Moines," which was not enjoying much success in its previously recorded bebop form. Sitting at the drums between takes of another song, I started playing around with a beat that I first heard on a Gabor Szabo album that Bernard "Pretty" Purdie played drums on (an oddity titled *Jazz Raga*; the tune was "Walking On Nails"), but I was using brushes instead of sticks, as Purdie had done. So I was just sitting there, amusing myself by playing and experimenting with this, when Henry Lewy came running out of the control room and yelled, "Keep playing that same beat!" Then he ran to get Jaco and we cut the basic track to "Dry Cleaner" in fairly short order — first take, as Jaco preferred — and the thorny question of how to record that blues was solved. Jaco wrote the horn chart and recorded it later at Tom Scott's Crimson Sound studio in Santa Monica (former home to the Beach Boys' studio, with lots of "hippie wiring" still extant by the time we were in there, according to engineer Hank Cicalo). That triplet ending? Jaco played it, as he had done for the intro, and just gave me a wink to cue me for the end.

However the album is judged artistically, I feel that it showed remarkable bravery on Joni's part to put her imprimatur on this music in the midst or arc of her pop album career. Joni has great artistic integrity. The album also marked an interesting point in the use of electric instruments to play jazz, the *Mingus* collaboration putting a spotlight on the musical sensibility and aesthetic choices made with electric bass and piano — and the success or failure of that — and put a spotlight on the whole jazz-meets-pop thing that still resonates today. It's not the easiest album to listen to, but I give Joni high marks for it. As far as I know, it began her musical relationship with Herbie Hancock and was also the starting point for the tour the following summer that would result in the *Shadows and Light* video.

By the way, that was supposed to be Weather Report on that tour. Jaco had helped to set everything up, and Joni and her management agreed to have Weather Report open the concerts with a set, to be followed by our backing her on the *Mingus* and other material. Well, as I begin planning for this great news I get a telephone call from Joe Zawinul.

"The Joni Mitchell tour thing is not happening. I told Jaco that he can do it because of his long association with her, but I don't want Wayne or you to do it."

"What happened?" I asked.

"I just told her we ain't no fucking L.A. Express." [*click*]

Thanks, Joe.

photo: Peter Erskine

So WR tours Europe that summer but not the USA, save for concert appearances at the Berkeley Jazz Festival and the first-ever Playboy Jazz Festival at the Hollywood Bowl. While Jaco is on tour with Joni and a terrific band consisting of Michael Brecker, Pat Metheny, and Lyle Mays with Don Alias on drums, I am getting to know my girlfriend Debbie Sabusawa very well, and we spend a wonderful summer together in L.A. I've done my first television-show recording session up in the ancient TTG Studio near Sunset and Highland in Hollywood. My high school harpist-friend Katie Kirkpatrick has recommended me for the date to composer Mark Snow (who would go on to fame with his theme and music for *The X Files* TV program) for an episode of the show *Family*.

I don't have a cartage company to haul my drums around town just yet, so I show up early and schlep my kit into the studio. Hey, this is the same place they recorded Frank Zappa's *Lumpy Gravy* and the *Basie Straight Ahead* album! I set up my drums and somewhat nervously await the recording session to begin. The commercial recording process and world are still new for me, and working with a click track (metronome in the headphones) is still a big fight for me, as I've done so much "live" playing versus recording work at this point. The rest of the small orchestra shows up and we begin, my drums in a small but open booth, and we're all wearing those old-fashioned Bakelite headphones like ham radio operators used to wear. When I hear my first "bumper" cue — that short piece of music that ends a scene and prepares the viewer for the TV commercial to follow — I laugh in appreciation and recognition. But I manage to miscount on one of the cues and play an isolated snare drum hit a beat early (on the "and" of beat 2 instead of the "and" of beat 3 of the bar). Snow does not hear it, but he asks the ensemble, "Everyone okay? Any mistakes or shall we move on?" I think that this mistake, minor though it may be, might cause a problem later on, and so I begin to raise my hand in guilty but helpful acknowledgement. From out of nowhere, a bass fiddle bow reaches into my drum booth and catches my upraised arm, pushing it downward with surprisingly great force. I look over to the direction from whence it has come and see that it is attached to the arm of bassist Buell Neidlinger, who is silently shaking his head "No" from side to side. I desist, we move on, and Buell is now happy.

We take a break at that point and I introduce myself to Buell. He asks me, "How is that bass player of yours? The one in that band?" (He was never willing to say Jaco's name out loud for some reason.) I laugh and say that Jaco's fine. Buell then asks me if I would like to join HIS band. I was a fan of Buell's work with Frank Zappa and the Boston Symphony Orchestra, and knew a bit about his history with Cecil Taylor's band in the '50s. And so I say, "Sure, I'd love to play in your band," but this news will come as a surprise to the band's current drummer, John Bergamo, famed instructor at CalArts, where Buell is also teaching.

A gig is in the works, and pretty soon I find myself in a recital hall at CalArts along with Buell, saxophonist Marty Krystall, harmonica player Peter Ivers, and pianist Don Preston, another musician whose work I admired with Frank Zappa. Since this is avant-garde music, everyone is acting pretty aloof and ultra-hip. Okay, I can hang with that. Preston is the most aloof, competing with Ivers for aloofness points. He's so cool that he brings a BEER into the gig and places it at the top of the keyboard range so he can reach it easily for refreshment. We're playing some free, beboppy swing, trippy music, and everyone is being pretty darn cool, but all of a sudden I notice a very un-cool franticism in the movements of Don Preston at the keyboard. He tears off his shirt and is desperately daubing at the keys of this once magnificent Bösendorfer piano; he has knocked over and spilled the contents of his Pilsner Urquell bottle directly into the keyboard action of the piano, and a small moment of jazz history is made: no jazz recitals will take place on that piano or in that concert hall for years to come as a result of this debacle. But I would go on to play for a few more years with these guys; I always enjoyed their free and iconoclastic ways.

Don Preston would call me shortly afterwards to make a recording at a small studio in Venice with my first electronic percussion equipment, the Synare pad (I had a few of them, and they can be heard on portions of the Weather Report *8:30* and *Night Passage* albums) while he played his full kitchen-wall-sized Moog modular synthesizer setup. We did some free-form improvisations. I still have the cassette dub from that afternoon. A few months later I called Don, asking him when I might expect to get paid for that session. "Paid?" he replied. I could only answer with a "Never mind…" Like I said, I enjoyed their free and iconoclastic ways.

Other live playing opportunities included some gigs at the legendary Donte's, Concerts by the Sea, and Lighthouse jazz clubs. Working with Joe Farrell leads to my getting to record an album with him in the famed Contemporary Records studio (which was really more of a shipping room with small playing area and even smaller engineering booth — but what a sound!). *Sonic Text* is the name of the album, and I still enjoy listening to it, with George Cables on piano, Tony Dumas on bass, and Freddie Hubbard on trumpet. FREDDIE HUBBARD! We get along well during those two days of tracking, and he kindly sympathizes with me when I read a review aloud of a just-released Weather Report album (the *Mr. Gone* disc) where the writer comments that there are 500 other drummers he'd rather listen to before he has to listen to me. I complain to Freddie that I can't even think of 500 other drummers (missing the intent of the hyperbole, I suppose), and Freddie says, "Damn — that's some cold shit. Aww, come on. Don't worry about that, man!"

The next time I would record with Freddie was on the George Cables recording *Cables' Vision* with Freddie Hubbard, Ernie Watts, Bobby Hutcherson, and others. We were back in the same studio complex where I had made my first recording with the Kenton band some eight or nine years earlier. I drove my drums to the studio and set them up, and was happy to see Freddie Hubbard, only this time Freddie decided to bust my chops. "Yeah… hey, ROOKIE! Heh, heh, heh, YEAH, alright there, then… ROOKIE!" And so on, like all day, and I figured that I didn't need an entire week of that, so…

The next morning I stopped by a liquor store on my way to the studio and purchased a bottle of really good cognac. As soon as I saw Freddie at the studio, I walked up to him and presented him with the gift-wrapped bottle, saying, "Here, Freddie, this is for you." He eyed me kind of surprised and suspicious-like, and asked me why I was giving him what was obviously a nice bottle of cognac. I replied, "Oh, for no special reason, man, other than respect for you." That did the trick and we were buddies from that day until the end.

One of the later times I saw Freddie, he stopped into the Catalina Bar & Grill in Hollywood to say hello — this would be in the '90s; I was playing there with Alan Pasqua — and when I asked him how he was doing he replied that he had just come back from a recording session for Cecil Payne, surprised to have gotten the call, however: "Man, I thought that motherfucker was dead!" We laughed, and he was in good spirits. In any event, the Contemporary Records association with founder Les Koenig's son, John, producing the dates and very kindly including me on these albums (Joe Farrell, George Cables, Joe Henderson), led to my own album. But there's more session history to discuss first.

29. Recording Session Stories

My very first experience in the recording studio was when I was 17 and a first-year college student. Our group, named Design, was made up of music students from Indiana University and the University of Michigan. Most of us knew each other from high school, and even though we'd only played a few gigs together as a band, we decided to make a recording to see what might happen. This was in early 1972, and it was a combination of rock, funk, and jazz: "fusion," in other words. We were really excited because the studio had an 8-track tape machine — imagine the possibilities! The result? A pretty cool tape that we could play for college girls that we'd meet over the next few remaining weeks of school — but that's about all we got from it. Hey, it still sounds pretty good.

A couple of months later I was standing in the middle of the large room at United/Western Studios in Hollywood, making an album with the Stan Kenton Orchestra. I have worked in that same room over the years, and nowadays it doesn't seem all that huge, but as an 18-year-old about to make his first professional recording, it was LARGE. There was and would be so much for me to learn about the art of making music, especially in the recording environment. I remember that I was self-conscious in regards to knowing that any take could possibly wind up on an album, and that I'd better play well every time. Still, I remember that I took chances while we were tracking; I couldn't resist the feeling that I might get lucky and play something really cool. When I listen to those moments now, however.... Well, those are the times I cringe. Live and learn.

That album was not something that the rest of the band really wanted to record — a DOUBLE ALBUM of national anthems arranged for the Kenton band by the very talented Bob Curnow, much in the style of the Ralph Carmichael-arranged Kenton Christmas album that I listened to so much in high school. But this was my first album and I was up to record anything. The band would schlep from Anaheim every morning following a late-night gig at Disneyland, set up and record for several hours, and then tear down, pack the bus, and drive back down to Anaheim, unload, set up, and play three or four shows there that night, and repeat the process for five days. Stan recorded like this a lot; a day off without concert or gig revenue was to be avoided at all costs, I guess.

The Kenton band recorded in Los Angeles or Chicago during my tenure with Stan; however, the Maynard Ferguson big band always did its recording work in New York City. One of the first times that we got to cut a track "live" and complete in the studio (this was the exception rather than the rule during the height of disco) was to record the Mike Abene arrangement of Sonny Rollins' "Airegin." We schlepped our instruments into the legendary 30th Street Studios of Columbia Records — the same room where Miles and Monk, Leonard Bernstein, and Glenn Gould, Tony Williams' New Lifetime, and countless Broadway show soundtracks were recorded. WHAT A VIBE, and WHAT A SOUND in that room. I took some time to walk around the room on my own, and I stood silently for several minutes just to get the "feel" of the room and its history. I've also done this at such studios as the Warner Brothers, 20th Century Fox, and MGM soundstages. I like to pay my respects to a place and its memories.

Mr. Gone was my Weather Report initiation, and I did drum, percussion, and vocal overdubs on the album as well as playing on "Pinocchio." But this did not fully prepare me for the real experience of being in the studio with Weather Report. A lucky accident while mixing the "live" tapes for the *8:30* album provided the opportunity: one of the engineers erased all 24 channels at a crucial edit point of one song, which ruined the piece and left us with too little material for a double album. So it was decided that we would go into the studio to record additional material. Back into the room with its carpet-covered walls and oh-so '70s lighting fixtures, I learned one of the secrets of WR's success: their operating rule was to always have some sort of a tape recorder "on" and recording all of the time whenever anyone was in the studio — meaning whenever the band was in the building; this was in order to capture any spontaneous bit of playing or musical exploration. So, a stream of musical consciousness was encouraged (as opposed to an engineer slating the tune, "Uh…okay… we're rolling! 'Weather Report, free jam,' take 2…"). This also encouraged and necessitated the creative use of editing, and that was how some memorable musical pictures were created. In fact, the title track to that album, "8:30," was initially captured on a cassette tape that was left running while Joe and Jaco started fooling around in the studio—

Jaco on my drums! I walked by the control room and heard them playing, and I rushed to the cafeteria and summoned the engineer to come and turn on one of the proper/multi-track tape machines. If you listen to that cut, you'll hear it go from black and white to full and glorious color; that's about when the real tape machine got turned on — my contribution to musical history! Anyway, we also recorded Wayne's tune "Sightseeing" during that week, and it's still my favorite thing that I've played on a Weather Report album. That album won a Grammy. We were on tour when the Grammy Award winners were announced; we didn't even know that we were nominated!

A funny story from *Mr. Gone*: Joe invited me to sit down, telling me that I could "sit down in the producer's chair" for a listen to one of the tracks. The engineer cues up the 2-inch tape of the title track that had a blisteringly cool Tony Williams drum track on it. Meanwhile, Jaco has cued up several lines of cocaine on a framed *Heavy Weather* gold album that he's taken down from a studio wall, and it sits partway on the mixing board and partway off the mixing board, as the mixing console is angled towards the engineer with a padded elbow rest to even things out. I start to sit down, feeling pretty lucky to be seated in the producer's chair for this rare listen, and I act the part of honcho by crossing one of my legs in exaggerated fashion. Of course, my foot hits the overhanging album cover with all of the blow on it and the drug platform goes up on end, flips into the air, and I hear the tape stop and the music goes "droo-o-o-p." The engineer, Alex Kazanegras, yells "You motherfucker!" as the drugs fall onto the floor, and I quickly follow them down on my knees, trying to salvage whatever I can of the precious white powder. Jaco later hits me up for a "loan" of $70 that I gladly pay in hopes of not getting fired for my clumsiness.

Other sessions in L.A. will include some film work for Henry Mancini and Patrick Williams, another couple of TV shows and, of course, the Weather Report and Jaco albums from 1979 to 1982, whereupon I followed Joe Zawinul's advice and headed east: "If you want to be a real jazz musician, then you have to live in New York."

peter...just found out that it was you
who said hello to me in studio D last
week....i offer my humble apologies
for not recognizing you...you looked
familiar ,but i didnt make the connection....i was pretty stoned and concentrating on dealing with michael
brecker and had shut out all other
things...please forgive me...
    i really dug the concert that we saw
at the SM Civic....the way that you have
integrated yourself into the group
and your contribution to the feel
and the sound ; just blew me away...
even the drum solo spots were exciting
to me....and i usually don't like drum
sbbos...your playing on joni's cuts
sound great and hopefully we will
continue that album next year...
...so hello once again and hope to
see you soon....

                    regards and happy
        holidays

A&M RECORDS INC., 1416 NORTH LA BREA AVE., HOLLYWOOD, CALIF. 90028

30. Go East, Young Man

The musicians of New York represented everything cool about professional music making as far as I was concerned, whether playing on recording sessions or jingles or television shows or Broadway albums or the New York Philharmonic with Leonard Bernstein. When I was a kid, I wanted to do what the musicians were doing. I wanted to be just like them and be able to do what they could do. I wanted to be Art Blakey, Shelly Manne, Don Lamond, and Sonny Payne. I wanted to be Sol Gubin, Saul Goodman, and Elvin Jones! Photos on albums showed musicians in Webster Hall or in the ballroom-turned-recording studio of the Riverside Hotel, or the legendary 30th Street Studio of CBS, or RCA's midtown studios — gentlemen in white shirts and ties. Mike Mainieri, vibist and founder of the band Steps (Ahead), told me that he and his jingle-recording cohorts helped to usher in the era where white shirts and ties were eschewed for tie-dyed T-shirts and fringed leather vests. And guys like Mainieri and Gary McFarland, with Warren Bernhardt on piano and a great drummer, Donald McDonald, along with such studio stalwarts as Chuck Rainey, Grady Tate, Bill Lavorgna, Bernard Purdie, Eric Gale, Ron Carter, Marvin Stamm, Jerome Richardson, and others, were the guys making the albums I was increasingly drawn to in the years before I went away to high school. My sisters had been dating plenty of jazz musicians who would bring the latest and hippest albums of the day to the house, including Miles and Coltrane LPs, but I liked this music that had other elements in it. Not just world, not just jazz, but with a pop backbeat. Think Beatles with really hip chord changes.

I've read that a person's musical tastes are pretty much cemented into place by the time that person is 15 years old. I suspect that this is true. I still love to listen to this music, as well as to the other recordings I collected during this formative time. Writer Jon Pareles asks: "Does love of music have a window of opportunity? Is there some moment in our biological program when popular music means the most, when we bond to 'our song'…the way baby birds bond to the nearest moving object?"

In any event, Mike Mainieri's music inspires me and keeps me company in high school. My girlfriend Anne and I hug each other to one of his songs, and I transcribe another to play on vibraphone for my senior recital. So imagine my thrill when I discover that Mike's son has come to one of the Weather Report shows in New York at the Beacon Theatre and suggests that Mike use me for an album he's producing of Japanese guitarist Kazumi Watanabe. I'm flown in for one evening's worth of recording, and the other musicians on that date include Warren Bernhardt on keyboards, Tony Levin on bass, and Michael Brecker on saxophone. We did this at Media Sound, a studio located in the building where Béla Bartók lived the last years of his life, the studio living the last years of its life there, too, as that locale is now a bar and dance club.

The session went well, and I am delighted when Mainieri calls again, this time to work on his next solo album. Others on the session that week include the keyboard players Don Grolnick and Warren Bernhardt, bassists Marcus Miller and Tony Levin, flutist Jeremy Steig, percussionist Sammy Figueroa, guitarist Steve Khan (who I know from my Maynard Ferguson days, the first professional New York rhythm-section studio musician to take me under his wing ["the click track is your friend"]), and my heroes Mike and Randy Brecker. We're recording in Power Station Studio A, the best room in the world then and now. For better or worse, I'm a change from the New York guys who normally work with Mike. My studio chops are still not nearly what they should be, but whatever I might lack in polish I make up for in genuine musical enthusiasm. I'm a fan of all of these guys, plus I'm a Weather Reporter — it's a good club to happen to be in. Every one of them plays great. Mike Brecker is truly outstanding, despite his being in the midst of some hard-core drug use at this point. The first morning, after we've gotten sounds on all of the instruments, we're still waiting for Mike to show up, and so a betting pool is created where the first thing Mike says will be either:
(1) I'm fucked;
(2) I didn't get any sleep;
(3) I can't find a reed.

We each picked the most likely thing Mike would say upon entering the studio. Imagine our collective pleasure and the guffaws that greeted Mike when he walked into the studio all of sudden, saying to all of us and no one in particular, "I'm fucked, I didn't get any sleep, and I can't find a reed!"

Don Grolnick and I hit it off really well during the week of recording. Still, I'm surprised to hear from him a few months later asking if I'd like to come to New York to work with his band at the Breckers' jazz club, Seventh Avenue South, for a week. Don had never led a jazz band, and this week-long gig in New York represented a real milestone for him. So he took a bunch of the money he had made and saved as a studio musician and invested it in having all of the music for this gig professionally copied, flew me in, put me up in a Manhattan hotel, and paid me well, plus put together a stellar band with such players as saxophonist Bob Berg, guitarist John Tropea, Marcus Miller or Will Lee on bass, and me. It was a fun week, the first of what would be many gigs at Seventh Avenue South. And as a result of this week, I'm asked to come and play with the kicks band that Mainieri started along with Mike Brecker, Don Grolnick, Eddie Gomez, and Steve Gadd known as Steps. They've already played and recorded in Japan. I fly back to New York for another week, and it's beginning to look like a move might be in order.

Meanwhile, life in Los Angeles has not been without its exciting moments. Jaco has been camped out in my rented home in the hills of Silverlake just east of Hollywood, during which time he has been overdubbing, mixing, tracking, and fixing, writing, and overdubbing some more, and mixing into the wee hours of the morning, and then coming back to this house I'm sharing with Deborah, sometimes turning on my stereo full blast at 4:00 in the morning to listen to his latest mixes of "Crisis" from his *Word of Mouth* album in the making — and Debbie as well as the neighbors have just about had it. I reach my limit when a vodka bottle gets thrown through a bedroom window one afternoon and Debbie says, "I can't take this anymore." She walks straight out the door and down the hillside to who-knows-where, and I'm late to a gig, so I stop looking for her and race over to the Music Center, where I play a very distracted concert. Jaco shows up telling me not to worry, that Debbie's come home, but I'm so angry at him that I tell him he has to leave. He follows me around the Dorothy Chandler Pavilion parking structure, where I can't seem to find my car, and all the while Jaco is walking five or six steps behind me. "I said I was sorry, man!" but I won't accept his apology. Maybe it's time to move to New York and change my scene a bit.

Debbie and I make the move. I'm still in Weather Report, and I'm still working with Jaco, and it looks as though I've got all of the scheduling worked out for the next few months so that there will be no conflicts of interest or calendar. Well, that was the plan, anyway.

photo: Peter Erskine

31. But First, Down South

Jaco's 30th birthday is fast approaching and he wants to celebrate it in style. *Word of Mouth* is complete, an album that was a long time in the making. In fact, Jaco was already planning his *Word of Mouth* album back in 1978 during my first tour with Weather Report. The band ran into the New York Philharmonic in Osaka, Japan, as we were all staying in the same hotel. Having gone to the opening concert of their tour, Jaco invited legendary flutist Julius Baker to his room, along with a couple of the Phil's esteemed percussionists, to play them some music and specifically to ask Julius Baker if he would consider playing flute on an upcoming album. Joe Zawinul stopped by the room, and while Jaco was preparing to ask Julius the Big Question, Zawinul was busy getting into a friendly argument with maestro Baker concerning who could get the "better flute sound": Julius on his flute or Zawinul on his synthesizer! Jaco pulled me out into the hallway, exasperated and saying, "I can't believe Joe is THAT rude!" But, to be honest, Julius Baker thought it was funny. And, of course, he agreed to play on Jaco's album; the orchestral tracks wound up being done in Los Angeles, and the L.A. Phil's Jim Walker as well as Hubert Laws did the flute tracks. The accompanying photo is of Jaco and me and New York Phil percussionist Arnie Lang, and, I remember the moment very clearly: Jaco was playing the opening vamp of "John and Mary" for Arnie. I felt lucky to be there, hearing the piece for the first time. Arnie merely turned and said to me: "This guy's never heard Aaron Copland, huh?"

As Jaco's posthumous website describes it: "On Jaco's 30th birthday (Decmber 1st, 1981), he held his own "surprise" party at Mr. Pip's in Ft. Lauderdale, Florida. This recording documents the birthday party concert with 11 tracks. The Peter Graves Orchestra and other Jaco favorites were brought together as The Word of Mouth Band for this spirited performance. Peter Erskine contributes liner notes for this release and is also the album's producer."

I produced the mix session that engineer James Farber should receive all credit for, with honorable mention going to recording engineer Peter Yianilos. I like to think that Jaco would have been pleased by the album's sound. The actual event was a wild and wooly affair; the recording captures the vibe pretty well and, if the reader is a fan of Jaco or Michael Brecker or Bob Mintzer or Don Alias — or me, for that matter — then the album is well worth hearing. There was a tremendous amount of energy and good playing that evening. I mean, check out "Invitation." Ferocious.

The next morning, Michael Brecker would enter rehab in south Florida, and a new era of sobriety would enter the musical universe I was traveling in.

Conrad Silvert © Conrad Silvert. From the collection of Ina Silvert Hillebrandt

32. Cue Now... I'll Take Manhattan

After the birthday gig, I return to L.A. to finish the pack for the move. There will be some more gigs with Jaco and the Word of Mouth band; the album is doing well enough despite Jaco's seemingly best efforts to derail its successful launch by alienating most of the staff at Warner Brothers. Wintertime is a heck of a time to move to New York, but move we do, subletting Warren Bernhardt's one-room studio that happens to be right next door to Steve Khan's apartment. I've made the move to New York!

The one-room apartment proves to be too small for Debbie, me, our cocker spaniel, Buffy, and my drums and newly acquired Oberheim OBX — a synthesizer (for composing), and Debbie decides that she should move out only eight months or so after we've made the move. Where I once imagined that we would be together for life, for some reason I don't fight her suggestion to move out. She'll go back to her family home in Chicago, and I'll eventually go back to my bachelor ways.

I forgot to mention that, during this time of our first having moved to New York, I have left Weather Report. In the middle of a Japanese tour with Steps in February, the best-laid plans of the upcoming summer touring schedule are bumping into reality: I get a phone call from Weather Report's management advising me that Joe and Wayne are determined to tour in the summer of 1982 despite earlier assurances that I could plan my '82 summer tour with Steps in Europe. And I'm enjoying playing this music with these guys. I've got a ton to learn, but the softer dynamic and, frankly speaking, nicer vibe of everyone is making a whole lot of sense to me. But now I have to make a decision, real quick. No help here. I think, and I don't think for too long and say, "Please tell Joe and Wayne that I'm going to tour with Steps this summer, so… I guess that means I'm leaving the band." To which management merely replies, "Okay, if that's your decision." I hang up the phone in my Japanese hotel room and I feel **FREE**.

I decide to go for a late-night walk and run into Michael Brecker in the hotel hallway. "Hey, Mike. Guess what?" "What?" "I've quit Weather Report so I can do the tour with Steps this summer in Europe!" Mike says, "Are you nuts?" and walks off.

Turns out that the Steps guys have a problem with commitments, at least as far as a band goes. What started out as an informal entity — a so-called "kicks" band — is risking evolving into a real band with long-range planning and commitments (that word again) and responsibilities, etc. Mainieri desperately wants the band to get to the next level, but Grolnick and Brecker are resistant. As a result, things are made worse by our having more and more band meetings to address this lack of commitment. Would have been simpler had we just shut up and played and took the gigs as they came, but bands are like personal relationships in that way.

Jaco had already made his departure from Weather Report, so I guess the writing was on the wall for me, but I hadn't made any plans one way or the other at that point. Still, the freedom experienced by leaving Weather Report felt really excellent. The other guys in Steps reacted more appreciably.

One of the things I most liked about being around Mainieri, Brecker, Grolnick, and Gomez was that they didn't scoff at the notion of my writing something for the band — contrasted with Zawinul who, upon officially welcoming me into the band at the end of our Japan/Australia/ Hawaii tour on a Honolulu hotel room balcony, looked towards the ocean horizon with me as we planned for the future. Anything was possible! Anything, that is, with the exception of my trying to write something for the band. After I had suggested that as a possibility, Joe's voice got sour and he cautioned me with a side-to-side shaking of the head (i.e., "no"): "You're going to have to be one hell of a writer to write for THIS band," and so that idea was put to rest for a while. But the Steps guys were cool with the idea and were already playing a tune of mine in concert. Okay, so it was a 12-bar blues in the key of C. But it was a start!

I've gotten ahead of myself. We're in New York and I'm writing music when I'm not traveling someplace. My in-town recording/playing career has not yet begun to take off aside from those Seventh Avenue South gigs — and I've got the chance to make my first solo album for Contemporary Records.

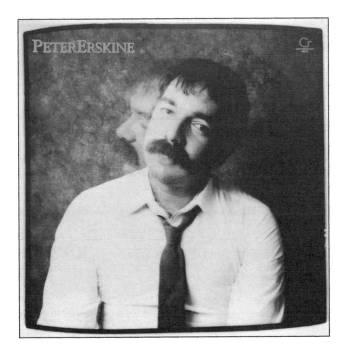

33. Peter Erskine: On the Record

The music I'm hearing and writing and playing has "Steps" all over it, and these are the guys I want to play on my album. Problem is, the band is getting ready to make its first record in the USA, and manager Christine Martin is shopping the band to the labels. I can't remember if a deal was already made by the time I'm getting ready to go into the studio for my own album or not, but a recording that's essentially "Steps" but not "Steps" is problematic, business-wise. I can't see any of this, as we've all been working together leading up to this moment, and I can only think of this in music terms. Debbie is working in Christine's office at this point, and she sides with Christine on the issue; I think this is where some sort of divide occurs in our relationship. Honest criticism of one another can be crucial in any relationship, but when it's time to stand by your woman or your man, well, that's the stuff of a real partnership — the kind of partnership I've enjoyed for all of the wonderful years of marriage to Mutsy, a state of wedded bliss that does not come overnight but does stand the repeated tests of circumstance and time.

Anyway, I'm going into the studio for two days of recording my first album, my girlfriend is treating me like I'm a jerk, and so is the manager for Steps. We try to come up with some band personnel workarounds, and so there are song limits imposed on who can do what. This is really complicating my first album experience, but guess what: this is what first albums are all about. The band includes Don Grolnick on synthesizer, Kenny Kirkland on piano, Mike Mainieri on vibes, Eddie Gomez on bass, Michael Brecker on tenor along with Bob Mintzer on saxophone, Randy Brecker on trumpet, and Don Alias on congas. The music does not sound like Steps, and I always knew that, but on paper I guess it didn't look so good. Regardless, we go into Europa Studios and record direct-to-2-track with multi-track backup. The only fault I can find with the album would lie in the weakness of my writing and playing in some spots, but the recording has stood the test of time pretty well. Famed photographer William Coupon, who has taken the photos of presidents and other world leaders, agrees to shoot the album cover.

The tracking is fairly painless — but being in charge of an album all of a sudden is like being a soloist in front of an orchestra for the first time or directing a film, all of them comparable to standing on railroad tracks with a train coming right at you while there's a tornado coming from the other direction, the telephone is ringing, and your pants are falling down. You hate what you just played, but you're not sure if what you played sucked or not, and why is the bass so loud, and who doesn't want to take a solo on the next tune? I want to end the first day early just as we're about to play "My Ship" with Randy Brecker, Mike Mainieri, Eddie Gomez, and Don Alias. It's all a bit too much for me to process, and I've had it (I think it was a phone call that did it this time around). So all of a sudden I say, "You know what, everyone? Let's call it a day and we'll see what we can get done tomorrow. Let's just CALL IT, okay?" Mike Mainieri calmly walks over to me with mallets in hand and says, "Don't be an asshole. Sit down and let's record this thing." We nail it in one take. Jaco would have been proud. It's still one of my all-time favorite tracks.

DownBeat magazine gives it a disappointingly lukewarm review. I dedicated the album to Deborah, but by the time it's released we're not together. I also dedicated the album to Joe and Wayne and Jaco but, as far as I know, none of them ever bothered to listen to it. As of this writing Kenny Kirkland, Don Grolnick, Don Alias, and Michael Brecker are no longer with us, but I'm grateful that their music lives on in a variety of places, my first solo album included. And here's something wild: photographer William Coupon has recently taken photos of my now-grown daughter Maya for her acting career. It's good when circles complete or overlap themselves. Sometimes it feels like my whole life is one big generously overlapping circle.

34. More Sounds in the Big Apple

I got my first "commercial" recording gig in New York when I answered a call to play orchestra bells and drumset on a jingle for a television commercial about pantyhose. Mike Mainieri did me the favor of strongly recommending me to the contractor who was hiring the musicians for that session; this guy was not familiar with me. So even though I agreed to do the date, I realized that I had no orchestra bell mallets in my possession, having not played the instrument since college!

The session was scheduled to begin at 10 A.M. the following morning at Automated Sound. At 9:45 A.M. I was two blocks down the street at Manny's Music store, pounding on the window for them to open up early so I could buy a pair of mallets (the bells were being provided by the studio)! I played drums with the small orchestra assembled for the date, and then I was asked to stick around for the orchestra bell overdub (cheaper for them to pay one guy doing both gigs rather than paying for a separate drummer and percussionist). The violin and flute players all left, and I positioned the bells in the center of the room while the assistant engineers placed the microphone in front of me and gave me a set of headphones. I noticed that the contractor came into the recording studio room and crossed his arms as he leaned back against the wall and stared at me as I was about to play this overdub. It was in the key of B (five sharps), on orchestra bells, which I had not played in 10 years' time. The tape began to roll and I started to play, thanking my lucky stars that I had practiced enough back in college to still be able to do this sort of thing. I got it in one pass, and the contractor came over immediately and gave me a hug, saying things like, "You can read! This is wonderful! I love a drummer who can read! Hey! You're a real musician! I love a drummer who's a real musician!" and so on. Three jingle dates later I stopped getting calls for marimba or bells and began working for this man exclusively as a drummer.

I learned a lot from doing jingles: professionalism, and being able to find the tempo and groove quickly in a piece of music (there's not a lot of time to spare in a 15- or 30-second spot for the groove to settle).

Another session that proved to be quite memorable was an album with Makoto Ozone, the prodigal pianist from Japan who played in Gary Burton's band. Gary was producing the recording, which was taking place in a very large mid-Manhattan studio (Clinton Studios), and guitarist John Abercrombie and bassist Marc Johnson were playing as well. One of the songs was a bit of an epic affair: very complicated melody and chords as well as structure, with challenging ensemble parts sprinkled throughout the piece. We rehearsed a few times in the studio and commenced to do a take. All seemed to be going quite well, and we had successfully navigated our way through the melody, guitar solo, interlude, and were deep into the piano solo when all of a sudden we heard "Oh shit!" and some out-of-time/out-of-key guitar strums; the universal indicator to STOP THE TAKE, right? Everyone groaned a bit, shaken out of our concentration and confidence in how well that take was going, and Makoto asked, "What happened? Why did we stop?" John Abercrombie, his face flushed with embarrassment, said, "Hey, I'm sorry Makoto, I got lost." Makoto demanded, "WHERE did you get lost?" Suddenly a voice appeared as if from the heavens; it was Gary speaking to us on the talkback mic that was being pumped through some very large speakers near the ceiling of this very large studio. And Gary said, "Makoto, if he KNEW where he had gotten lost, then he wouldn't have GOTTEN lost!"

photo: Peter Erskine

35. Common Denominator

Referring to when your playing is brought down to the lowest level of the circumstance, whether that be the poor playing of one of the other musicians or the tune being counted off at the wrong tempo, or something else just not being "right." We are usually our own worst enemy...

I was always highly dependent on the playing environment I was in. You know, good bass player, life is good; bad bass player, life's a drag. One late evening in New York, as I'm getting to know Mike Brecker, we wind up at Kenny Kirkland's loft and a jam session evolves out of the hang, just Michael on tenor, Kenny on a real beat-up upright piano with missing keys and notes, and me on a less-than-stellar drumset. No bass player. I obsess on that as soon as we start playing. No bass player. This would all sound a whole lot better if there were a bass player. I'm not in the moment or playing anywhere near my best; I'm playing so-so because there's no bass player, and I'm allowing that to prevent this from going anywhere. For too long I've been the kind of drummer who only sounds great when the band sounds great. We stop after a while and Michael looks over at me and says, "That's interesting." I ask, "What's interesting?" and he continues, "What's interesting is that I've never played with someone who, on one hand, can sound so incredible and yet, at another time, sound so bad." Of course, I reacted with surprise and hurt at his candor; I thought we were friends! He saw this right away and jumped in with, "I didn't say that to hurt your feelings; I just find it interesting, that's all." A sober Michael would handle this sort of thing with more sensitivity, but this Mike was telling it like it was and like he heard it. Food for thought.

And then I got it. Traveling down to Florida a year or two later to visit Disney World, I'm taken to the jazz club there where Zoot Sims is appearing with the local rhythm section, and the local band does not sound very good on this occasion. They sound bad, in fact. How will Zoot react to this? ZOOT SOUNDS GREAT. ZOOT SOUNDS LIKE ZOOT. And that's when it hit me that it is essential for any real musician to be able to play at a particular level of competence no matter the circumstance. That's the ticket: to have enough of a voice and enough faith in music and in your own sense of musical self and abilities that it doesn't matter.

It takes time for these lessons to take root and grow, to take hold and become a solid part of our fiber and being. Too often we're borrowing good advice and not yet living it. That's what growing older is all about, I suppose. And it's going to take a minute getting used to not being on the bandstand surrounded by Weather Report.

Meanwhile, when I think of people I admire, Mike Brecker's name is always at the top of the list.

36. Steps Ahead & New York City

Early in the band's career, a name change is necessitated due to the fact that some bar band in North Carolina already has the name "Steps" registered, and their buyout price is equal to the entire budget that Elektra/Musician has allotted for our debut album. Hence: Steps Ahead. By this time Don Grolnick has tired of the band meetings and demands for commitment; he begged: "Please, let's just keep booking gigs like we always have in the past, and I'll be there for them. Don't ask me to commit to leaving these other things I enjoy doing" (like Linda Ronstadt and, later/again, James Taylor). Things happen for a reason, I suppose, and so Don leaves and we need a piano player.

Eddie Gomez and I both volunteer the name of a young Brazilian pianist, Eliane Elias. We do a demo recording for Eliane along with Mike Brecker, which Mainieri agrees to produce. It's pretty much a done deal by the time we listen back to the first song. She's a great player, and she will go on to enjoy a fabulous solo career as pianist, composer, and singer.

Michael Brecker is studying composition from a classical composer and is dealing with a neck hernia as well as with his new-found sobriety, meaning that he's burning his candle at all ends by going to meetings while the band is on tour, etc., and already I'm marveling at what this guy has taken on.

Randy Brecker and Eliane fall in love and decide to get married.

We've made the album and are touring it when we can. These tours go better than the very first Steps tours, where no one connected the name of the band to the identity of any of the players in the band. And even though the new moniker for the group is still taking some getting used to, the music is catching on. The most popular tune by far is our opener, "Pools," composed by Don. And since this is a musician's musicians band, we are getting a lot of fans that play musical instruments — in other words. a lot of young guys with notepads. Young professionals are taking notice of the group, too, of course. One of Woody Herman's sidemen arranges "Pools" for Woody's big band, only he cannot remember the name of the song or group when he announces it on-stage, so he supplants the proper titling with, "Here's a tune by Pete Erskine and his Hot Five, and it's called 'Soup.'"

Eliane leaves the band to have a baby. Warren Bernhardt, Mainieri's keyboard partner for many years (and in many a band including White Elephant, L'Image, etc.) joins the band and we make what will be my favorite Steps Ahead album: *Modern Times*. Pre-MIDI but post-Weather Report, the band hits its creative stride and peak with this album. Blessed with a decent budget that grants us enough time in the studio but still forces us to be clever and non-indulgent, we spend long hours and all-nighters to craft this album, and we really feel like we're on the verge of making it as a group.

Coinciding with this is our producing of music tracks for a Jane Fonda exercise record. Her first two releases are huge hits, and this third album might just help us get our big break to a much wider audience. We recycle some music (or vice-versa: my composition "Now You Know" starts off as "Stomach, Legs and Butt," so-named for a series of ab, thigh, and buttocks exercises). The album and video are titled *Prime Time*, aimed for an older audience. Jane Fonda meets the band at the press conference/release party, unaware that Eliane is no longer in the band. She looks the band over and her only remark to us is, "Where's the woman?"

We go out on tour. Warren has been a studio musician for so long now that he's not sure he enjoys the rigors of the road, while Eddie Gomez has been a touring musician for so long that he is sick to death of the whole thing. This new music is requiring more and more equipment to be carried around in order to play it live. This is back in the days of being able to wave a $100 bill in front of a skycap and all excess baggage worries would disappear, but we still experience difficulties traveling with so much gear. Carnets and mismatching serial numbers on amps, vibes that get flown to Indiana while the band arrives in Utah, and so on.

Christine Martin, who meanwhile has discovered a then-unknown Stanley Jordan playing guitar on the streets of New York and made him a star, has gotten fed up with our prima donna ways and complaints and threatens to quit. Remember that big-band rule about ultimatums? Well, they don't work too well with small groups, either, and the band votes to accept her resignation, and now we're really on our own. Which is too bad because Christine did so many good things for us, and it was really fun to have someone to complain to or about!

The band makes a change from acoustic bass to electric when Eddie's finally had enough and the young, talented Tom Kennedy does a touring stint with us, but when we decide to change the line-up from keyboard to guitar (this band is becoming good at hurting peoples' feelings), Warren and Tom are let go and we schedule a series of auditions. Guitarist Chuck Loeb, fresh from working with Stan Getz's band and hot on the New York studio scene, grabs the guitar chair, while Weather Report bassist Victor Bailey kills it during the audition process — he's really great! Victor brings some much-needed young blood as well as soul into the group, as well as a fresh bit of Zawinul-inspired attitude. (When Mike Mainieri gives Victor some music direction that amounts to his telling Victor to listen to some folk albums in order to get the right vibe for a tune, Victor tells him, "You'll have to loan me some of your folk albums then, 'cause ain't none of that stuff in my listening library.")

We begin to cut the album that will become *Magnetic*. Grolnick is brought in to play, and we insult him by the fee we offer. Warren is brought back to play and I enthuse, as producer of my composition's overdub, how great he sounds, only to hear him mutter to the microphone during the taped count-off, "Yeah, well, if you like it so much then why did you kick me out of the band?" Chuck Loeb plays a terrific solo on one of Brecker's tunes, but it's a bit too "jazzy" all of a sudden and so we bring in Hiram Bullock, which hurts Chuck's feelings, of course. But we are all treated to Hiram's wonderful sense of philosophy when, as the last guitar note of his one and only take is ringing out, he asks everyone in the control room "So, was that everything you ever dreamed of?"

The band is a three-way cooperative at this point, but we all go our separate ways for the most part to work on our own tunes — never a good sign. With more than half of the album under our belt, we do a tour of Europe while playing the new music, and then we fly to Japan for the 1985 Madarao Jazz Festival.

photo: Ebet Roberts

37. Madarao, Japan

By this point in time I've had a number of bachelor adventures in New York and abroad — lovely women all, and apologies for the short shrift this book gives to the multitude of muses in my life. More about discretion than dereliction of duty, I am grateful to all who have held my hand.

One woman who may not be so receptive to this entreaty would be my live-in girlfriend, Mami, who flew from Japan to move in with me in my one-bedroom/two-story co-op apartment on 29th Street in Manhattan. It's a great place, and she and I have a lot of fun playing house, but my being away for much of the time with Steps Ahead is not good for our fledgling relationship. I'm afraid we both go our own ways without admitting to it — hmmm, similar to what's beginning to happen in the band. By the end of summer '85, the band flies to Japan and spends the first night in Tokyo, preparing to train and bus it from there the next morning to a ski resort in Nagano prefecture known as Madarao. That following morning, as I'm standing in the lobby, a Japanese woman comes up to me rather quickly and, looking me right in the eyes, she asks, "Peter, do you remember me?" And I, who normally hates that question and can't remember most people's faces and names very well after repeated introductions, I just blurt out, "MUTSY!" as though seven years' worth of time has elapsed in mere seconds from when we met during my first Weather Report tour.

Background: I had made the mistake of telling Mutsy about my girlfriend when I first met her — "mistake" in that I knew pretty quickly how strongly I was attracted to her, and knowing enough about the Japanese that she would never consider my attentions as anything other than scandalous or lecherous. Nevertheless, I could not help myself by that tour's end and I bought a dozen roses for her from the New Otani Hotel flower shop. This amounted to a lot of money in those days, especially for a not-so-incredibly-well-paid sideman, but I was happy to do this, smiling at the thought of presenting her with these beautiful flowers. Little did I think or realize that touring bands receive flower bouquets from fans all of the time in Japan, and so when I chose a quiet moment before the band's final concert appearance in Tokyo to present the flowers to her —

"Mutsy, these are for you!" — she merely accepted them and casually remarked, "Oh, thanks," and walked away. No kiss. No eyes filled with that soulmate-recognition-mirrored effect, she just walked away. "Hmmm," I thought, "THAT didn't go as planned." So that was that. Mutsy later realized that I had gotten those flowers for her and that I did not find them sitting around the band's dressing room. In the meantime, she had gotten married — to a drummer! — and I went on to love and live with two different Japanese women; I can only think that both of us were practicing for the real thing when it would finally come along. Destiny took my hand that morning in Tokyo, and destiny had the most beautiful smile in the world.

The festival is located high up in the mountains, but this does not prevent the temperatures from reaching incredible highs (ski resorts tend not to have hotel rooms with air conditioners). I'm in love and I don't care. But I don't know if she is feeling the same way about me. Victor Bailey finally solves this riddle for me when he points out, "Hey, you notice how she's TOUCHING YOU every time she walks by you? Check it out, man; I think she likes you." Sure enough, her next pass by me includes a soft touch of my arm, and all of a sudden I get it. Whoopee! We're in love, even though we don't know it yet. The beauty of the Nagano mountains combined with a full moon and too-little time that we have to steal away, all of these elements conspire to form a heady brew of dumbstruck love, and somehow I know my life has changed forever.

I fly back home from Japan — having sent a flower bouquet to Mutsy by Japanese FTD this time — with love in my brain, smile, and heart, but also a heavy knowledge in my heart because I know that I will have to confess this change of heart to Mami as soon as I get back to the New York apartment. The conversation goes like any of those conversations go: not well. I resigned myself to sleeping on the couch and telling Mami that she was welcome to stay there as long as she needed to — I would be traveling much of the time anyway — but that she had to go. But we're scheduled to visit my parents down in New Jersey the NEXT DAY, and I insist that we both go. So we take the bus from Port Authority to one of the Atlantic City casinos where my parents meet us. We all go to my parents' house. I can't wait to tell my Dad about Mutsy, while Mami and my mother carry on an awkward conversation. I think Mami has broken the news to her but isn't getting much sympathy; my Mom is happy at the news. The visit lasts for a day or two. And so…

Mami stays at the apartment in New York while I go to Europe to tour with John Abercrombie and Marc Johnson. I'm daydreaming about Mutsy the entire time. Imagine my shock when I get a letter informing me that she's called the New York apartment to leave a nice message for me, but a Japanese woman answers the telephone and Mutsy is terribly confused and hurt by my deception.

More fences to mend.

My propensity to live a double life — more accurately to live the life where I am while maintaining that other life where I was or normally would be, etc. — is getting complicated. But this is more important to me than anything in the world, so I explain everything to Mutsy. Bless her soul, she's an understanding and forgiving woman.

Mutsy and I finally meet face to face during a series of rendezvous, including my flying out to L.A. where she has taken part-time work as a translator for a Japanese animation company. (Mutsy was one of the most famous music-biz interpreters in Japan, having worked for Stevie Wonder, Queen, Earth, Wind & Fire, Rod Stewart, John Denver, Sting, and even Frank Sinatra, who personally requested that she do his on-stage translation during his shows in Japan.) I've neglected to mention the other best part of falling in love with Mutsy. Her son Taichi! And while long-past warnings of an instant family echo faintly in my ear ("Don't marry into a ready-made family," according to one of my Kenton bandmates), I'm delighted and scared at the prospect.

We finally are able to plan a trip where she and Taichi will visit me in New York, from where we will ride the bus to visit my parents in south Jersey. We are met again at a casino and drive to my childhood home. I'm proud as punch of the two of them; meanwhile my father is asking Mutsy all sorts of questions about her health and religion, and then my mother asks: "Oh, you read Japanese of course, right? Could you please tell me what this says?" and she leads us both to a nightstand by the bed where Mami and I slept during our swan-song visit. Scrawled into the paint and wood by deeply-etched ballpoint pen ink and impression is a letter "to the next woman," which basically says, "This guy is a scumbag and his parents are bastards and he's going to do the same thing to you that he's done to me." Mutsy is still getting to know me, she's just met my parents, and my Mom is standing there smiling, waiting to know what the inscription means. Mutsy translates as follows: "She says that she's really sorry that things didn't work out so well."

With that, my parents have both fallen in love with her and Taichi.

38. Tachikawa to Santa Monica

Former site of the largest U.S. airbase in Japan, this is where Mutsy grew up and where she now lives with Taichi, and where I must travel to court her and realize our destiny. My trip winds up contributing to costing me membership in Steps Ahead due to the *Magnetic* album's late but now rushed completion schedule — that, and my opportunity to work once again with Joe Zawinul, who has invited me to participate in what will be Weather Report's final album.

All of that aside, I feel marvelously at home and at peace in Japan. There's no question that I want to spend the rest of my life with this woman and this child. And when she becomes pregnant with our baby girl, that seals the deal.

Meanwhile, there's that final Weather Report album to make. I love being back in the company of Zawinul and find working with him a much more pleasant task these days. I'm more confident, and he's in an interesting place. It soon becomes apparent that the band is shutting its doors for business, and that this album is a swan song — hence my involvement. Joe looks to a familiar hand to help chart his next course. That will become "Weather Update," a clever name that is all but reviled by most people who resent the use of the word "Weather" anywhere in a new band's name that doesn't have both Wayne and Joe in it.

Guitarist Steve Khan joins the band along with me, plus Victor Bailey and Bobby Thomas, Jr. It's an important transitional vehicle for Joe to get from WR to his "Syndicate" bands, but we don't amount to much more than that in the fusion history books. The one-chord groove, vamp thing is starting to take center stage in Joe's musical universe. At one point of the tour, after a concert in New York, I bring some old VHS tapes of Weather Report from 1978 that my father shot of the band in concert (with direct sound coming from house engineer Brian Risner's board mix; this video has made it to the Internet several times over), and we play it during an overnight bus ride from New York to Washington, D.C. Joe turns and says to me, "You know what? We were actually playing better tunes in those days." We finish the tour on the West Coast and plan to start anew in the New Year with a new band. So for that reason and more, Mutsy and Taichi and baby and I will live in Los Angeles, which represents the halfway mark between Tokyo and New Jersey. Mutsy's father has just passed away, but her mother is very much alive, as are my parents at that point. We go house hunting in L.A. and almost land a place in Glendale. When we mention this to our mutual friends Darlene Chan and Peter Donald, they almost yell out loud, "Glendale? Uh-uh, you guys are going to live in Santa Monica!" and they hooked us up to their real estate agents, who found us our dream home in two days. We have lived there for 26 years. Small, but wonderful. When my brother, who I hired to move my stuff from New York to California, drove up to the house with the moving truck — knowing how much we were paying for it — he drove right past it thinking, "This can't be the place." He was used to Vermont home prices. Welcome to L.A. In addition to my brother helping unload the U-Haul truck, I've consigned a crew of USC drum students to help in return for future drum lessons, Mutsy, Taichi, and I have just gotten off the plane from Tokyo, and we're all set to begin our new lives as Californians and as Erskines.

39. What the Hell?

As soon as we settle in and start living as Santa Monicans, I read an interview in *DownBeat* magazine where drummer Dennis Chambers mentions that Joe has invited him to join his new band. This is one of the more unpleasant ways to find out that you're out. I go to my Macintosh 512K computer and print out a letter on its ImageWriter printer that mercifully decides not to eat up reams of paper in the process this time around, and I mail my thoughts off to Joe.

L.A. mail is quick. The next day the phone rings and I pick it up and I hear without warning or "hello": "What the fuck is with this crazy fucking letter?!" I reply (now knowing how this game is played), "What the FUCK is with this crazy fucking bullshit in *DownBeat* magazine?" to which Joe then meekly says, "Okay, man, okay... How you doin'?" and we talk. As pissed off as Joe could make me, it was never easy to stay angry at the man for too long. He was a genius as far as I was concerned, and geniuses — even boorish ones — get wide latitude in my book.

So any Zawinul-related enterprise is now out. I book myself fairly solid European tours and New York gigs, and I spend a lot of time flying and playing all over the place, mostly Manhattan, Italy, Germany, England, and France, with John Abercrombie's trio or the powerhouse band Bass Desires with John Scofield and Bill Frisell, put together by Marc Johnson. The house payments are demanding, and I've yet to sell my co-op in New York. So we really work hard to set ourselves up as family and to make ends meet, and Mutsy is doing so much of this while pregnant. Now, in addition to the touring, I've got a composing gig for a play up north in Solvang, California — everything seems to be happening at once — *A Midsummer Night's Dream*, directed by my high school friend Jack Fletcher. The birth date for our daughter comes just as planned, and that morning in May, 1987 ranks as the single greatest moment in my life. Welcome, Maya!

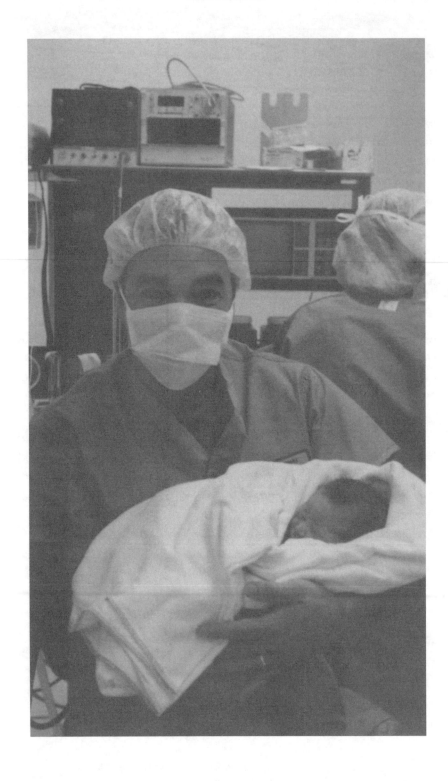

40. And Baby Makes 4

Diapers and feedings and naptimes and walking around the room at midnight humming the theme from "Davy Crockett" (a pentatonic melody that works like magic with most crying babies — try it!). Shouldn't I be playing a gig somewhere?

Zawinul had been saying to me for some time, "You will play better once you are a father." He was right. Everything simply makes better sense and has more meaning. Note choices are more important while being completely less important. "There are no bad notes." It's simpler to negotiate gig fees, too. Now I have a reason to ask for more money and the guilt monkey stays away, though I did hear about one European producer's response to a fee request: "Who does this guy think he is, RINGO STARR?"

The Abercrombie and Bass Desires groups have each made a pair of albums for Manfred Eicher's ECM label at this point, and I'm involved with more and more free-lance ECM album work, all of which will lead up to my being offered the chance to make a solo album for the label. None of this would have happened without my having worked with Kenny Wheeler and the indulgent assistance of one of the tour bookers, Nick Purnell. Nick is one of those kindhearted guys that easily gets overlooked or pushed around because he's too nice and too sensitive to deal with pushy or arrogant people. I'm pushy, and Manfred Eicher asserts himself without apology. Nick gets me a record deal with Manfred, almost lands himself a job at the label but gets pushed out of the picture by Manfred's rudeness — that shark-poking madness that is supposed to rule out the weak from the strong. (These Germanic people and their Nietzschean perspectivism!) In any event, by Nick's good graces and confidence in my music I am led to an ECM album deal that will last for four albums, plus incredible work opportunities with Kenny Wheeler both in a large and small group setting, composition commissions, and the inspiration ultimately to start my own record label. Just wanted to mention all of that as a big thank you to Nick.

Nature takes care of itself, and the puzzlement of wondering how we'll manage in that unimaginable future, or the amazement from looking back and seeing everything we did to the point of getting tired just thinking about it, it all makes sense and it all gets done and we all survive; as Joe liked to say, "We're all just doing the best that we can," and if you couple that with Jaco's admonition to "pay attention," then it all makes sense because we were doing just that. Having a baby in the picture will do that for you. It will also make you wonder what you used to do with all of that spare time. As my friend Jack Fletcher reminds me, "The universe is right on schedule." This has become my favorite saying. I'm also scheduled to deliver this music for "Midsummer Night's Dream"!

photo: Peter Erskine

41. The Play's the Thing

The written word, especially those written by Shakespeare, seems to inspire more compositional flights of fancy than anything else I've tried, and since I don't have the necessary technique to be able to sit and write without inspiration, I count myself as fortunate that so many plays come down the creative pike from Jack, and from these come the songs I will use for my solo albums.

Director Jack Fletcher and I met up in Interlochen, Michigan, when I heard the sounds of the Don Ellis big band coming from his dorm room, thinking at that point that I must be the only high schooler hip enough to be into this music. Even though Jack was a theatre major — his parents well known and acclaimed in the theatrical world — his passion was in drumming; even though my major was music, my passion was for things theatrical and/or cinematic. Perfect match. He hips me to the finer production points of Cyrano de Bergerac while I tell him about Elvin Jones and Bernard "Pretty" Purdie. Years later, during a visit to my New York apartment, he will ask me if I'd be "at all interested in scoring a production of *Richard the Secon…*" "Yes, I'd love to do it."

I write most all of this on my own but am not confident about the scoring I have done for French horn, and I'm planning to have Jerry Peel come to the studio to multitrack the end-of-show hymn. I'm so impressed by the work of a college student I've met recently in Columbus, Ohio — a young trumpet player-arranger named Vince Mendoza — that I send him the music I have scored and ask for his corrections and voicing suggestions. What comes back in the mail is an "I can't help it, had to fix it" rescoring of the hymn that is absolutely correct and brilliant. Counterpoint and voice leading exemplar. Welcome, Vince Mendoza.

This begins a series of associations that will intersect and overlap over the years. If nothing else, I become known as a great dot connector. I am also known, to myself at least, as someone who benefits from the kindness of friends and ridiculously talented people, and if nothing else I know how to spot talented people a mile away.

The world of scoring for the theatre opens up a universe of musical possibilities for me. Zawinul hears my *Richard II* score and tells me that I write "in the Viennese tradition," which is thrilling to hear from him, especially since he introduced me to the music of Erich Wolfgang Korngold back in the Weather Report days. My second score, this time for *Midsummer Night's Dream*, garners an L.A. Drama Critics Circle prize for Best Original Music Score, and our next collaboration in San Francisco, *Twelfth Night*, will earn a similar award there. Vince and I begin a collaboration that continues to this day.

I used the theatre music on my albums *Transition* (which has a front cover that's later voted as one of the worst album covers of all time, but is a good album nonetheless, featuring a very young Joe Lovano; that album and subsequent New York promo gigs will help land Joe his record and career-making deal with the Blue Note label); *Motion Poet* (probably my favorite solo album, it features a great sound and wonderful arrangements by Vince plus great playing all around. It also features an ambitious arrangement of Zawinul's "Dream Clock" from the Weather Report *Night Passage* album. This tune cost the most to record but seemed well worth it, and I could not wait to play this for Zawinul when I traveled back to L.A. from the mixing session. His only reaction after hearing it: "It's too slow. Come on, let's have a drink!"); and *Sweet Soul* (which begins with an exquisite quartet rendering of the ballad from William Walton's score for *Henry V*, "Touch Her Soft Lips and Part." Normally done as a strong chamber orchestra piece but not a jazz ballad, I am glad to put this piece on the map, while Lovano, Kenny Werner, and Marc Johnson play breathtakingly beautiful). Then the ECM era begins. No more arrangements from Vince, but I will ask him to contribute some compositions — and I might even try penning a couple for these albums myself. I will continue to work with Jack Fletcher over the years, providing music for several more of his Shakespeare play productions while he provides Vince and me with album and song titles. Other theatrical opportunities will present themselves in the form of a books-on-tape collaboration with actors John DeLancie and Leonard Nimoy (*Alien Voices*), actor Greg Itzin (*President Charles Logan* from TV's *24* series), in several Andy Robinson-directed plays (Andy played the Scorpion killer in the first *Dirty Harry* movie), and so on. My favorite moment working with directors like Jack and Andy would be their patience with the actors, giving them the necessary time to discover an emotional truth about their character or part. Were it always so with music making!

42. The ECM Recordings

The inspired idea to work with John Taylor and Palle Danielsson results in four finely attuned recordings that create their own niche in the realm of recorded music. These are unlike any other recordings I've made or heard. Somehow, sitting in the "leader" seat creates a delicious sort of vulnerability, and while I hate the feeling at the time I also recognize that the birthing process has to be like this. "Machiavellian" does not begin to describe or do justice to the machinations that Manfred Eicher is capable of bringing to the creative process. That's not meant to be taken as a criticism, by the way. The man has a strong vision. Musical X-ray eyes like Superman's, only he is not necessarily fighting for the American way. In fact, Manfred has an antipathy common to many Europeans regarding the way we do things as a culture and as musicians. Jan Garbarek does his best to explain some of this to me during a post-concert hot chocolate soiree in Paris, while Manfred and drummer Daniel Humair argue about something having to do with jazz and American music in general.

If nothing else, Manfred — like Zawinul — is a good button pusher. He's also a genius when it comes to sound.

John Taylor is a brilliant musician and prolific composer. The trio is naturally assumed to be "his," but it is not and for a simple reason: setting aside the fact that my name was enjoying some marquee value while we were booking tours, I can at least lay claim to the guiding esthetic principle that would serve us well for most of our recording and touring work, and that was to treat musical events as non-events.

Anti-playing, as it were. Whereas Mike Brecker was intent on the band hitting a homerun or getting the music into "5th gear" for pretty much every tune, I was more interested in exploring the other side and seeing if we could create a counter-tension and resulting (or relative) musical strength by going the opposite direction. This was accomplished by lots of post-concert discussions, usually in the touring van as we headed back to the hotel. These were the perfect guys to do it. Palle Danielsson was a terrific sport about all of this and was game to try anything. Both of the guys are great, and it's really the top quality of their playing that made the trio sound so good. But the band definitely has a specific tone to it, and that was where my name came in; other trio collaborations by John and Palle, for better or worse, just don't sound the same. This is all said with pride. (The leader has to take care of all of the business stuff, too.)

The first album is not without its hiccups. Things are going smoothly enough until we reach this new tune of mine that has a spare and bare melody. "Perfect," I'm thinking, "for the ECM sound" we're getting in Rainbow Studio. We're recording with all of the instruments in the same large room, a sonic strategy that forces the musical direction to go where it happens to go: drumming choices and dynamics must needs be specific and careful as hell! This is compositional improvisation at an all-new level, and if I'm not careful, I risk getting another Manfred "your drumming sounds like Billy Cobham's drumset being pushed down a spiral staircase" comment — which he made during one of the Kenny Wheeler album dates.

Back to my tune: We play through the song, I'm liking the vibe, but it needs a bridge. Nick Purnell is there and he helps me to craft one. I am feeling a bit on the spot, and Manfred must be able to sense this. We figure out how to play the rest of the song and create a form, and so we decide to record it. First take. The sustain rings out to infinity, and we all take off our headphones and smile at one another and nod our heads towards the control room where we'll listen back to the song. By this point Manfred has got the newspaper propped up in front of his face, always a bad sign (especially when he uses a Norwegian newspaper, seeing how he does not read or understand Norwegian). I ask him, "How was it?" and he lowers the paper and merely gives me a shrug. I venture further: "Shall we play it again," to which he says, "What...for?" To which I can only start laughing, and I say, "Let's listen to it!" My final verdict: "Fuck it, it's good!" By the next day's mixing/mastering session at album's end, Manfred agrees and "On the Lake" makes the album. The title track is a sketch of John's that we decide to run down. The song has that kind of sound and vibe that makes me immediately realize that I'm not going to play the bass drum even once during the entire tune. "Of course," I think as we're playing it, "Manfred's probably going to start the fucking album with this tune." And he did. And that's much of how *You Never Know* was born. Add some brilliant Vince Mendoza tunes, one of them named by my daughter Maya: "She Never Has a Window."

I still enjoy listening to these albums, and many people became very fond of them. They are sonic adventures. My father was never enamored of these albums, though, as there wasn't enough drumming on them for his taste   him and a few others, probably. (Once, while getting ready to go onstage at a *Modern Drummer* festival with a U.S.-version of the piano trio, I am advised by one of the show's producers just before we're announced, "Oh, and Peter, don't play too much of that sensitive shit.") It's a long way to travel for me, but we persevere as a trio, and we tour and record for some time in Europe. But the fourth and final album is no fun.

I'm sending copies of the tunes to John but getting no response. "Is John's fax machine working?" I wonder. "Yes" comes the reply, and so I don't think much beyond that and travel to Oslo from L.A., arriving in the late afternoon. I go from the hotel to the studio for a private evening rehearsal with John and Palle. "Let's start with this tune of mine," I venture. John then does his best Art Carney/"Ed Norton" imitation, looking at the music but not able to bring himself or his arms far enough down to play the keyboard. He tries and tries again but is not able to bring himself to play. Finally, after performing this pantomime several times, he turns to me and says "Peter, this would work perfectly in a Clint Eastwood film."

"Hmm. Oh yeah? Which one?" and John readily replies, "The one with the bridges in Madison County. After all, Peter, you HAVE been living in Hollywood for some time now, and..." I'm defeated. I can't believe he's pulling this. I finally suggest that John play one of his new compositions, and after he runs it down I say, "You know, that would work terrifically well in an Arnold Schwarzenegger film," and it's all downhill from there.

The next day Manfred asks me what's going on with John, and I have no idea what to tell him. We finish the album, somehow, and that is that for that trio. By this point, I thought that Manfred and I were getting along real well.

Enter Alan Pasqua and Dave Carpenter, my American saviors. No need to travel, and these guys swing and they'll play my tunes and trust them and not worry about trying to be too clever with the music. Of course,

Manfred expresses no interest in recording this band, and so I decide to make a trio album on my recently-begun Fuzzy Music CD label — a move that Manfred seems not to have been too pleased about — and that's it as far as any other ECM work goes. But I'll always be grateful for having gotten to play with Palle Danielsson and John Taylor.

43. Competition

Recently, I went down to the swimming pool in a hotel in Europe, and it was filled with young parents and little babies: it was a baby swimming class. I was expecting an empty pool, so that was a very big surprise. But what truly surprised me was how much I enjoyed being in the pool with all these little babies, and how fearless they were! A slightly older baby — a girl, who was maybe one-and-a-half years old — was much more tentative and fearful compared to the newborns who were just so happy to be in the water. I thought: It's interesting how fear comes along in your life and creates uncertainty and doubt and unhappiness. When you get much older, you lose that fear; maybe you get another kind of fear, the fear of dying, and then you accept that, too. Fear is the troublemaker, I think.

Quite a few years ago I was invited to appear at *Modern Drummer* magazine's drum festival, a two-day affair held annually in New Jersey; this was one of the earlier events. I was flattered and pleased to get the call, entered it into my datebook, and then pretty much forgot about it. A couple of weeks prior to the festival I got a call from the magazine's managing editor who was handling all of the programming and logistics for the show. He informed me that I would be following Dennis Chambers, and I thanked him and hung up. Dennis was pretty new on the scene at the time, but I was already one of his biggest fans. Talk about prowess! This guy was the Mike Tyson of the drum world (back in the days when being compared to Mike Tyson was not such a bad thing). However, the thought of having to follow Dennis in a drum solo environment was, well, intimidating! And so I turned to my wife and told her that now I was not really looking forward to traveling back east to New Jersey to do this show. She asked me why, and I told her that I had just found out that I would be following Dennis.

Mutsuko: So? What's the problem?

Peter: Well, you see, Dennis is just… He's just so strong.

Mutsuko: Hmmm. Use his strength to your advantage.

Of course, you could watch the film *The Karate Kid* and figure out the same thing, but when my wife said that to me, good ol' "Mr. Lightbulb" lit up above my head.

Could I possibly "out-drum" Dennis? No. I couldn't, I can't, and I never will. And, heck, I wanted to be able to enjoy his performance as much as everyone else there, too. So, I decided on three things: One, prepare to sit back and enjoy his great drumming, even if it was five minutes before I would go on. Two: Approach my solo piece in an opposite manner from what I figured he would do; i.e., I knew Dennis would be slammin', so I started off my set with a pair of brushes and played as simple and as softly as I could. And three: Practice anyway!

Dennis DID play great that day. And I enjoyed every bit of it. I also managed to enjoy every bit of my own solo spot, because I was determined to. I was not out to be better or to get more audience response; just determined to try my best and to make some music on the drums. I should add that Dennis and I are very close friends, and I am grateful for his friendship as well as for the fact that we seem to have a mutual-admiration society going.

Okay, so maybe I was clever enough to follow my wife's advice. Her wisdom would prove to be the saving grace for the day. But I was also inspired by the sense of good old-fashioned competition. I WANTED to do well and to show what I could do: who wouldn't? So, part of what I did was to create a musical balancing act to what the audience had just heard; but my competitive juices were flowing. In other words, competition need not be considered a dirty word. A sense of competition is a healthy thing: it motivates us to strive, to excel, to become better, and in some cases to survive. It may help prove us to be fit enough to do what we do, and to do it enjoyably and with confidence. Meanwhile, after Dennis' amazing performance, I started my one-hour presentation by simply playing the brushes, and then I let the music take me to where it was going. This involves LISTENING to the music — even when it's just yourself; the sound of the drums and the sound of the room and the motifs that you play and the variations that you can come up with are all interconnected, and if you connect these things to your imagination, then there's no time or reason to experience fear or insecurity. It becomes ALL ABOUT THE MUSIC.

As a young drummer I was always worried what other people thought of me, just like most drummers and most young people worry about. But I had more anxiety, perhaps, than some. My psychiatrist father sent me to a psychologist, and I read the report years later: the psychologist was concerned about my anxiety, considering how much and how well I was accepted. Growing older yet joining all of these bands as the youngest member, I usually felt that I had something to prove, and I was very aware of people listening to me as such: maybe enjoying it, but half the people maybe in judgment or jealousy: Why does HE have this job? You acquire defensiveness to deal with that. And while I would always show respect to older drummers (without fail, even if I didn't like the way they played; they were older, they'd been doing it, they deserved respect — that was an important part of the tradition), I wasn't always so ready to "give it up" to my colleagues. You know, competition.

So a few years ago, when my son was in high school, he came home and he said, "Dad, can we talk?" and I said, "Sure." He said, "Can we go into the studio?" "Of course!" So, we go to the privacy of my studio and I'm thinking, "Wow, I thought we already had this discussion, but maybe, hmmm, something's come up." I'm wondering what he's going to tell me, he's struggling to speak, and I say, "Come on, tell me, what's going on?" He finally said, "Uh, okay. My good friend Matt came up to me and said, 'No offense, dude, but Jeff "Tain" Watts is a better drummer than your old man!'" So I smiled, and I said, "Yeah, well… I agree." "DAD! NO!"

I continued, "It's okay, it's okay." He desperately said, "B-but you're more sensitive, right?" and I said, "Well, that depends on who you ask, son, but don't you worry about your Dad. Your Dad is doing just fine."

A few weeks later I'm in Copenhagen at the airport with a Steps Ahead reunion band, and we run into Branford Marsalis's band. And there's Tain. So we give each other a hug. Now, some years earlier Jeff and I had played a concert together in Japan that was pitched as a drum battle. At the end of our set, when we were bowing and shaking hands and giving each other a hug, Jeff whispers into my ear as we hug on stage, "I won." Now this is some funny shit, and of course you don't forget something like that. So I see Jeff at the Copenhagen airport and I tell him about my son and his best friend, leaving out the more sensitive part, the story basically ending with my agreeing with the friend of my son: "Yeah, Jeff's better." So Jeff is looking at me, and I'm looking at him as I tell the story, and when I get to that part in the story, he says, "Get the fuck outta here." And I said. "No, man, it's true," and I gave him a hug. We said good-bye, and walking to my gate was the lightest I'd felt in years. This remarkable lightness of spirit... It was really interesting to me that I felt this way.

A week later we are in Munich, and we're soundchecking in the basement of the hotel that has a very large jazz club, The Bayerischer hof. It was a big summer festival with a lot of bands: Chick Corea was there, but he had the night off, Branford was there with the night off, too, and so during our soundcheck there's Jeff and one of the other band members. Normally, if I was rehearsing and Jeff Watts was sitting 15 feet away, I would become self-conscious. But instead it occurred to me: what a nice thing that he's here! He could be walking, shopping, taking a nap, or drinking a beer. Instead he was here, giving me his energy! I felt even freer by this, and I realized that if I'm playing and someone's listening — it might be in judgment, but usually it's just great that they're listening. If they like it: fantastic. If they don't, then maybe there's a reason they don't. All I can do is play the best I can play the music. Technically you try to pay attention and do it well, but you just try to play the song. Concentrate on the arc of the song, not so much on the performance, and the result will be more compositional than otherwise. In contrast, one of the other members of the band was made to feel very self-conscious by this other musician of that same instrument. He was having the worst time. The monitor wasn't good, the lights were wrong, the sound wasn't right, the instrument... And I thought: the same circumstances, but this musician is having a terrible time, because of fear. It completely chokes your circulation, it chokes your thought, and it chokes your ability to do what you do.

When my students are asking me what to do when it's not feeling good, I say, "Just take a deep breath, simplify what you're doing, and really try to feel gratitude for the existence of these other musicians you're playing with, as well as gratitude for the ones in the audience." I guess this plays back to what Jaco said to me all those years ago: "Have fun." Of course, Weather Report was a very competitive atmosphere.

44. Life Goes On

Valentine's Day is a celebration of love and, by extension, life itself, for what is a life lived without love? And on this day, by one of the cruel ironies of life, my family found itself spending the afternoon of this year's St. Valentine's celebration at the site of a freshly dug grave where the father of one of my daughter's friends was to be laid to rest. While everyone in attendance tried their best to feel some joy in the remembrances of a life well lived, there wasn't a dry eye on this windy hillside. The sermon reminded us that "life goes on." It got me to thinking about some of those very big questions that are at the root of our very being.

Growing up means that we learn to confront and accept the loss of those whose lives have touched us. Since moving to California in 1987, I have enjoyed the growth, companionship, and support of my family. And during this time, I have also felt the sting of loss that is, regretfully, a sad and simple fact of life. A few short months after my daughter was born, I received a telephone call from a musician colleague that informed me that my friend Jaco Pastorius had died. Much has been chronicled about Jaco's struggle with his personal demons, and in that light, the news did not come as a huge surprise; it was the phone call I was dreading but half expecting to come someday. Such phone calls always come too soon, however. Over the years, more telephone calls or emails would announce the deaths of such stalwart drumming colleagues and friends as Jeff Porcaro, Carlos Vega, John Guerin, or my best buddy in New York, Don Grolnick, or my parents, or saxophone colossi Bob Berg and Michael Brecker. Or Joe Zawinul. But I don't wish to dwell on the hows and whys of death. Rather, I would like to focus on the notion that a person's being and soul really do live on. This is not a religious tract, though I leave it to the reader to instill his or her own sense of values and spiritual perspective into whatever I write here. Free of any particular adherence to dogma, then, I press on and offer the following.

Is there a heaven? There are certainly plenty of promises, as well as jokes, about the place. But seriously, folks, I believe quite strongly in the existence of heaven, for I see and feel its presence around me on a daily basis. For example: any and every time that one of us listens to a recording of Jeff Porcaro playing with his band, Toto (or on any one of the hundreds of recordings he made during his all-too-brief life), we are sublimely reminded and graced by the poetic and energetic life force of Jeff's essence and being. At those moments, Jeff is as every bit alive for the listener as he could be. Think about it. Every time we hear and intelligently understand what Jeff is saying to us, it's as if he is speaking to us personally. Same with Carlos on a James Taylor recording; or John Guerin on that big band recording he made with Thelonious Monk and Oliver Nelson (titled *Monk's Dream*, though John is not properly credited on the album).

I was speaking about Valentine's Day. That night, I went to a club to hear a band from New York that's known as the "Fab Faux," a clever play on the expression the "Fab Four," used for the Beatles when they first stormed America and the music world in the early 1960s. My good friend Will Lee is the bassist in the tribute band, and they put on a show that was astoundingly good and fun and exciting and moving. Good fun to hear Beatles' tunes "live." It was moving in the sense to think on the day's events, and in the midst of all of that glorious music, smiling at the thought that the work we do in our lives does indeed live on to touch the lives of our loved ones and, possibly, countless others. John Lennon was murdered in New York, George Harrison died of cancer in Los Angeles, and yet their youthful spirit and thoughts and beings were completely alive in that Hollywood club on Valentine's night — and on your radio or CD player or mp3 device or just your memory of their music! How often do I think of God? More often than I think of the melody to "Penny Lane"? The *Magical Mystery Tour* probably wins, hands down.

Will Lee and his lovely wife, Sandrine, came to our home for breakfast the next morning on their way to the airport. Conversation went from myriad Beatles tunes to the music of others, including our dear departed friend Don Grolnick. Will told me, "Not a day goes by that I don't think of Don." Which reminded me of something Don said while he was sick and certain of his own death; I'm paraphrasing here, but in essence Don expressed his assurance that Heaven did indeed exist as long as his presence was in the memory of those who knew him and/or his work. Of course, it does not surprise me that such a gentle and good man would be in Heaven, but it is comforting to know it for certain.

It is the charge of us who survive to see another dawn each day that we honor the memory of the kind and brave souls who have pioneered and lived and loved before us. They have taught us how to interpret a melody, or how to play a rhythm, or how to laugh at one of life's many absurdities. Life lessons. Good deeds. Mistakes. The sum of a man's or a woman's life can take years to absorb and understand, but we must always appreciate the sacrifice, wisdom, love, and humor that our fallen comrades have left to us.

The late singer Mel Torme was once flying coast-to-coast on an airplane, seated next to the very much alive and wonderful drummer Jerry Marotta. (Don Grolnick told me this story, in fact.) And the conversation they had turned to such matters as I've touched on here, as well as some likely mundane diatribes about this or that. And while I don't know the bulk of what was said, I do know the closing remark that Mr. Torme offered to Jerry: "Take it from me, Kid, every day above ground is a winner!"

Good advice, Mel. Thanks! In memory, then, of some of the musical heroes and friends whose lives have touched mine: Stan Kenton, Shelley Manne, Jaco Pastorius, Mel Lewis, Buddy Rich, Jeff Porcaro, Carlos Vega, John Guerin, Don Grolnick, Bob Berg, Michael Brecker, Joe Zawinul, and my parents, Lois and Fred Erskine, I offer words of love and thanks. The days with thoughts of you are, indeed, winners.

45. Plays Well With Others

I got called to work on the first *American Songbook* album of ballads for Rod Stewart. I show up and the producer Richard Perry asks me if I have a wooden bass drum beater. I said, "Yes, but we're playing standards, right? I wasn't planning on using it." He said, "I'd like you to use it," so I put the wooden beater on my pedal. We were running down the ballad "These Foolish Things" before Rod arrived. I was playing a typical smooth, legato brush feel, and the producer stops the band and says, "What's with the zzzz, zzzz (mimics brush sound) thing? Break it up more. Go zzzz, zu zzzz, zu (sings long sound on beat 1 followed by short sound on beat 2)." I played it and he said, "Yeah, that's it. Now add the bass drum when you stop the brush (i.e., on beats 2 and 4)." I said, "You mean like this?" and by this time everyone in the band is looking at me kind of weird. He said, "Yeah, that's great." So now I'm playing this beat like an idiot. Rod Stewart shows up and we start running the song with him. He soon stops and says, "Just a sec' lads." He goes into the control room, and I can see him saying to the producer, "What the fuck's the drummer doing?" Then the producer is in my headphones saying, "Uhhhh, just go back to what you were originally doing."

There were a couple of times during my tenure with Weather Report when I truly just wanted to pack it in and go home; it's easy to get tired of the touring, the rigors of traveling, and working and eating and socializing with the same people, day and night after day and night — especially tough when your efforts are being criticized or (from your point of view) not being appreciated. But I would always remember two things: (1) these people knew more about this music than I did, and (2) plenty of musicians come and go; the ones who "stay" are the ones who stick around. I wanted to be sure I was one of those people, because I was (and am) still learning, and being in Weather Report was the best possible educational opportunity that I could hope for. Besides, a day or two would go by after a rough gig, and all would be well again or even better.

Life lessons. The next generation is always 'round the bend. Passing along the knowledge and the tradition…

Mr. Peart and a few other well-known rock guys. Why do they choose to study with me? Some want to learn a little more about jazz, others come just because they're curious or having some issues, oftentimes dealing with self-confidence, or they just feel in a rut. So a lot of my drum lessons are more like counseling than mechanical sessions. Sometimes I've got to be like one of those characters in a martial arts movie: I've got to hit the student in the head a couple of times, metaphorically. I have to slap some sense into them — whack! — even if the point is to treat sitting at the drumset much like dealing cards at a friendly game of poker — smooth and relaxed — versus guiding a 747 jumbo jet into its parking spot at the airport gate.

Whack!

That said, it takes a lot of listening to be able to hear this music in order to speak it. I stopped teaching privately for a while because it was becoming too frustrating, and I tried to explain it to my wife as follows: "It's like I hear a knock on my door and open it, and there's some guy with a loaf of bread and a bottle of wine, wearing a beret, and he says in an Inspector Clouseau-accented voice, 'I want to be French!' Just like that: 'I want to play jazz.' I'm glad that Neil is serious about the study of jazz and drumming. I'm also glad that he's from Toronto and not Montréal. Neil has my highest respect for the drumming he does with his band, Rush, and for the qualities he exhibits as a human being.

I've had the pleasure of touring and being part of many bands and various artists' backing ensembles over the years. Some of the more notable groups include Steely Dan (doing their first tour in twenty years) as well as Joni Mitchell when she toured the USA with orchestral accompaniment, and Diana Krall when she toured the USA, Canada, and Europe with her quartet.

The Steely Dan call was a complete surprise. I had worked with Walter Becker in the studio on several albums, but never expected that he and Donald Fagen would think of me for their band. The call went like this: I had just returned to my hotel room in Sardinia, Italy, after a concert with the ECM trio, and I said aloud to the empty room, "This is the only kind of music I want to play for the rest of my life!" Cue: telephone ring. It was my wife, who said, "You'll never guess who just called." So I agreed to meet the band in New York City for three-and-a-half weeks of rehearsal for a summer's worth of touring. The band's management sent me two cassette tapes' worth of songs to learn, and I created cheat sheets of the basic beats for each tune (I couldn't remember "Hey Nineteen" from "Bad Sneakers" when it came to the drum beats), shrinking and laminating my carefully-notated parts for handy reference. I also practiced these most basic of beats with a metronome set to mildly different tempos so that I could feel the necessary confidence to "own" any tempo that Donald Fagen might count off at the first rehearsal onward. Fortunately, I gained his full trust and confidence thanks to this bit of preparation, as well as by watching his left hand when he played the Fender Rhodes electric piano; my bass drum foot stayed in sync with him, and for the rest of the tour it was "Hey band... WITH THE DRUMS!"

I suspect that both Donald and Walter were hoping for a bit more jazz voodoo on that tour than I was willing to impart; the recorded drum parts seemed so perfect to me that I could barely stray from the original patterns and beats (though I would never claim to being able to play with the pocket and funk of mssrs Porcaro, Gordon, Keltner, Purdie, Marotta, and Gadd). All in all, a lot of fun to be part of a big rock-and-roll tour.

As the drummer, I was responsible for counting off the songs, and I used a metronome for that purpose. While Donald and Walter were not so picky when it came to interpretation (much to my surprise), they were absolutely nitpicking when it came to tempo (which should come as no surprise to anyone who has worked with a vocalist). During the lengthy rehearsal process, we would practice tunes at decimal-point tempi (118.5 BPM [beats per minute]), but were able to convince the guys to stick to whole numbers.

Speaking of "Hey Nineteen" and 118 BPM: after a couple of weeks of touring, I noticed that, when the band played that tune, the horns had a tendency to push the time a bit, and so I thought it might be a good idea to bump up the tempo from 118 to 119 BPM. And so I did, in Cincinnati, without telling anyone and thinking none were the wiser. The next afternoon in St. Louis at soundcheck, Donald and Walter walked onto the stage and called for the band to run "Hey Nineteen." Then they both turned to me, looking up at the drums on the stage riser, and said, "Oh yeah, felt kinda...FAST last night." I replied, "Wow, that's really something that you guys noticed," and they countered with, "Well, did you do anything different last night?" I said, "Uh, yeah, I changed the tempo from 118 to 119. That's remarkable that you could tell!" They laughed a bit and then said, real serious, "Yeah, well... DON'T DO THAT AGAIN."

My kids both got a big kick out of my doing the tour. I was very glad and remain grateful for having made the acquaintance of the late saxophonist Cornelius Bumpus.

Touring with Joni Mitchell was luxurious in that we played the Vince Mendoza arrangements for orchestra all across the USA, traveling with Joni, Vince, producer Larry Klein, concertmaster Ralph Morrison, saxophonist Bob Sheppard, bassist Chuck Berghofer, and myself. Guest artists in various cities included Herbie Hancock, Mark Isham, and Wallace Roney. Joni sang her heart out every night. What a thrill.

Diana Krall's quartet, including Anthony Wilson on guitar and either Christian McBride or Bob Hurst on bass — with an excellent production crew! — was a lot of fun for me, especially when we focused on her own tunes. It felt more "new" to me than when she turned and returned to the music that made her so popular in the first place. It's always fun to feel part of something that's fresh and being put together for the first time. Lots of audiences though, I noticed —whether at a Steely Dan or Joni or Diana concert — were half "there" and half very much not there at all, and I could see in their far-away eyes and smiling faces that the music was taking them back to a comfort zone of when they were younger and discovering the world around them with much of this music as a soundtrack to their lives and loves. And that's okay. But, that said, it's more fun to play music that's new and being created on its own terms — not subject to the expectations of a record company, a bandleader's spouse, or an audience of balding baby-boomers and their used-to-be-hippie wives. Wait, I just described myself.

Time to be in charge of my own thing...

FUZZY MUSIC

After being a sideman and working for other bands and leaders and waiting for one record company executive or label-owner after another to consent to my entering the studio to realize my own next project, I started my own record label. Just like a lot of other things in life, when you want something done and you want it done the way you want it done, then do it yourself. I should say "we" started our own label, as this venture is entirely a team effort between me, my wife, and some musical colleagues. It takes a fuzzy.

My dad had always wanted me to make a recording with my cousin Joey. He's a singer, Italian but kind of like an Irish tenor, with a lovely voice, and he could sing ballads real nice. In other words, he's not a jazz singer. My father said he'd really love it if Joey and I could record something. So I put a band together with Frank Collett, Sarah Vaughan's pianist for many years, and bassist Dave Carpenter, and we made an album. What do you do with an album? First, you shop it. "Hmm, sounds nice! How old is he?" "Well, he's just retired as a DC-10 captain for Continental Airlines, and…" "Too old, sorry." Then you decide to release it yourself for your own amusement. I had just been reading a book about Fuzzy Logic, so I thought, "Hey, let's call the label Fuzzy Music." We printed up some CDs by mail-order but didn't really know what to do with them. We made another couple of albums, and by this time we thought, "Let's see if we can start selling some of these." It was a vanity label with lofty ideas. Maybe we could become a means for other artists, because we were all running into the same thing: begging producers or the guys that wore the suits at the record label companies, "Please let me do a record," but their timetables might be months away from your moment of inspiration, or they weren't interested, or they would disappear and become unavailable. So hey, we'll do this ourselves, make the music we want to make when we want to make it, and it won't disappear forever.

And we got better and better at it. It was always kind of a kitchen tabletop operation, where we'd get orders, pack 'em up in a box, and send them off. Come to think of it, we still do it this way. Only now, more and more of our music is being listened to and purchased online by way of digital downloading. Most of our fans, the fans of the music I play, seem to be interested and supportive of the music and they're happy to download it. I wouldn't even know where to find a free tune on the Internet, because I just don't do that. If I want a tune, I go to iTunes, buy it, and download it. Thankfully, we have a fan base that operates the same way.

Fuzzy Music has remained a vanity label in part because I felt we really couldn't do justice to what other artists deserve, expect, or need. I was at a business meeting — a friend of ours knew some really smart businessmen and invited them to this meeting at our house — and I told them about the record company and my dreams for a better world, etc. One of the guys finally asked, "What does Peter Erskine want to be when he grows up?" And I went, "Huh?" And he goes, "This is all nice and good, but what you're talking about isn't business." Then another guy adds in, "Well, maybe that's a good thing. You're doing what you want to do, you have a passion, and you believe in the music. You don't want to get people like us involved, because as soon as you get us involved, we're going to start demanding, 'Why didn't you do this? Why didn't you do that?'" And I told them, "Yeah, I've got enough other things to think about; I don't really want to have to worry about meeting other peoples' expectations." We put out the recordings and hope for the best!

We finally got smart and began investing in a publicist, which has been a great help. It hasn't increased sales ALL that much, but the visibility has improved and, besides, the whole idea of doing this is not so much about making money as to get the music out there. It's my business, but it's funded in great part by my drumming and other activities. Since most of the recordings we do are collaborative projects, we need very little money to put upfront because we can record in my home studio (Puck Productions). Everyone makes more money as a result of being a collaborative partner. I build the spreadsheets and databases, so when I get the sales statements, all the composers get their royalties, and then the performers get performance royalties each time an album is sold or a song is downloaded — it all adds up. So it's a fair fight and it feels good and it's fun. I mean, we're not CBS, but we've got a pretty good catalogue now, and what we do is respectable. We are survivors. Our titles remain in print; we now have twenty of them to show for our efforts. And we're Grammy nominees. Like Dorothy said in *The Wizard of Oz*: "There's no place like home"!

Speaking of the movies, one of Fuzzy's latest CDs is *Standards 2, Movie Music*, which was recorded in the same acoustically rich and challenging hall in La Jolla, California with some state-of-the-art stereo microphones. The band this time around is Bob Mintzer on tenor, Darek Oles on bass, Alan Pasqua on piano, and myself on drums and producing. The album came out so good we're already planning a follow-up, and maybe we can include "Over the Rainbow" on that.

Our most ambitious project to date would have to be *The Avatar Sessions* — no relation to the movie but recorded in New York's famed Avatar Studios, formerly known as Power Station, where I made my final recording with Weather Report and first recordings with Mike Mainieri, Steps Ahead, and others. This time around it was Tim Hagans writing for and leading the Norrbotten Big Band from the very far north of Sweden, all of those musicians flown over to Manhattan for the express purpose of making this album, joined by guests Randy Brecker, George Garzone, Vic Juris, Dave Liebman, Rufus Reid, and myself. It's the best large ensemble playing I've ever done. Thanks to the support for the arts that European communities and states offer their artists. Without Europe, the state of American jazz might be in peril. Like Michael Jackson said: "We are the world."

The time and talents of several friends deserve mention: Our design team of Mark and Connie Beecher back east have been the brains and creative brawn behind most of our album covers, with West Coast-based designer Kio Griffith doing his share of cover designs, too. Mark is currently the President of the National Association of Rudimental Drummers. We are fortunate to have him on our team. Recording, mixing, and mastering engineer Rich Breen is the sonic epicenter of Fuzzy Music. We occasionally broaden out to include recording techniques or philosophies from such people as Dan Atkinson and Kent Fuqua who have pioneered the use of the KMF Stereo Microphone (more accurately, Fuzzy Music has been pioneering its use in two of our recordings). Weather Report engineer Brian Risner has recorded tracks in my home studio for the label; Rich Breen assisted on a Weather Report album done in Chicago's Universal Recorders, same studio where I made two albums with Stan Kenton! Pianist and musical soulmate Alan Pasqua has appeared on most of our albums; Interlochen classmate Bob Mintzer is on *Standards 2, Movie Music*. Kenton bandmate Tim Hagans directs two of the big band titles, and so on. Our friends help. You can also find copies of my instructional books and DVDs at our website www.fuzzymusic.com Here are two of our CD covers...

THE AVATAR SESSIONS

RANDY BRECKER PETER ERSKINE
GEORGE GARZONE TIM HAGANS
DAVE LIEBMAN RUFUS REID &
THE NORRBOTTEN BIG BAND

THE MUSIC OF TIM HAGANS

peter erskine
alan pasqua
darek oles
the interlochen concert

46. Diary of Two Film Sessions

As my wife exited her office and entered the kitchen of our home, she had that happy/excited-almost-mischievous look that I've come to know as meaning "some good news has come our way." I asked, "What's up?" and she answered with another question: "Guess who you'll be working for next week?" "I give up," was my enlightened reply. "For the first time, you're finally going to be working with John Williams!"

If you've seen the *Star Wars* or Indiana Jones films, *E.T.*, *Close Encounters of the Third Kind*, *Jurassic Park*, *Superman*, *Saving Private Ryan*, or *Catch Me If You Can*, you're familiar with this man's music. His website biography starts: "One of the most popular and successful American orchestral composers of the modern age, John Williams is the winner of five Academy Awards, 17 Grammys, three Golden Globes, two Emmys, and five BAFTA Awards from the British Academy of Film and Television Arts… (he) has composed the music and served as music director for over eighty films…"

Interestingly, I first became aware of his music back in the day when he was "Johnny Williams," a jazz pianist (Juilliard-trained) and writer of music for television. He composed a piece for Stan Kenton's Neophonic Orchestra in the mid-1960s titled "Prelude and Fugue"; I must have been all of eleven years old when I first heard it — a haunting, challenging, and swinging work that Stan later told me was "the best goddamned piece of music that's ever been written for this band!" Of course, I have enjoyed his film music along with countless other movie fans over the years; call me an admirer of the man's work. What would I be playing? Would this be an orchestral or small jazz group date? Which drumset should I have the cartage company bring? I had no idea, but I finally got this much information from the contractor: "The ensemble consists of you, two harpists, two percussionists, a celeste player, and a couple of Japanese musicians." Since I knew that John Williams was working on *Memoirs of a Geisha*, I figured this must be the film. Would I be improvising or reading? This was a period film. Why call a jazz drummer for this particular film date?

I found out on a Saturday morning as I entered the cavernous recording soundstage at the old MGM studios (now SONY) in Culver City. My drums were being set up in the drum isolation booth at the rear of the soundstage; I joined my cartage guy, and after exchanging morning pleasantries he pointed out that I might be playing "only the tom-toms today; there's four mics just for the toms." "Okay," I thought. "Toms will sound good." I then walked to the control booth to say hello to the engineer, Shawn Murphy. Shawn speculated that I might "not be playing any drumset at all today." When he saw my puzzled look, he continued: "I think you'll be out in the big room, playing some of those Japanese taiko drums." Wow. Cool! I sat in once with a taiko drumming group. Very large sticks and a different attitude were required to play those drums. How "Japanese" was I feeling this morning? My two percussionist colleagues for the day were the always excellent Alan Estes and Mike Fisher. The taiko drums all belonged to Mike.

Soon the composer entered the room, and we were introduced. "Maestro!" I beamed as I shook his hand. John was very cordial, insisted that I call him "John," and then suggested that we look at the music we were going to play. Spread out on four pages was a fairly non-stop litany of eighth notes, laid out in 6/8 time with a few rests as well as sixteenth-note flourishes here and there. John, in his soft voice, suggested that I might want to approach this as a sort of "Japanese Buddy Rich," and I instantly knew why I had been called — not that I'm a Japanese Buddy Rich, but because I had a drumset player's sensibility while being known as a good reader. My only question, after we had chosen which of the many taiko drums would be best suited for the three-drum part, was if he wanted me to "exceed the speed limit of the eighth-note pulse" during the cue; not having played it (or viewed the scene to which the music would be added), I was fishing for some info so as to guide any improvisational forays. He thought about the question for a few seconds and suggested I not overdo it too much. It turns out that the part he wrote was almost perfect "as is," but I could add a normal sense of musical shading and phrasing to it — using dynamics as well as a bit of added velocity now and then — to make it both my own as well as the film's. It was challenging to read and play but great fun.

The music was consummate John Williams stuff: sparkling and ingenious, wonderful just to listen to but even better to hear while watching the cinematic scene play out on the large screen. The director, Rob Marshall, liked it; John liked it; Shawn the engineer liked it; but John wanted to get it even better. I was loving every second of all this: THIS is why I studied and practiced in school; THIS is why I learned how to read and how to play in legit as well as jazz ensembles; THIS was the big leagues; THESE guys were the New York Yankees of film music.

A couple of favorite moments: Maestro Williams had the harpists change their parts for one scene, and when they played this new arrangement for him, he smiled and said, "Yes, that's going to look real good." The other came from my being able to recount the Stan Kenton anecdote to John during a mid-session break, letting him know that Stan regarded his piece as the "best goddamned piece of music ever written for (my) band!" John came up to me at the end of the day to thank me for that. I guess we all like to know that our work is appreciated.

Several years later I was fortunate to be called to play again for John, this time for the Spielberg film *The Adventures of Tintin: The Secret of the Unicorn*. The ensemble was larger, the drumming much more quiet — on a 1940s period kit with calfskin heads, playing brushes — and the requirement of the music called for zero interpretation; the "swing would result from the absolute mechanical perfection of the performance." I never played anything like this before in my life, but the results were magical once the band clinched the piece.

Film music can be some of the most thrilling stuff to record, especially when you're in the presence of Hollywood legends.

photo: Peter Erskine

47. Back to the Classics

A cold blust'ry wind blows upon the crags 'bove Edinburgh. Settled comfortably inside my hotel room, I reflect upon the last few days' adventure I shared with the BBC Scottish Symphony Orchestra and soloists, rehearsing and performing Mark-Anthony Turnage's 80-minute opus "Blood on the Floor." Even though I have played this piece numerous times over the ten years since its premiere, I still find myself challenged each time in new ways by its volatile complexity.

First, a little something about the composer (the BBC website says it well): "Turnage is one of Britain's most successful living composers whose communicative music reflects a range of interests and concerns, including jazz, the arts, politics, and everyday life. He has worked closely with various orchestras, music groups, and jazz musicians, with whom he has made significant recordings of his works." I can add that Mark was born in 1960, is a keen football fan (Arsenal being his favorite team), and has been responsible for my being able to enjoy working as an improviser in the symphonic setting. He is, in my opinion, one of the great musical geniuses of our time. He is also a fun guy.

A brief history of the work: Mark began "Blood on the Floor" as a single-movement work, inspired by the Francis Bacon painting of the same name. He later expanded it to become a nine-movement suite for orchestra and jazz soloists, which was premiered at London's Queen Elizabeth Hall on May 30, 1996, by the Frankfurt-based Ensemble Modern, conducted by Peter Rundell and featuring solo performances by guitarist John Scofield, British saxophonist Martin Robertson, and myself on drums. It is described as "a masterpiece of contemporary sensibility" and has been performed since its premiere by orchestras in Berlin, Hamburg, Vienna, London, Birmingham, Amsterdam, Helsinki, New York, Los Angeles, Glasgow, and Oslo. As I have played nearly every one of these performances, the piece should present no problems, yet a testament to the vitality of its inner construction is that it still manages to bedevil me. If you are at all familiar with the rhythmic construction of contemporary written (or "classical") music, you'll know that most modern composers avoid the use of a simple 4/4 meter but will instead write the music in combinations of 3/8, 5/8, 7/16, and so on. The challenging bar of 7/16 aside, much of this music could be written in 4/4 more often than it is. In fact, when I was a young student and aspiring orchestral percussionist, I used to listen to many works by Bartók, Stravinsky, Bernstein, and Varése that seemed to me to be in 4/4 for the most part. I heard most of the metric complexities as a sort of jazz-over-the-barline expression. That made the most sense to me when I was a kid, and, to be honest, it still makes a lot of sense to me today. However sophisticated they might seem on occasion, jazz and pop music are an expression of tradition and experimentation. While both types of music have flirted with metric complexity, they usually confine themselves to simple 4/4 or three-quarter metric schemes. Dave Brubeck and Don Ellis pioneered the use of compound meters in jazz, and the influence of Indian music soon made itself known across a wide cultural spectrum in the 1960s. Meanwhile, classical composers were trying to get the gist of syncopation as heard in ragtime and early swing music. Instead of relying on syncopated accents within the 4/4 context and counting on the non-jazz musicians to feel those syncopations "correctly," they resorted to displacing the barline in order to create a new sort of rhythmic tension. (Of course, this was true for non-jazz-inflected music as well; witness Stravinsky's "Rite of Spring," etc. If the use of odd-times in musical circles, circa 1913, is news to fans of Rush or Dream Theater, then I encourage them to check out some early 20th-century classical music!)

The confounding issue of barline placement and interpretation exists in Mark's music; hence, these thoughts: Does a barline exist on paper only, or is it meant to be perceived and heard by the listener? For starters, I think that the barline is first and foremost a tool that enables composers to construct their music; it also allows them to inform the musicians (and conductor) how to navigate through the music. In simple metric settings, the barline functions as a handy sort of punctuation mark like a comma or a period. When the metric construction becomes more specific and complicated, then the barline seems to function not only as a signpost indicating where each new succession of "one" is, but it also seems to serve as a sort of "devil's advocate." What does this mean? Since players will often phrase rhythms and phrasings dependent on the written "one," an artificial or contrived sense of accent is engendered by the use of shifting meters. It's almost impossible to not breathe anew and phrase as the barline commands. This can lead to some exciting if quirky rhythmic complexity. However, my job as a drummer requires me to create a musical arc or horizon that best serves the music. Imagine if, after every accent in a piece, the drummer consciously (or subconsciously) shifted gears; this might work for some parts of a piece, but not for the entire work. The drummer as well as the listeners will all tire from this formula. (I once pointed out to Mark that a complex sequence of meter changes all added up to several measures of simple 4/4 time if redrawn, and he replied, "Oh…yeah.") Of course, the genius to much of this music IS the metric complexity! What's a drummer to do?

The solution is to step back and try to get a bigger picture of what's going on musically. I'll admit to having redrawn some of the barlines in this piece so that I could better play it as a drummer, giving the work the type of contemporary jazz feel the composer is wanting from the rhythm section while still serving the needs of the ensemble. This is otherwise known as "cheating." It's probably best for listeners to not be aware of the barlines as they're hearing the music. Unless you're playing for a dance crowd (or an uncertain band), you can probably enjoy getting away with obscuring some barlines in written music. Bottom line: if it feels good, do it; just don't get lost!

QUESTION: How do you prepare mentally for a big performance? ANSWER: I will spend a lot of time aurally "imaging" the music that I'm going to play, especially if it involves written notation, as in when I am playing with an orchestra. (I get called to play a number of contemporary pieces that call for drumset soloist with orchestra.) I do my homework. So, there's not a whole lot to get nervous about. Kind of like a downhill racer on a ski course. There's plenty of improvisation along the way, but you know the way because you're prepared. Following a conductor is just a different type of ship to steer, and there is no better training for it than experience. If you and the conductor are on the same wavelength in terms of tempos and dynamics, it can be a lot of fun. You just have to pay attention and watch the baton.

Classical conductors are different from most jazz and pop conductors. With jazz and pop conductors, when the baton reaches the lowest point of the motion, that's where the beat is, but with classical conductors it's all on the "up" stroke. One of the secrets of conducting, according to

Stefan Ansbury and Vince Mendoza, is that the smaller the conductor keeps his motions, the better the band will play in time. I've seen Michel LeGrand do this to magical effect. When the motions get too big, everything starts to slow down. I've seen that with some big names in the biz who don't really know what they're doing. What good conductors can do with a piece of music, night after night, in terms of the subtle changes they make, is extraordinary.

Every summer in London's Royal Albert Hall, a series of concerts takes place that are formally known as The Sir Henry Wood Promenade Concerts presented by the BBC, or more simply known as "The Proms." A famous premiere took place there in 1995 during the final night of The Proms, an evening normally reserved for crowd favorites and patriotic tunes. Sir Harrison Birtwistle's composition "Panic" was played by the BBC Symphony Orchestra with soloists Jon Harle on saxophone and Paul Clarvis on drumset, and they all found themselves on the front pages of the nation's newspapers the following morning. "Panic," as the name implies, is a piece with some rough edges; Birtwistle is dedicated to very contemporary music, and the Union Jack flag-wavers didn't like that one bit (imagine you're expecting Kenny G but get Ornette Coleman instead). It took a few years for the excitement to calm down. The BBC decided it wanted to revisit the music, albeit with different soloists. I was pleased but surprised to receive the invitation to come to London for this (drummer/percussionist Paul Clarvis is an excellent musician and friend, one I had written to earlier that year in order to compliment him on some of the fine film music work I'd heard him do). In any event, I got the call and took the gig. Birtwistle's music takes some getting used to, a bit like the man himself. Born 1934 in Lancashire, his character is gruff and outspoken. When I was introduced to him at the first and only rehearsal, I schmoozed him with a complimentary but sincere, "The piece is brilliant," to which re responded, "IS it?" Nice guy. Martin Robertson played the alto saxophone, and we were accompanied by the BBC Scottish Symphony Orchestra conducted by Martyn Brabbins. When one of the BBC musicians complained that the music was too loud, he bellowed, "TOO LOUD? If you were worried about the music being too loud, you should have learned to play the fucking recorder!"

Even though I had a lot of rhythmic reading to do — notated responsibility — I was free to improvise during vast portions of the piece. The improvisations would usually take place within a repeating "box" while the saxophone and/or orchestra carried on. It took some careful concentration to keep pace with the score. At one point I walked over to a second drumset that was facing the brass section, where I acted as a second conductor. If this seems like a lot to put together in one 90-minute rehearsal, you're right. Lesson? DO YOUR HOMEWORK. Studying the part and score ahead of time saved me from a lot of panic during rehearsal.

The concert was a success. Our piece was paired with the percussion concerto "Veni, Veni, Emmanuel," composed by James MacMillan and performed brilliantly by Colin Currie; it was inspiring to hear him play. I hope Sir Harrison enjoyed my drumming on "Panic." It was a bit more bop-oriented in performance than I had originally intended, but that was due to receiving the sad news that day of Max Roach's passing. I did my best to honor the music, and to honor the father of jazz drumming on the stage of Royal Albert Hall. I was lucky enough to meet up with legendary bassist Jack Bruce following the Proms gig, and we enjoyed a couple of get-togethers before I left England. He had played the Royal Albert Hall two years earlier when Cream made their historic and triumphant return there. In any event, I am grateful for Mark-Anthony Turnage returning me to my classical roots. As of this writing, he is composing "Erskine — Concerto for Drumset and Orchestra." It will be premiered by me with maestro Stefan Blunier and the Beethoven Orchester Bonn. **Yes, Beethoven!**

48. Flying to Japan Again

Typing this 38,000 feet in the air above the Pacific Ocean, I am seated inside of a Boeing 747 jet that is flying me, along with my musical colleagues Alan Pasqua (pianist) and Dave Carpenter (bassist), to Tokyo. More specifically, we are flying to Narita Airport. After passport and customs clearance there, we will have a one-and-a-half hour bus ride before we reach the hotel. One week ago I was on a jet, too, flying from Frankfurt, Germany to my home in Santa Monica. That trip began at 5:00 A.M. when I checked in at the Bremen airport for my first of two flights. At least today's trip is only one flight — one long flight.

Sometimes I like to nap when I fly. I like to read, do crossword puzzles, and listen to music. I will usually drink plenty of water, and I'll use my computer to watch DVDs or do some work — like typing this chapter. In Japan right now it's 1 P.M. tomorrow. The body clock tells me it's 9 P.M. tonight. By the time I get to the hotel in Tokyo, I should be in some kind of shape. Crossing the International Dateline is "all in a day-and-a-half's work." And what is the occasion for this formidable journey? A gig. More specifically, a two-week engagement with Japanese jazz star and saxophonist Sadao Watanabe. "Have sticks, will travel." Still doing this after 40-plus years of touring.

Why?

Well, it's good to work. I feel very fortunate to be able to make a living and make my way through life by making music. It puts bread on the table and pays the rent. It also affords me the best chance to learn and to grow; there's always something new to learn.

Nearly two weeks into the trip now, and I have had a ball playing bebop with the group, meeting many Japanese friends and fans, and sampling some delicious Japanese food. But the best part of the trip has been the learning experience. A sampling of that is as follows: On the second night of the gig, the band was having some difficulties with the sound onstage. As much as I preach being a proactive player — and that is certainly important in the creative department — I am a reactive player by virtue of being a drummer who perceives the role of drummer as accompanist and enabler. Concentrating so much on a seemingly endless array of adjustments to try to make things the best they could be, Sadao could easily see that I did not appear to be having too much fun. I've never been a good poker player, especially on the bandstand, and so my guise was not as genuinely endearing to the audience as it might otherwise have been.

These jobs are especially important to Sadao, now that he is in the autumn of his musical career years (Sadao is 70). And since many of his friends were coming, he wanted the concerts to be as enjoyable as possible for all concerned. And so he sat down with me after the show, and we discussed a bit of life philosophy over a couple of beers. He taught me a lovely Japanese expression, "Ichi go, ichi ye (ee-chee go, ee-chee yay)," which translates roughly to, "Today is the first time we meet, and today might be the last time we meet." It is, perhaps, a uniquely Japanese sentiment, but it has application to all who might be open to its meaning. An encounter with another being, whether on a musical or personal level, is a fleeting moment in time. Its beauty lies in the transient nature of its passage in time. And yet, we all know that such fleeting moments leave a taste in the memory that can be quite evocative. And so, reasoning would have it, why not make the very most out of every chance we have to interact with another, musically or otherwise? Put another way: life is too short not to have fun.

photo: Peter Erskine

I might be prejudiced, as my wife is from Japan and I have had a love for the country and its people for many years, but I will say with certainty that the Japanese people are, as a whole, some of the most polite and aware people in the world. Their awareness is specifically centered around harmony, or "wa." What could be more musical than that? Walking throughout the city of Tokyo, one will encounter gestures of humility and care that is, quite frankly, refreshing and inspiring. People pay attention to what they're doing, and since the "what" that they're doing involves other people, one will experience a sense of generosity that the rest of the world could sorely use. Sure, there are impolite and brusque Japanese people; there are some jerks anywhere in the world. But "wa," a vital part of the Japanese psyche, pervades and prevails in the Land of the Rising Sun.

FOR IMMEDIATE RELEASE: *LOS ANGELES, March 28, 2011*

Vitello's Jazz Club Hosts Jazz Relief for Japan/Concerts & Fundraiser Event With Support From Local Jazz Community

Vitello's Jazz Club in Studio City in association with the Los Angeles Jazz Society asks the Los Angeles jazz-loving community to come out and support the victims of the recent earthquake and tsunami in Japan. Musicians and fans will be coming together on Saturday, April 9 for an all day/all night concert event that will raise funds for the Japanese Red Cross.

Music will be provided by Los Angeles' finest, including the Yellowjackets featuring Russ Ferrante, Jimmy Haslip, Bob Mintzer and Will Kennedy; the Grammy-nominated trio of Alan Pasqua and Peter Erskine with Darek Oles; the Wayne Bergeron Big Band; the POEM Quartet comprised of Alan Pasqua, Darek Oles, Peter Erskine and Bob Mintzer.

Grammy-nominated vocalist Denise Donatelli will also be performing, as will the Vitello's All Stars featuring Bob Sheppard, Larry Koonse, Tom Warrington and Joe La Barbara. Attendees will also be treated to "Jazzcomedian" Franklyn Ajaye; Japanese vocalist Takako Uemura; THE TRIO with pianist Terry Trotter and bassist Chuck Berghofer; cajon master and percussionist Alex Acuña; pianist David Arnay; guitarist Mitchell Long; bassists Larry Steen and Kevin Axt, drummers Aaron Serfaty and Ray Brinker; plus the top combo and big band from USC's Thornton

School of Music. Noted jazz radio personality Dick McGarvin will serve as host and emcee for the event.

Performances will begin at 11:30 A.M. and continue until 11:00 P.M., and those attending will enjoy the delicious Italian cuisine of Vitello's. There will also be a silent auction featuring an array of items donated by music celebrities as well as by various musical instrument and electronics manufacturers, with all proceeds going to the Japanese Red Cross.

While the earthquake and tsunami disasters have left us all speechless, the gift and power of music has inspired these talented artists to donate their time, their talent and their voices to this relief effort.

An event like the recent earthquake and tsunami in Japan is one of those "thousand year" occurrences, something of unimaginable horror and magnitude that's not supposed to take place during our lifetime. And, yet, it has happened. But the response of the Japanese people has inspired the world beyond measure. The extended jazz community, in particular, has found a resonance in all of this and a calling to help as best it can. Most all of us share a deep connection with Japan in one way or another: as a place of repeated visits, a land of inspiring grace and beauty; a people who love the music we're hearing today; our best friends in art, industry, commerce and even, in some cases, love; a source of poetic calm in a world that's carpool-laning to madness. The secret for this especially deep connection or sense of recognition may lie in the Japanese concept or word "wa." Wa, in Japan, means "harmony," and the prevalence and importance of wa throughout Japanese society provides an easy explanation for the stoic and selfless response we have seen from the people there these past few weeks. It makes sense that jazz society "gets" this in its gut, heart and soul, and so the response from everyone associated with the presentation of the music, the raising of funds and the giving of gifts has been beyond expectation, hope and belief. You all know who you are. To every artist, volunteer and gift-giver, we offer our profound thanks.

Here's to a brighter tomorrow in the Land of the Rising Sun.

D.S., Coda, etc. Sometimes, life is like a drum chart.

April Williams: thank you for Vitello's and for making this event possible. We raised $17,000 in one day, in a relatively small jazz club. I like to think that this helped in some small way in Japan. I know that it helped all of us who were there.

photo: Peter Erskine

Saturday, April 9, 2011
Vitello's Jazz Club, L.A.

49. Me and Japan

The most casual of readers will have noticed that Japan figures prominently in my life. I first visited in 1974 with the Stan Kenton Orchestra, but have been drawn to the country and its people for much longer. Was it the book of Haiku that I received from my older sister when I was young that triggered my interest? The beauty of our Eurasian-looking "cousin" Evelyn who was actually German but seemed Japanese to me when I was a child and infatuated with her? The girl in high school I had a crush on?

Whatever the reason, I've found myself drawn to Japanese women most all of my life, and I wound up marrying the most beautiful one in the world as far as I'm concerned. Japanese art. Japanese esthetics. Japanese manners. Japanese attention to quality and excellence. I admire most all things Japanese to the point of extreme prejudice.

My father noticed this early in my marriage to Mutsy and was disturbed enough by it to write me a letter that, in essence, served to remind me that the Japanese had, after all, bombed Pearl Harbor and that I shouldn't forget that.

"Dad, hi, it's Peter. I just got your letter. Are you putting me on?"

"Peter, the Yellow Peril…"

"Dad! LISTEN TO YOURSELF!"

Unlike other dogmatists who have just uttered something really dogmatic, he stopped and said "Whoa…waitaminute, er…wow…far out, you're right…." And he looked back into his childhood and the prejudices his mother laid onto him re: the Orient, etc. Even though December 7, 1941 was a date that would live in infamy and was traumatic to all Americans of my father's generation, he realized that he was not thinking big, not thinking right. My father adored Mutsy and Taichi and now Maya, but he had this old bee in his bonnet.

And so we visited Japan together, first opportunity. I took him with me on a John Abercrombie Trio tour of Japan. AND HE FELL IN LOVE

WITH THE PEOPLE AND THE PLACE. We had a ball during that tour. He learned to speak Japanese, and he even braved some sushi — without ketchup, I might add.

The next thing we know, Dad is constructing torii gates around his property and buying antique Japanese this-and-thats for decoration and for just, I imagine, some feel-good presence. His embrace of Japan was not only an expression of the love he had for my family, but the greater love he wanted to find, and did find, in humanity. In Japan, he found himself.

photo: Peter Erskine

Maybe that's why I like it so much here. It feels like home.

50. Life 2

While presenting a jazz drumming class at an East Coast university recently, I was asked, "How has your drumming changed from when you were a younger player?" Hmmm. How best to answer? Should I provide some sort of specific assessment of my musical evolution? Perhaps a comparative analysis of my stylistic growth would suffice. Highlight the changes in my influences as my listening and perceptual horizons became broader? Or maybe I could simply discuss what I do now as compared to what I didn't do when I was a young professional (or vice-versa).

My answer surprised me as it spontaneously formulated itself in my thoughts, and it was spoken aloud after only a moment's hesitation. "When I was younger, I played as though my life depended on it. Now, I play as though someone else's life depends on it."

Interesting, huh? I think back on gigs past when I put everything into the music, meaning literally everything, including energy, sweat, and notes. I used to be soaking wet by the end of most sets, and I saw this as a natural and necessary part of the musical curve. Obviously, whatever the music might have lacked in subtlety or finesse was more than made up for by enthusiasm and muscle. But this left a lot to be desired, most especially on my part. I began to sense that I was fighting the instrument as much as anything else, and so I looked towards a new technique and higher aesthetic to guide me to a better place musically. My playing life depended on it! But now, I would play more for the song. This all goes along with the teachings that "less is more" and "there's power in surrender." Zen and the inner game of paradiddles; less ego, more art. And so on.

I came up with that reply at a drum clinic on a Monday and played a concert that night (with the excellent big band at New Jersey City University); I received lots of positive comments from folks who were at the workshop and concert. I flew home from New York to Los Angeles on Tuesday, and found myself in Capitol Studios early Wednesday morning for a big band recording session with a young vocalist from Canada. The first track was a typical and enjoyable big band arrangement to play, written by the excellent Sammy Nestico of Count Basie fame. The next tune was more of a hybrid piece, half pop and half big band, and the song called for the drums to be hit hard. And I got into it. Meanwhile, I forgot the mantra of the last dozen years that has helped me through innumerable gigs and sessions: "Jim Keltner, Jim Keltner, let the mic do the work, Jim Keltner," etc. And so I am physically pushing myself along with the music. I'm also receiving a bit more direction from the producer than I'm used to getting. The combination of these things plus the apparent demotion from being a guest star back east to being a studio drummer back home is all starting to add up. Coupling my intense concentration to "nail" the tune in as early a take as possible while keeping an eye on the clock (as we had three tunes to finish in as many hours), I exalt when the rhythm section crosses the finish line of a great take. Everyone could hear it, including the producer. Yet, he wants to do it again. By this point, I'm sweating and huffing and puffing, and I'm wondering why on earth he would want or need for us to do it again. And so I step out into the main room from the drum booth and simply announce that I am not going to play it again, at least not right away, but that I will be taking a break and that they all can do what they like. This is generally considered to be out-of-bounds behavior when working on a studio call. But I was entirely confident that the music was there, and that the take was what they wanted or what they WOULD want as soon as they heard it and realized it. By the way, I had also protested that I was "banging the fuck out of the drums" and that I needed that break. Fair enough, right?

Long story short, the session wound up being fine, the take in question was recognized to be "the one," and everyone was happy. But I was disturbed by my actions. I certainly wasn't hitting the drums THAT hard; why did I feel at wits and body's end?

A possible answer came to me that very evening as I watched a film with my wife, an excellent movie titled *Infamous*. This is the second film released in as many years that concerns the penning of the book *In Cold Blood*. The movie is based on the book about the author Truman Capote by George Plimpton, was written for the screen and directed by Douglas McGrath, and stars Toby Jones and Sandra Bullock. Ms. Bullock speaks at the end of the film as longtime Capote friend (and author of *To Kill a Mockingbird*) Nelle Harper Lee: "I read in an interview with Frank Sinatra, in which he said about Judy Garland, 'Every time she sings she dies a little.' That's how much she gave. It's true for writers, too. You hope to create something lasting. They die a little bit when they write. And then the book comes out. And there's a dinner. And maybe they give you a prize. And then comes the inevitable American question: 'What's next?' But the next thing can be so hard, because now you know what it demands."

I recognized something about art and myself in this speech. Whether smart or not, whether art or not, I most often find myself giving the proverbial 110 percent when I play. Contrary to my knowing that drumming is not brain surgery and that I need not perform as if my own life (or anyone else's, for that matter) depended on it, this seems to be something that I can't help but do. Perhaps the "someone else's life" is the music after all.

I've written often about the generosity of drummers when it comes to sharing their knowledge. What I haven't emphasized, perhaps (until now), is that the greatest gifts we can receive from other musicians rarely have to do with matters of musical technique. In fact, the topic of drumming per se was a total conversation-stopper whenever I would chat with the late, great Tony Williams. On a couple of occasions when I went out to see and hear Tony play, I was blown away by his drumming (of course), and felt compelled to compliment and thank him — the best way, I thought, to show my respect for him. Tony would always be warm and welcoming (we met when I had first joined Weather Report, and he was friendly and supportive towards me) whenever we would encounter each other. For whatever reason, however, his eyes would dim immediately as soon as I brought up any mention of his drumming. He simply wasn't interested in hearing anything about that. (Matt Wilson told me a wonderful story about a friend of his who went up to Tony after a set that Tony played, and began his question to Tony with the usual "thank you for the music" expression of gratitude and respect, along with the appropriate accolades, etc., but then followed with the question "Tony, how can I play those fast tempos like you do?" Looking up in exasperation from whatever he was doing, Tony bellowed: "PRACTICE!")

Back to my last encounter with Tony: I had read an interview with Tony in *Modern Drummer* magazine where he spoke at length about taking time off from drumming so that he could study musical composition and orchestration. Tony was very proud of this, and with excellent reason: his composing and orchestrating skills were in full blossom, the result of all of his earlier musical training, experiences, and recent dedication to those art forms. And so I began my conversation after his set with a comment about how inspiring it was to read that he (Tony) was so earnestly studying composition. His eyes lit up, and we got into a wonderful conversation about counterpoint, orchestration, film scores (Tony and I shared an enthusiastic appreciation for the music of Hollywood composers Max Steiner and Erich Wolfgang Korngold), etc. We were chattering away like two enthusiastic kids until I made the mistake of somehow bringing up his drumming, and he immediately got that far away look in his eyes. I excused myself to give him some between-set space and never saw him again after that.

I don't know why Tony was like this with me; former Williams group trumpeter Wallace Roney seemed surprised when I mentioned this to him, claiming that Tony was always eager to talk drumming with other drummers. Perhaps we all seek out in others what our instincts tell us to. In any event, I do know that if Tony and I had exchanged small talk about the drums, it would have been pleasant and memorable, simply by virtue of the legend he was. But to have enjoyed his attention, speaking about matters that carried him away from the — dare I say it? — humdrum of drumming, well, I'll always be grateful for his confidence and enthusiasm about this other side of his artistry and humanity. Tony's first orchestral endeavor and final album is titled *Wilderness*. Tony was dedicated to music, and the drumming world lost its conscience, the guiding light that was to carry us onward after Max Roach and the like. Tony was beyond genius and his drumming is beyond time.

Little-known fact: Tony was not happy with the way he played on the original Weather Report tracking sessions for *Mr. Gone*. According to Zawinul, Tony flew back to L.A. with his drums at his own expense and went back into the studio to play the tracks that are now heard on that album.

51. More Talk About Life and Art

FROM AN INTERVIEW WITH HUNGARIAN JOURNALIST MARCZELL KATALIN

Cegléd, Hungary

Best Western Aquarel Hotel

16 May 2010

P.E.: John Abercrombie was one of the most instructive musicians, and the time period spent with him one of the most valuable for me. Learning how to let go more and become a more fluid player became job number one because the devices I was used to using didn't work with him. So I began to learn not to play out of muscle habit, and to change my touch, even my awareness of time. A lot of the music we played — John, Marc Johnson, and myself — had very flexible time: we would speed up and slow down and do all sorts of things to stretch the fabric of the music. But the only way this would work, from my point of view, was if we had a strong core of understanding about time. The most expressive poets have a good understanding of how language works on a basic level, even though their approach may not be formal or even abstract. Any work of art relies on an inherent structure or structural integrity. A Zen painting with just two or three lines, simple though it may be, is a complex series of forces at work that make the Zen piece of art beautiful compared to when just anyone puts two lines on a piece of canvas.

[I'm pausing a lot between thoughts here.]

M.K.: It's not easy to talk about!

P.E.: Yes, it's like the old joke: talking about music is like someone trying to dance about architecture.

In terms of teaching, much of what I'm doing with my students with requiring them to approach their drumming in the most basic of terms and getting them to think about time is meant to be a process. When you strengthen your inner clock, you learn to respect the spaces between notes.

I do a demonstration in my classes, an exercise from theatre director Peter Brook that he writes about in one of his books. You get ten people, and you give each one of them a single word from the most famous speech in *Hamlet*: "To be or not to be, that is the question." So one person says "To," the next one "be," the third "or," and so on. All words come out like this without fail when you say "Action!": "To…be…or…not… to…be…that…is…the …question." And you say: "Okay, there was a steady rhythm there, but it's not at all musical. "To be…or not to be…" So, real musical rhythm comes when you listen to the note that's been played before you, and you know when and where to place your note — and you listen to the note that comes after! This is how ensembles swing or rock or funk or whatever. It's really all about listening and having a strong enough understanding of where the beat is. You can intentionally pull on the fabric of time, pushing at the edge of the tempo. This could be achieved even harmonically: Ron Carter was a very good example, the way he played with Miles (Davis); that's what he would do: push the pitch of a note, and depending on where he placed it — and the way Tony Williams responded — this all contributes to creating a lot of surface tension. And it is tension that requires resolution of some sort: tension – release – tension – release… Almost like a heartbeat! This is why poetic music is ultimately much more satisfying than marching bands or disco, because in most of that music there's no syncopation, it's just (beating on the table: beat — beat — beat — beat). There's not a whole lot there besides the pounding pulse. Music requires a steady beat, but it also needs flexibility. Time awareness is not about trying to play like a metronome. If I play precisely, it's because I try to play with clarity and I try to choose my notes very well. Some players do it other ways — I'm not saying that my way is the right way or the only way, it's just the way I like to do it — and the way, I think, a lot of other musicians like. The most common compliment or comment that I get from other musicians is, "Wow, you made that very easy for us to play!"

M.K.: I talked to a bass player you played with when you were in Hungary last time: Viktor Hárs. He told me when you played with the Budapest Jazz Orchestra, you prepared everything so well that it was almost impossible to make a mistake. And I asked him: What can Peter Erskine do that other drummers don't? And he said: "He does what others do, but what he does is in its place."

P.E.: All I'm trying to do is to listen, but it's also an architectural approach, let me put it that way. And some drummers don't do this, and it's fantastic that they don't. They play very expressively in their own way.

I always try to be aware of the arc, or shape of the piece of music, and I think this is why, ultimately, I have some of the most fun playing in a large ensemble. It's a nice playhouse to be in. Trios are great, I love trios. I'm one of the few drummers who like to go so much back and forth between these two vastly different-sized ensembles. Another drummer who does both is Jeff Hamilton. He has his big band and his trio. His trio thing is very much like the Ray Brown Trio — great stuff but not really my cup of tea. I like trios that have a lot more mystery, and arc not so what's the word? — so obvious or arranged. I like what we *don't* say, that's more interesting to me. So it's almost anti-drumming in that context. Which again takes us back to the whole time awareness thing. It's what you don't play that makes everything else work. If you play everything, supply every bit of information, there's nothing left for the imagination of the audience! You're playing a form of musical pornography at that point, right?

M.K.: Is there a willing audience for that kind of music?

P.E.: For pornography? Sure. For poetry? That, too!

M.K.: But it's not easy for everyone to listen to that kind of music, to be in it!

P.E.: No, no, but you're inviting them into the discussion. You're respecting their intelligence. You know, in jazz clubs where people want to have a drink or eat dinner, or talk [all of the time], it's tough. You're spending time selling the music or ignoring the audience as much as possible. But we do have some clubs, actually one or two in Los Angeles, where people really come to listen. And it's always the most fun to play there. Unfortunately, one of them is situated on the second floor of the building, so I have to carry my drums upstairs. But it's worth it, because people really come to listen, so you all become part of the evening.

However: if you want to hear good Puccini, you go to Milan — and, if you want to hear really good jazz, you go to New York! When I was in Weather Report, I said to Joe that an opportunity has come up for me to move to New York, and I realized that this would probably put an end to my being in Weather Report, and Joe said: "Hey, man, if you really want to be a jazz musician, you have to go to New York, so this has to happen at some point for you." And so our parting was quite amicable in that way. He was very happy that I went to New York, because he knew it was going to be good for me.

M.K.: So you decided to become a jazz musician after Weather Report?

P.E.: Well, I think I've always wanted to be one, but I realized when I was in Weather Report and I was also doing other session work, that I was unable to play the way I wanted to, the way my hope or imagination wished or heard inside my brain. And I had to get out of playing in such a loud band, and had to start working with musicians who were presenting different challenges, and also more of an invitation to write music and to make those kinds of mistakes I felt I couldn't make onstage with Weather Report. WR was a very improvised thing but also a big show. And it was difficult to play this music that had so much flexibility but also had so much volume; the old Weather Report wasn't that loud. So basically, I had to get myself in a situation where I wasn't playing with so much muscle. And because the level of competition is so intense in New York, if you survive, you have to become a better player. And it was my good luck getting to work with John Abercrombie; I felt he really was the gateway for me. Becoming part of the ECM family for a few years, working with Kenny Wheeler, Dave Holland, John Taylor, Palle Danielson, and Marc Johnson, of course — they really became the essential part of the process for me trying to learn how to listen.

I remember one recording session with Manfred Eicher; Manfred could be a very demanding producer. We just finished an album with the band Bass Desires, and we came into the studio after a tour and were playing really well, we knew all the music — you know, we sounded quite good. And then I stayed in Oslo to do an album with Gary Peacock, Jan Garbarek, and Palle Mikkelborg the next day. So we begin and recorded the first tune, and when we listened to it, the drumming sounded terrible to me! And I couldn't figure out why, only knowing that it sounded like someone doing a really bad imitation of Jack DeJohnette or Jon Christensen. Manfred saw my reaction and he came over to me, pulled me aside, and said, "It's going to be okay, just listen. All you have to do is listen, and you'll know what to do." So that was one of those great lessons: I can't play what I think I'm supposed to play; I should just play what the music tells me to play. There's a big difference. And of course, many drummers play what they think they're supposed to play. Especially at these drum events; I find myself doing it, too. […] take a deep breath: what do I really want to hear if I listen to this back? So it makes it easy to give good advice to my students: It's simple: play what you would like to hear. Don't worry about someone else's expectation. Some of my colleague professors say: "Play more like this or that drummer!" My approach is quite different from that.

M.K.: No imitation?

P.E.: Imitation is an important part of it. And you have to listen to these guys, but I say, "I don't want to hear you play like Jeff Watts or whoever. I want to hear you play like you. So what vocabulary will you use, and what choices will you make, what is the song telling you to do?" Now, if you're doing repertory, playing a Basie chart or something from the '30s, like a Fletcher Henderson chart, then you play it in that style and try to use that vocabulary — and you'll learn a lot by doing that. But listening will bring any musician his or her own voice quicker than anything else — listening and playing.

I was touring with Palle Danielson and the great British pianist John Taylor, and in the midst of our concert tour we played at a so-called "drum meeting" in Prague. The other musicians there were all drum clinic soloists. John and Palle had never seen anything like this, and it made absolutely no sense to them. "Why are these people playing like this?" Good question: I don't know — I guess to show off.

M.K.: But at least it wasn't pornographic…

P.E.: Yeah, it wasn't pornographic, but it's not much different from going to a shopping center and there's someone demonstrating a karate move, where he can break nine bricks at one time. That's really amazing, but — who cares?

The reason for my visit to Hungary was to be present for the opening of the Peter Erskine Lifetime Achievement exhibit at the famed Drum Museum that is located in the city of Cegléd. Here is a portion of the press release:

The Drum Museum in Cegléd, Hungary recently unveiled a lifetime achievement exhibition honoring the work of drummer Peter Erskine, titled "40 Years at the Top." Present at the gala opening on May 14 were Peter Erskine, museum founder and curator Sándor Kármán, the Cultural Attaché for the U.S. Embassy John O. Balian, plus a crowd of 200 persons in the City Hall of Cegléd, which is located outside of Budapest. Cegléd is often referred to as the Mecca of drummers due to the fact that it has hosted Europe's only drum museum since 1992, and the International Drum and Percussion Gala that has been organized in its sports arena since 1993.

Erskine donated a large collection of instruments and memorabilia, spanning his entire career as drummer, recording artist, record producer, musical instrument innovator, composer and educator. Erskine is also the founder of Fuzzy Music, a CD label that has come to represent what an artist-owned label may achieve.

It was nice to not be dead for something like this. Seriously, it was all very humbling and quite nice.

photo courtesy of the Drum Museum , Cegléd, Hungary

52. USC

I have been teaching drums at the University of Southern California's Thornton School of Music since 2002. The big news now at USC is that we are teaching beginning drumset as part of a new degree requirement: all popular music performance majors are **REQUIRED** to master basic drumming techniques and drumset beats. We teach eight students at a time in a drum lab setup, much like an electronic keyboard lab where the instructor will have a headset and communicate with students individually or collectively. This class is fast becoming one of the most popular music courses at USC. In one semester's time enrollment grew from 16 to 64 students, and we're adding more sections or class times every year. My books *Drumset Essentials, Volume 1* and *Time Awareness for All Musicians* are the textbooks for the class. The history of contemporary music is so intertwined with the development of the drumset and drumbeats, and we're teaching all of that.

My private students are all great — excellent players and inquisitive students. The school's jazz department is a strong magnet, and it has been attracting some terrific players. I asked one of them once why a particular recording was so good; the recording in question was Keith Jarrett's "Common Mama" on the album *Expectations* with Paul Motian playing drums in a hypnotic and compellingly modern way; "uncommon" would be a word for it. But my student does me one better: "It's great because Paul Motian is letting the music do all of the work."

I'm getting paid to teach, but I feel as though I'm the one who's learning.

However, I can get impatient with some of my students. I'll say, "Yeah, your drumming is fine; you're doing all the right drumming stuff. And I'm sick of drumming like that. Let's make some music, and don't just play what you're used to playing. Don't keep reacting the way you always react because when any instrumentalist — drummers, especially — start feeling uncomfortable, they start sounding very much like the way they did in high school. You know, 'Oh man, what am I going to do?' And you can get beyond that: you don't have to fall back on the stuff you know. Don't play what you know; play what you don't know."

I am proud to teach with my colleagues Ndugu Chancler, Roy McCurdy, Alan Pasqua, Bob Mintzer, Patrice Rushen, Alphonso Johnson, and drummer and percussionist Aaron Serfaty. We have a great dean who supports us, and a better-than-ever jazz school.

53. Whither Jazz Goest?

On a recent morning I was enjoying a cup of coffee in the kitchen of our home, my wife sitting across the table from me, also with cup in hand. We were about to walk our dog, but somehow the conversation underway steered itself towards matters of musical aesthetics, and your faithful correspondent was off and running in the talking department. When my wife asked, "What's so bad about an artist like Kenny G if he manages to get people more curious or interested about jazz?" I replied, "Fair enough, but shall we brew another pot of coffee while we're at it?"

I continued: "This is a legitimate question, though it seeks to legitimize an aspect of musical philosophy that has more to do with business than with art. Whatever your stance might be on 'commercial' music, 'smooth jazz' and the like, there's no shame or argument in the fact that this is a music that's designed to be enjoyed (or consumed) by the greatest number of people possible. And while I cannot get inside the head of musicians who choose this path, I should not doubt their musical sincerity. At the same time, it would be disingenuous for such musicians to deny that commerce is somewhere in the forefront of their creative impulses. That is not a crime, but I do consider it an upside-down way to make music.

"Regardless of motivation, let's assume that a percentage of the improvised-music listening initiates who are digging on, say, Kenny G, decide to explore more in the way of instrumental sounds. My educated guess is that most of these listeners will seek out more of the same types of music that function as an ambient soundtrack for their life, as it were; music that makes, at most, a two-dimensional demand on the part of the audience. But, for the sake of argument, let's say that many smooth jazz listeners decide to pursue the 'jazz' part of the equation with some good measure of effort. What then?

"Well, if a Kenny G fan found his or her way to my own music, I should be pleasantly surprised and grateful for the attention. Whether my music would prove to be of entertaining interest or not to that person would have to be seen. I'm not at all confident that the preparation provided by exposure to 'smooth jazz' would work in anyone's favor in this case. The aesthetic choices between these two schools of music making are worlds apart. If you cherish unpredictability or space in your music, or the intelligent use of counterpoint, or bounce in your beat, then smooth jazz will usually miss the mark by a mile. Let me make clear: I do not doubt the potential intelligence or patience of these imaginary listeners, but their finding my music would most likely be the result of any number of circumstances NOT related to the fact that a Kenny G introduced them to the grooviness of 'jazz,' smooth or otherwise. So I find the suggestion that art which is half-way honest, authentic, or competent might possibly have a positive impact on art that is otherwise created with discipline, spontaneity, and a good measure of craft to be a curious proposition indeed."

Espousing my jazz musician's well-honed sense of musical mistrust on my kitchen stool-turned-pedestal, I heard myself saying all of this stuff and immediately wondered aloud, "What is it about these smooth jazz musicians that riles the aesthetic fur of so many jazzers?" Well, some musicians are simply envious when they see the cashing-in success of music that does not (in their opinion) aspire to any sense of vision or greatness but is merely an expression of (arguably) mediocre aesthetics and/or abilities. All discussion of which, admittedly, will have very little effect on the people creating or listening to smooth jazz. (It's a circular argument. Oh, did I mention that my name once showed up on a list of eligible drummers to vote for in a Smooth Jazz Listeners Poll, based on my having appeared on a couple of particular albums? Yikes.) Psychology 101 instruction teaches that a person may express hostility at something or someone that has traits that are recognizable in them on a latent (hidden or dormant) level. In other words: successful smooth jazz musicians might represent that which us otherwise-artistic types might fear the most (or is it the annoyingly curly hair and the dopey-looking embouchure these guys all seem to share?).

I submit that a good part of our artistic conscience nags at every compromise we make along the way. We start out with the highest of aspirations and the best of musical intentions, however we're wired or taught. And then… Well, LIFE comes along and causes you to change your plans. Life demands adaptation. Living in society demands the ability to negotiate and compromise. At what levels do we exceed our self-made promises? Does the "pure" jazz musician exist? And what was I doing in a Hollywood recording studio last week playing drums on a country-music commercial for Toyota trucks?

I turn to saxophonist and writer Dave Liebman: "To begin, it is necessary to make a distinction between art and craft. Craft implies mastering technique to the degree that a craftsman is competent enough to skillfully reproduce the artifacts of the given art form. For a jazz musician, this means that one can sound convincing using the rules and customs of the music — no mean feat, by the way. Art, on the other hand, utilizes and transcends mere technique to communicate the personal feelings of the artist in whatever manner (s)he chooses. As Aristotle wrote: 'The aim of art is to represent not the outward appearance of things, but their inward significance.' For me, craft is a stage along the way, whereas artistic expression represents true individual freedom and the overall goal."

I like to consider myself a craftsman as well as an artist, one who is still on the path towards becoming a better musician. I try my best to aim high when it comes to those things that matter the most to me (my family, my music, my ethics, and my friends). I'm a husband, father, and a professional musician — one who enjoys the variety offered by the free-lance musical life. Like a doctor who has sworn to obey the oath of Hippocrates, I shall always strive "to do no harm" in my dealings with people or with notes. Each experience informs the next. My advice: Don't be afraid to try out different kinds of music as a player or listener. But always keep your eyes and ears on the musical prize that honestly feels right to you. You'll know it when you hear it.

I've been working on a pet theory of late, one that attempts to explain when and where music took a bad turn, or put another way, why the music I hear today does not seem to have the magic of the music I heard when I was young. Lest the reader think these are the ramblings of a mid-life musical malcontent, I wish to assure one and all that I am still a fan and lover of music. But a palpable change took place in contemporary music, just around the time I was beginning to make a name for myself in the world of music. Am I being nostalgic? Let's see where this goes...

The world was a different place not so long ago. It wasn't as easy to find something new, different, or unheard, like music-seekers today who have the World Wide Web at their fingertips, and I applaud the democratization of information access. But wait a sec; we did have the radio, with 24/7 jazz stations in just about every major city. We had television, too, with a fair amount of jazz on it from time to time. And we had The Beatles on *The Ed Sullivan Show*, their 1964 appearances and the song "I Want to Hold Your Hand" helping to lift America out of its post-Kennedy assassination funk. There's some magic for you. One thing that made the sudden discovery of new music so wondrous was that it was not on demand. One could not download a song; one had to wait by the radio or TV (or go out to the nearest vinyl album shop) to catch a listen. Hearing a good tune was much like finding a four-leaf clover.

Meanwhile, jazz had been undergoing some groundbreaking changes. Without attempting to offer a definitive mini-history of the music, the following chronology should prove accurate and useful: after the Second World War and out of the Swing Era came bebop, where rhythmic, harmonic, and melodic conventions were challenged and turned on their head. Different "schools" of modern jazz developed, characterized by the hot bop playing of Charlie Parker and Dizzy Gillespie in contrast to the "cool school" of the early Miles Davis and West Coast groups. Some of the great bop drummers were Kenny Clarke, Max Roach, Art Blakey, and Philly Joe Jones. Post-bop came into being by the forays made by explorers like Sonny Rollins and John Coltrane, followed by Wayne Shorter (with Miles Davis, who again was at the forefront of the musical vanguard), Eric Dolphy, and Freddie Hubbard; some notable drummers in all of this included Roy Haynes, Elvin Jones, and Tony Williams. Other musical giants of the late 1950s/early 1960s included Thelonious Monk and Charles Mingus. The avant-garde was (literally) making noise in the late 1950s, where conventions of the norm were deemed "square" and irrelevant; Ornette Coleman led the charge.

Parallels can be found in the worlds of visual and literary art, and modernity was busting out all over. America was rebuilding as much of the world as it could after World War II, out of generosity as well as in its own interests and image, while most of us were being taught to "duck and cover" should a nuclear missile find its way into our neighborhood. Racism was still overt in this country, but change was underway. Martin

Luther King, Jr. had a dream, The Beatles wanted to hold our hand, and Sly & the Family Stone were getting ready to take us higher. Pop music crossed over from safely-packaged/produced fare to experimental soundscapes. Young people everywhere started asking more and more questions: of their leaders, of their parents, of the system, and of the very society they were in. Music was right there alongside, not attempting to provide any answers, but fueling the questions with more of its own.

This is my guess: As older jazz styles merged with the new, and jazz collided with pop and rock sensibilities, music found itself in a cornucopia of genres. Free jazz met free love. Man, anything was possible. Recording technology was just getting to the point where musical searching could take place in an environment where a lot of new things were possible: multi-tracking, electronic effects, the separation and joining of instruments combined with the layering of sounds upon sounds, etc. What a laboratory! And each new recording seemed to herald yet one more advance into the unknown. As such, chances were pretty good that every new album purchased would deliver something new, something never heard before, and something that seemed to say, "Here is what's possible, but we're not really sure yet."

Music was asking questions. Upon hearing the recording *Now He Sings, Now He Sobs* by pianist Chick Corea (with Miroslav Vitous on bass and Roy Haynes on drums), I felt that I had been lucky enough to receive a postcard from the future that said "here's what's possible." The first couple of Weather Report recordings said the same thing to me. Even the titles of the songs reflected the mystery of not knowing: Corea's "Steps – What Was" to Weather Report's "Unknown Soldier" to Corea's "What Game Shall We Play Today?" Each new listen was a shared experience with the composers and musicians on recordings from this era (mid-to-late 1960s to early/mid-1970s).

It seems that by the time America had pulled itself out of Vietnam, we began, possibly, to tire of asking so many questions. We wanted answers but didn't want to think too hard to get them. Music obliged. It only took a few years to go from the syncopated boogaloo funk that challenged straight-laced/white collar/corporate imperialism to the relentless and mind-deadening pulse of disco that pounded the beat into each listener, turning anyone into a dancer. Jazz tried merging with this, most often with musically dismal results. A neoclassicism emerged, jazz started sounding suspiciously like bebop and post-bop all over again, only this time the music and its media messengers (a/k/a the critics) were TELLING us that this was how jazz was supposed to sound. Music stopped asking questions. While all of this was happening, a lot of jazz got smoother and slicker, and most every musical venture began to appear as if it were driven by money rather than by art.

Disclaimer: the above is a highly truncated, bastardized, and biased history of recent music.

This brings me to an interesting point, best expressed by the late Canadian percussionist and composer John Wyre. John was a great musician: timpanist in several major orchestras and a founding member of the percussion group Nexus. He organized many world percussion symposiums and musical get-togethers. He explored sonic landscapes in his improvisations and compositions. John cared deeply for all of those good things that were possible when people and sound were brought together. In a documentary film that was made about John, *Drawing on Sound*, he quotes an ancient Chinese proverb: "The bird does not sing because it has an answer; it sings because it has a song." Hearing John utter these words in the film brought back tremendous memories of this great person. John defined himself as an explorer, but one who was more interested in the journey than the destination or outcome. In other words, his music was always about asking questions. Like John and our fine-feathered friends, shall we strive to create the kind of music that we must create while leaving the answers to those who listen?

54. Wayne

photo: Peter Erskine

The first time my parents came to see a Weather Report show, I introduced them to the band onstage during our afternoon soundcheck. At some point I glanced over at my mother, who was engaged in conversation with Wayne. She was smiling her big, beautiful smile while Wayne spoke, looking very animated and happy. "Good," I thought, "they're getting along really well and she likes Wayne!" About a minute or so later she walked over to where I was standing and, still smiling, said in a very low voice, "Is that guy for real?"

Wayne was (and is) the Mysterious Traveler.

Interesting thing

One interesting thing about Wayne was that, in all of the time I was in the band with him, he never once referred to Miles or his time in Miles' band to serve as any sort of example, musical or otherwise, to us; meanwhile, he never failed to mention Art Blakey at least once a day when we were on tour or in the studio. I found that fascinating. Wayne was the quietest member of the Weather Report quartet, but easily the most profound when he wanted to be.

Scene: The University of Weather Report. This freshman class of 1978 is taking place on a Shinkansen ride from Tokyo to Osaka. The guys have noticed some heavy-handedness and slack in the way I'm hitting the drums; not enough "snap" to the sound or the beat in enough places to warrant their concern — something that Joe would comment on immediately following a performance, but not Wayne, who seems to always be watching but not saying anything during one of these post-mortems. At any rate, I am telling a story to Joe, Wayne, and Jaco, who are standing around me in the snack-bar car of the train, and when I get to the part of the story where I say, "And just like that," with a mild slap of my hands, muted in part because I do not wish to disturb any others on the train, Wayne reaches out and stops me, rewinding the story a few seconds so he can go, "Not like that, like THIS," and he whips one hand towards the other so that he produces an intense slap of the hands while looking triumphantly at me. "Like this...," I repeat as I, too, slap my hands with tremendous vigor and velocity. Wayne smiles, nods his head, and backs away.

Meanwhile, here I am every night getting ready to play a duo with Wayne Shorter. Mind blowing! What am I doing up here playing with Wayne Shorter? Enjoying it, that's for sure. But I had a lot to learn. For example, Wayne would launch into a rhythmic figure while soloing, and I would hear it and then play it in unison with him. This occurs on the *8:30* live album that we made, and while mixing the album, it was just Joe Zawinul and me in the studio with the engineer listening. Joe is standing by these big speakers, I'm standing next to him, and we're listening to the track. Wayne and I are playing on the tape, and Joe turns to me and says, "Sounds good." I feel proud. Then, just at that moment, Wayne did this whole sequential ascending pattern thing, and I caught it. Zawinul hears that on the tape, turns to me with a really sour look, and says, "Uhm! Too bad you had to do that."

Later, during a rehearsal, Wayne stopped playing when I did the same thing, and he said, "Don't do that." I began to understand that the role of the rhythm section is not to play in unison, but to provide the constant as well as the contrast, or counterpoint. So if the soloist starts playing syncopations, maybe you can do counter-syncopations as long as they don't get too busy. Or just keep doing what you're doing, because the soloist is cutting across the grain: that's what makes it cool. Imagine the rhythm section is a bright blue background, and the soloist cuts a brilliant red diagonal stripe across it; it makes no sense for us to turn red. (Drumming for me is all about balance. You're balancing dynamically, but you're providing a counterweight to things, and if something is happening in the band, you're either providing a steady pulse or coming up with rhythmic counterpoint that makes the stuff dance.)

When I joined Weather Report, my only thought at the time was to play my heart out. This quality, combined with enough experience to be able to pull off most of what I could hear inside of my head, stood me well during those first heady weeks of touring. The four of us — Joe Zawinul, Wayne Shorter, Jaco Pastorius, and myself — were thoroughly enjoying the newness of it all. Every relationship, however, be it between members of a band or a man and woman, undergoes the dynamics of change, and so it was, as I entered the second phase of my tenure with the group, that I had to learn how to become a more mature and contributing member of the ensemble. Joe, of course, began telling me more and more about myself: how I looked when I walked ("You take these funny little steps when you walk, man. You should learn to take bigger steps; it will make you a better drummer!"), how I paused too much when I spoke; my stroke on the drumset; my sense of time; and the velocity as well as the veracity of my beats — all "fair game" for discussion. And, as proud as I remained throughout all of this, I also realized and knew that these musicians knew much more about all of this stuff than I did. And so, I listened.

Throughout all of this and for all of their association, Joe and Wayne were the yin to the other's yang. And all of us benefitted.

photo: Shigeru Uchiyama

55. From Fearless to Self-conscious

Weather Report performed an intensive soundcheck every concert day on tour. The purpose of most soundchecks is to check the sound; our soundchecks became rehearsals, most of which morphed into what Jaco called "the drum lesson." Joe had this or that idea about how something I was playing could sound better, and he was not too shy to tell me! Trying to incorporate his suggestions out of respect as well as some sense of professionalism, I began thinking of all of the "do this" and "don't do that" demands. I went from being fearless to cautious, encouraged to discouraged, spirited to perfunctory, and so on. Being in the middle of the storm, though, did not make it easy for me to spot the spot that I was in! Meanwhile, Jaco and the band's crew were wondering, "What's happening with Peter?"

And so it was that, during a soundcheck, after Joe had made his umpteenth suggestion to me about how to play something, Jaco came over to the drumset and said, "Hey man, don't THINK so much; just CONCENTRATE!" What does that mean? I understood it right away on several levels, but will boil it down to two meanings here: One, LISTEN to the music; don't think about what or how to play, just LISTEN and then you'll play what you want to hear; Two: rediscover the magic that music brought to you when you first began to pay attention to it and when you first began to play.

This turned out to be excellent advice. I was able to return to a natural state of musical energy and enthusiasm in the band. Plus, like any good advice, it would prove to have a timeless and universal quality to it; i.e., it qualified as a "truism." I find myself quoting it nowadays to my students.

Jaco, giving advice to anyone about to listen to part of any new recording we made: "Fasten your safety belts."

Jaco said a LOT of things. Once, as I began to gain some weight, he cautioned me not to get on a trampoline and jump too high, lest someone come along and paint "Goodyear" on my side! Another time he was less humorous and more blunt; when I encountered Jaco in the airport just before we departed for the ill-fated tour of Japan with the Word of

Mouth Big Band (where and when Jaco's illness manifested itself beyond anything anyone had seen or expected), shocked by his crew-cut appearance with pieces of electrical tape on his face (to "hold my face together," as he later explained to me) — I greeted him with a quiet, "Hi, Jaco," and he replied, "Hiya, Fatso."

Back to Joe and the weight thing: running into Zawinul a few years ago, I said, "Hey, Joe," and he replied by poking his finger into my belly and asking, "What's that?" I explained that Mutsy and I had joined a health club and that I was working with a trainer, doing a 45-minute workout routine, and so on. He looked at me and said, "Oh yeah? Since when: TOMORROW?"

Funny guy. And then he said, 'Wayne and I are talking about putting the band back together for a tour, but I'm not going to call you. I'm going to call Paco because you play different now." I could only say "Thanks," because I did play differently by then, as I do now.

I started finding that the dynamic area I liked to work in was not always so loud. I simply didn't like the way I played, and the way playing loud made me play. I also learned how to make musical choices that were not only best for the music but true to my own values. I finally found my own voice. A couple of times I've run into some players who felt that I wasn't giving enough or I wasn't listening. I'm listening incredibly intensively when I play; that's all I'm doing, and I make the choice. "Yeah, I hear what you're doing, it's cool." And I think it's cool because I'm doing what I'm doing. I'm not going to comment on what they're doing or play the obvious. The Wayne thing. It's gotten to the point with more and more of my drumming that it has everything to do with space and less with playing. Kind of like anti-matter, only it's anti-playing. Not suitable for all occasions, but when it's right, man, it's right!

56. Weather Report Drummers

The Percussive Arts Society holds its annual convention in autumn, with 1997's musical festivities taking place in Columbus, Ohio. I took an early flight from Los Angeles to get there for the opening day, and what a flight! Other passengers included Louie Bellson, Emil Richards, and Ndugu Chancler. I quickly ran into more drumming legends and heroes when I arrived at the convention hotel: Ed Thigpen, Vic Firth, Arnie Lang (New York Philharmonic), Alan Abel (Philadelphia Orchestra), Bill Platt (Cincinnati Symphony), She-e Wu (marimba soloist), Dave Weckl, Omar Hakim, Chester Thompson, Billy Martin, and the man that would join me in a presentation to the PASIC audience at the close of the conference, fellow Weather Report alumnus Alex Acuña. Apologies for other legends whose names I have omitted; it seemed like everyone was there!

Two highlights were the Weather Report drummers panel, where Alex, Omar, Ndugu, Chester, Skip Hadden, and I discussed our work with the band, its recordings, etc. Rick Mattingly moderated this panel; the hour's time went by too quickly. Hopefully, we'll be able to have more reunions of this sort. The second highlight was the clinic that Alex and I gave on the final day of the conference. The ballroom was packed, and there was a positive sense of excitement in the air. This was more like an actual Weather Report gig than a clinic. We had prepared some play-along tracks — the antithesis of what Weather Report was about, admittedly, however… Since we wisely chose NOT to practice with these tracks beforehand, we were experiencing the music "live" and in the moment at the exact same time as the audience. Of course, getting to play this music with Alex is a drummer's dream. And so, we took chances, we had a lot of fun, we made some great music and, I hope, some great memories for the people who were there.

Speaking of the other Weather Report drummers…

I take my hat off and bow in respect to all of the drumming brethren who have shared the chair in Weather Report with me. It was not an easy gig, but it sure was hip. Alphonse Mouzon started the ball rolling, and I thought he was the perfect fit for the band. But then, so was Eric Gravatt, probably the hippest drummer to have played with the band in my opinion; there was a quality to his playing that seemed to reach out to the cosmos. A lot of drummers contributed to the band's growth, touring and recording in the years following Gravatt's departure, including Herschel Dwellingham, Gregg Errico, Ishmail Wilburn, Skip Hadden, Darryl Brown, Ndugu Chancler, Chester Thompson, Alex Acuña, Steve Gadd, Tony Williams, and, following my tenure, Omar Hakim. Their combined recorded legacy forms a history of modern American music unlike most any other imaginable.

My favorite WR recordings? In addition to the first two albums (*Weather Report* and *I Sing The Body Electric*), I love *Mysterious Traveler, Heavy Weather,* and *Sportin' Life*. My favorite composition is Zawinul's opus "Unknown Soldier"; like the best of the music from the late '60s and early '70s, it speaks from one time to another, reaching backwards and forwards in musical and emotional space.

A salute to everyone who weathered the storm!

photo: Peter Erskine

57. Stormy Weather

Speaking of stormy weather — as "right" as everything was about the band and its successes during the years I toured with Weather Report, there was plenty of dysfunction to go around. One lamentable aspect of Joe and Jaco's perfectionism in the studio was that every album took longer to complete than planned for, with the post-production overdubbing, editing, mixing, and artwork process lasting right up until that album's release tour was set to take place. So we always seemed to be behind in terms of promoting the album. Worse, the band would begin an arduous tour often in the poorest of health, having come straight out of the confines of the studio with its attendant late hours, drinking, etc.

By the time we had finished work on *Night Passage*, Joe was absolutely exhausted, but this did not fit in with his self image of tough guy, hard drinker, and so on. He began this tour occasionally giddy, but more mean and short-tempered, to the point where all of us were walking on eggshells around the man. There was no pleasing him or curbing his nastiness. It speaks volumes about Jaco's character as well as his relationship to Joe that Jaco had enough balls and sense of what's right to assemble the band and crew following an early concert during this tour, somewhere in Norway as I recall. And there took place a remarkable scene: The entire Weather Report band and crew were standing in a large circle, with Joe and Jaco in the center, Jaco addressing Joe, pointing out his behavior and demanding that Joe stop it once and for all: "You're RUDE, Joe. You've been acting like a rude motherfucker for a while now, and it's got to stop." We all stood wide-eyed and in silence. Finally, Joe said, "You're right." More silence. And then he continued, "And I would like to apologize to everyone here, right now." It was time to put that in the past, and we continued to tour and play some of the best concerts I remember the band giving.

It seemed that Joe would try to even out the score —out of earshot of Jaco — coming up to me and saying things like, "You know what? Jaco sounds like a trombone a lot of the time," or, backstage, "Jaco's solo lasts for another four minutes? I'll see you in five minutes," and he would disappear to the dressing room.

I don't remember Wayne ever being or seeming mean-spirited.

Despite the competitiveness or edginess to much of the band's humor, we all knew how to have a good time and enjoy each other's company. We laughed a lot, we cheered each other on, and we looked out for one another. Joe came to Jaco's rescue a few times to get him out of a jam, usually a result of something Jaco had said to someone. Jaco didn't have much of an "edit" button. But that's part of what made him so great. His impulsiveness is the stuff of legend. Once, immediately following a concert in Antibes, France, while the audience was still cheering, Jaco suggested we run onto the beach just behind the stage and into the Mediterranean — without our clothes on, of course. This seemed like a really cool idea, and I'll never forget how much fun it was to come up from under the water and still hear the people cheering. Jaco loved the water as much as he liked doing crazy things, and sometimes the two likes were well-met fellows.

photo: Peter Erskine

58. Three Views

photo: Norman Seeff

What should the music be called?

Just for the record: Weather Report always rejected the word "fusion," claiming the band played "modern American music" and "we don't fuse nuthin'."

Be that as it may, jazz-rock and fusion are handy terms; jazz-rock sounds a bit dated and faded, though, like an old pair of bell-bottomed pants. Maybe fusion is better, but I tend to picture Billy Cobham as soon as I hear the word.

How different was playing in Jaco's Word of Mouth Big Band from Stan Kenton's a decade earlier?

Jaco's band contained many brilliant soloists. While Jaco was honoring the traditions of different bands, he was busy inventing his own large ensemble style. Stan's band was largely dedicated to playing for young, aspiring musicians at schools, or older people at dances.

When the music morphed into "smooth jazz," why didn't it die?

I don't think that the music that Miles played, that Weather Report played, et al, morphed into anything of the sort. The roots of "smooth jazz" come more from MUZAK than anything else — Percy Faith with an R&B beat. It is music that essentially aspires to nothing. Meanwhile, Weather Report's music sounds as fresh as tomorrow.

The last time I saw Jaco...

Was at the Seventh Avenue South jazz club in New York City. He was holding his bass the same way I remembered when we first met: not drunk and not arrogantly angry at the world. He seemed subdued. In fact, he was on medication that was calming him down. And he told me, "You know, I burned so many bridges these last few years that I just decided to go ahead and burn every last one of them so I could simply start all over again." Aside from the ubiquitous, "Hey, Man!" he would always offer, those were the last words I remember him saying to me.

The last time I saw Wayne...

Was backstage at Disney Hall; he and his quartet were about to play in concert with the Los Angeles Philharmonic. Mutsy and I met Wayne in his dressing room to say hello and wish him well. "Have fun!" right? Always self-conscious about giving fellow players their space, we leave somewhat quickly. As I look down the long passageway between the dressing room door and back where Wayne is seated, he leans into view and yells down the corridor: "Big BANDS!" and that's been our last conversation to date.

photo: Peter Erskine

59. Two Deaths

photo: Peter Erskine

Jaco Pastorius and Joe Zawinul, the two baddest cats in the universe, are gone.

Only a few musicians of the highest order are recognized by their sound, and Jaco ranks at the top of that short list. And only a few icons, musical or otherwise, are known worldwide by their first name only; mention "Jaco" anywhere in the world and you are greeted with intense passion about the man, his music, and his legacy. There's no question that Jaco left us many years too soon. But his musical impact couldn't have been stronger. Music was not the same after Jaco came on the scene. It was almost 25 years ago as I write this that his physical presence left us, murdered in Florida. We all miss Jaco, and can only begin to imagine what musical riches he would have brought to us during these last 20 plus years (and beyond). Yet his musical message remains as vibrant now as when we all first heard his magical tone and unearthly rhythmic prowess.

We used to tell a lot of jokes in Weather Report. Jaco was the best joke teller of all. Some of those jokes were about the kind of band that was in Heaven (or in Hell). I know that the band in Heaven has never sounded better than it's sounding right now, and something tells me they're playing "Liberty City" or "Three Views of a Secret" as we celebrate and mourn and celebrate some more the gifts of our friend Jaco Pastorius.

"Birdland" is on the set list, too; you know it.

Josef Erich Zawinul was known simply as "Zawinul" to his many fans, "Joe" by those who knew him, and "Brother Joe" by those who loved and worked closely with the man. Joe Zawinul was uncompromising when it came to most everything in life, most especially when it came to music. "It's all about the music," he would say. And even though he held lively discussions about politics, history, food, literature, or sports, he never stopped thinking about his music. He demanded much from his colleagues as well as those he listened to. But he was also a kind and generous man — a teacher of the highest sort. During the years I spent working with Joe, he never failed to include a life lesson (that would always relate to music) to his bandmates He was our leader and our mentor. He was the "Mysterious Traveler," and he never stopped touring or working. His musical vision kept growing all of his life, tempered only by the focus he brought to it. He followed his own path. Unlike most jazz stars in the twilight years of their careers, he never took part in joining up with others in some sort of an "all star" band. His band was always an all-star band as far as he was concerned, and he brought out the best in all of the musicians who were fortunate enough to play beside him. I am grateful for his music, and for his appetite when it came to life. I am grateful for the seriousness that he brought to the art and craft of creating music, and for his incredible humor. And I will always be grateful that I could call him "Brother Joe."

60. Musical Salute

The best way to honor the memory of great musicians is to play their music. And what better way than to present Joe Zawinul's music in the famed Concertgebouw concert hall in Amsterdam, with Vince Mendoza arranging and conducting the Metropole Orchestra along with former Zawinul colleagues Alex Acuña, Victor Bailey, Amit Chatterjee, and myself, plus keyboardist Jim Beard and lead trumpeter Derek Watkins? I'm happy to report that I cannot imagine a better or more successful program than what was enjoyed by the standing-room-only crowd.

Vince arranged the big band versions of Zawinul's music that Alex, Victor, and I premiered a few years ago with Joe and the WDR Big Band (Nathaniel Townsley plays drums on the *Brown Street* album of that music, which came out recently). This Concertgebouw incarnation of Joe's music, however, involved the Metropole Orkest, an incredibly talented group that is part jazz band and part symphony (with strings, woodwinds, and percussion). Vince did a lot of writing leading up to our meeting at the Metropole rehearsal facility in Hilversum. Alex and I flew direct from the NAMM Show in southern California, while Victor arrived from New York and Jim Beard from Helsinki. Vince was already working with the Orchestra by the time the rest of us got there.

Weather Report was an organic music, most often composed as it was being improvised (for what is improvisation but instant composition?). The first task with some of the songs, like "Nubian Sundance" and "Jungle Book," was to find consensus on where beat "one" was! There was a lot of back and forth about this during the transcription process, including which meter should be chosen: 3/8? 3/4? 6/8? Was Joe thinking in 5/8 and then 2/4 when he came up with a particular part, or was that an edit on the album? I gave Vince my best advice on a good many of these questions earlier when I was on vacation in Japan. My colleagues in the Netherlands were not in total agreement with some of my metric suggestions, but we learned the tunes as they were notated (at this point there were too many musicians' parts to change).

Amit Chatterjee of the Zawinul Syndicate band played some great guitar and sang in Hindusthani style as well as in Joe's "Zawa-speak" mode.

Keyboardist Jim Beard added his own take to the Zawinul sound and formed a perfect bridge between the two worlds of the present and past. It felt like home to be playing again with Victor and Alex. The members of the orchestra were all keen and alert participants. Most of the music played itself, but there was room for some discussion and discipline on how best to play this or that song in order to maintain the proper essence of the music: to honor the man by properly honoring the music. I truly feel that we connected to Joe's spirit, and it was his spirit that connected all of us to one another.

We repeated the process the following year in a rousing afternoon performance at the North Sea Jazz Festival; highlights from both concerts have been assembled for *Fast City, A Tribute to Joe Zawinul*. This, for me, was a more successful revisiting of Joe's music than a previous attempt in Studio 4 of the WestDeutscheRundfunk in Cologne, Germany. The WDR Big Band is one of the best big bands in the world and was my big band home for several years. Other drummers could also lay claim to that distinction, Mel Lewis having been the first prominent guest drummer to work regularly with the band (others including Jeff Hamilton, Adam Nussbaum, John Riley, and Dennis Mackrel). The first time I worked with the band was on a project with Kenny Wheeler, and I played with them many times afterwards in conjunction with Vince Mendoza. Since the band is made up of lifetime appointees, some of the old-timer players leaned towards a pensioner's penchant for slacking and/or whining. And since the band had to fulfill its music duties for German TV as well as for the more idyllic and idealistic world of pure music, i.e., American jazz, I don't blame them for whining some of the time; only thing is, none of us Americans enjoyed their whining on our projects (and, half of the time, it was the expatriate Americans in the band who were doing a lot of the whining). All of that said, some of my favorite musicians in the world play in that band, including bassist John Goldsby, pianist Frank Chastenier, and lead trumpeter Andy Haderer, one of the finest lead players anywhere.

Victor, Alex, and I were brought in as guest artists for this first Zawinul music tribute, with Scott Kinsey playing keyboards, to be joined by a very-much alive Joe Zawinul for the concert. Joe showed up the evening before the concert, after the band and guests had been rehearsing the music for close to two weeks. This is my first chance to revisit the music of Weather Report, to experience that "if I'd known then what I know now" opportunity, and I'm making the most of it — shading the music the way I like and the way Vince's excellent arrangements invite me to do. We've been firing on all cylinders the last few days, and so playing the music for Joe should be fun. Studio 4 is packed with guests and members of the press. Zawinul arrives from the airport, and he's been drinking. After a few words of welcome, Vince counts off "Night Passage," which starts off in a Marty Paich-like/West Coast small big band feel, intimate, relaxed, and swinging. Joe immediately comes over towards the drums and reaches towards me with imaginary drumsticks, saying, "No, Peter, this is not a Weather Report beat; play more like this, man!" Instead of my smiling and telling Joe to fuck off, or even just thinking "fuck off" while smiling authentically at the ridiculous picture of his staggering swagger, I react like a long-lost relative who has returned home for a Thanksgiving dinner fully expecting that things will be different between him and his family now that he's grown-up and become successful on his own. But NO! Aunt This or Uncle That or Grandma or even Mom or Dad knows exactly which button to push, and it gets pushed no matter what, and you're young and stupid again. Everything is all self-conscious and I can't play, and I don't know whether to be more upset with Joe or with myself for feeling like this. I'm back in the middle of having just joined Weather Report, and Joe is telling me how to play. It's embarrassing, but I don't wish to make it more so by saying anything, so I just stew until I get back to my hotel room after rehearsal. "I can't believe what just happened," I begin in an email to my wife. Mutsy is really upset with Joe and very supportive and understanding of me. Vince drops me a nice note. I don't know how I'll be able to stand seeing Joe the next day at the concert, much less make music with him.

And, of course, when I run into him outside the concert hall the next afternoon, he merely says, "Peter Erskine! You sounded great last night, my friend!"

Aaaaaaarrghhhhhh!

Am I Charlie Brown, and is Zawinul Lucy in "Peanuts," pulling away the football whenever I go to kick it? The concert, by the way, was great.

The ultimate Joe-got-me-angry moment, by the way, occurred on tour with Weather Report when the band was playing in a number of venues where the lighting rig was closer than usual to the bandstand, resulting in hotter than normal stage conditions, especially at the end of the show. Those lights got really hot and we're finishing up an almost three-hour show, playing loud and in double-time, i.e., really fast. So I asked Joe if it would be okay that I show him the sign for us to agree onstage for the "last time around on this vamp" so I could give it all I had and not run out of whatever little bit of steam was left. He smiled and shrugged, and I was foolish enough to take that for a "yes." So that night we're playing this end piece, and I'm giving it all I've got, and I make eye contact with Joe and give him the sign to end the vamp this time around. He just smiles and leans into his keyboard rig, and I hear him get really loud. We don't end the tune, which means we have to play this vamp for another couple of minutes full steam ahead. Now I'm really angry. Pissed. Smacking the drums and cymbals as hard as I can, cursing Joe and shouting out epithets in rhythm as I pound the skins. And when Joe is satisfied by all of this, he signals, "Okay, NOW we end the tune!" and he does, and the rest of the band follows — but I don't. I keep hitting away, cursing, and I wind up on the snare drum alone, smacking it and still cursing Joe. The show is supposed to be over and I know this, but I can't stop and, besides, what I'm doing actually sounds pretty cool. Just then I sense a presence in front of me, so I open my eyes and look up, and there is Joe's face mere inches away from mine. He has climbed up onto the drum riser and is perched precariously on edge, and now when our eyes meet he yells, "Yeah, Yeah, YEAH, YEAH, YEAH, YEAH, YEAH!" And I finish.

I'm not sure what has just happened. He comes over to me backstage, extends his hand, and says, "Thank you, man."

The next day Joe proclaims that I have graduated.

photo: Shigeru Uchiyama

Interlude

A well-known German musician who played the Lyricon — one of the early electronic wind-controlled synthesizers — came backstage to visit Weather Report in the band's dressing room before a concert in Europe, circa 1980. This fellow had particularly long hair and a full beard, all the more striking in appearance because he was a midget — a German hippie midget. He must have been a good player because Joe and Wayne both greeted him with a sincere and smiling welcome, and they conversed with him for several minutes while the rest of the band was getting ready to go onstage. Finally Joe suggested to him, "Listen, why don't you go out to the front of the house now and get into your seat so you can enjoy the pre-show music and we can get ready for our concert." The Lyricon player smiled most agreeably as he said his goodbyes and bounded out of the dressing room. I was impressed by their congenial hospitality to this guy.

Zawinul waited a few beats after the door closed, then began to take a sip of cognac with a plastic cup in his left hand while making a cutting motion, waving his flattened right hand towards his beltline telling us, "You know, I've had it up to HERE with that motherfucker…"

photo: Shigeru Uchiyama

61. Quasthoff

I received an email that began, "Dear Ladies and Gentlemen, We are a music production company from Germany and will be producing a jazz album with the classical singer Thomas Quasthoff. Thomas Quasthoff has won three Grammys up to now and is about to record his first jazz album with German trumpeter/producer Till Brönner."

"Who is this Thomas Quasthoff?" I wondered, and so I asked a couple of classical music colleagues for input. Their replies were over the top in terms of enthusiastic respect for this singer. Wow. He must be good; but a classical singer making a jazz album?

Thomas Quasthoff describes himself as follows (taken from biographer Michael Harder's television documentary): "1.34 meters tall, short arms, seven fingers — four right, three left — large, relatively well formed head, brown eyes, distinctive lips; profession: singer." This apt description leaves out a few details, the first and foremost being that Quasthoff possesses one of the finest voices of this or any age. He is a remarkable man with musical knowledge and abilities par excellence. He was also born a Thalidomide baby; that is, his mother took Thalidomide while she was pregnant. The drug was sold and prescribed during the late 1950s and '60s to pregnant women as a sleep aid and medication to combat morning sickness. Inadequate testing was done regarding the drug's safety, however, with the devastating results that nearly 10,000 children were born with severe malformations. Thomas is more than just a bit sanguine about all of this: "I am lucky. Everyone can see my disability." He elaborated in an interview: "For me, my disability is a fact and not a problem. I'm not living the life of a disabled person. For sure, I have to handle some things differently from other people. But it's not so different from the life of someone who is not disabled. In any case, who is really not disabled? I am in the lucky position that everyone can see it. But if you are never happy, if you are only concerned about money or success, this is, in my opinion, also a kind of disability."

But all that I really know about him musically as I enter the recording studio in Ludwigsburg, Germany is that he is a singer with a great reputation. As I'm preparing the drumset for recording, I notice a smallish figure approaching me; my peripheral vision suggests that a young child had entered the studio. Imagine my surprise when the richest of baritone voices emanates from that tiny body: "It's good to meet you!" We shake hands, and thus begins an adventure that I can honestly say changed my life.

The next morning began with my watching a DVD documentary about Thomas, by filmmaker Michael Harder, titled *The Dreamer*. Harder had given it to me the evening I arrived; he was there to film the recording sessions. Watching the story of Thomas' life and art, I was moved to tears by the beauty of his voice and the triumph of his spirit. Hailed by leading conductors and loved by audiences worldwide, Quasthoff is a star in the realm of lieder (art song), oratorio, and even opera. He also seemed like a person with a terrific sense of humor. But could he sing jazz, and could he hold up to the rigors of making an album in the studio (a different process from performing a recital)?

I met Thomas and the band — which included my old Steps Ahead buddy Chuck Loeb on guitar, Dieter Ilg on bass, and pianist and arranger Alan Broadbent — for breakfast in the hotel restaurant. Producer and trumpeter Till Brönner was also there, along with his brother Pino, who was coordinating everything. I was glad to be able to sit next to Thomas, and he told me some of his story: of how he was denied admission to the music schools in Germany because he could not play an instrument (singers must also play an instrument, such as piano, to gain acceptance into the music studies programs there), and of various prejudices he had encountered in his homeland. He has a high regard for the open acceptance that he finds in America; nice to hear something good about our country for a change these days.

The true test in the studio, however, is in the music. Hidden from one another by sound-damping walls, connected only by means of microphones and headphones, we began to play the program of American standards chosen for this album. Great songs. How would Quasthoff sing them? To be honest, most classically trained vocalists tend to sound pretty stiff and out of their element when they attempt to sing jazz or popular music. Perhaps this is the key to Thomas Quasthoff: he apparently does not accept the notion of being "out of his element," in life or in music. Simply put, he made the songs his own, with enough of a stylistic debt to some of the great jazz singers like Johnny Hartman (whose album of standards with John Coltrane set THE standard for male vocal ballad renderings in jazz; some wonderful playing by Elvin Jones on that recording, by the way!), Billy Eckstine, Ella Fitzgerald, even singers like Bobby McFerrin and Stevie Wonder. Quasthoff knows his stuff, and it was immediately apparent that he was not just visiting these songs, but that he had lived them.

Alan Broadbent fashioned some terrific arrangements that had me playing sticks, brushes, easy swing, and New Orleans-style second-line grooves. On the first day, we cut some basic tracks along with Thomas for an orchestra to dub onto, arranged by Nan Schwartz. Gorgeous stuff. The second day featured a smallish big band comprising of some of the best horn players in Germany and Holland. We covered a lot of musical ground in two days' time, an arduous task for the most robust of singers. That Thomas could manage this without having had the prior experience of working in a studio with headphones, working with musicians whom he'd only gotten to know at breakfast, and to get all of his takes "live" with the band (almost no fixing afterwards) is a testament to the guy's talent and guts. One outstanding feature, thanks to his classical training and vocal excellence, is that his pitch was always spot-on. Speaking frankly, most singers I have worked with in the studio — and these are famous vocalists who have thousands of hours of studio time under their belts — tend to sing "flat" a fair portion of the time when they're wearing headphones. Not sure why this happens, but it sure didn't happen with Thomas. This man can sing.

He did his homework, that's for sure. Stylistically, rhythmically, melodically, he covered it all with nuance and perfection. Perhaps the song titles, chosen by Thomas, reveal the affinity between the singer and the stories he was telling: "There's a Boat That's Leaving Soon For New York," "Watch What Happens," "Secret Love," "You and I," "Ac-cent-tchu-ate (the Positive)," "I've Grown Accustomed to Her Face," "Can't We Be Friends?" "Smile," "They All Laughed," "My Funny Valentine," "What Are You Doing the Rest of Your Life?" and "In My Solitude." Thomas told me that he chose the songs for their relevance to his life. The CD, *Thomas Quasthoff, The Jazz Album*, was released by Deutsche Grammophon. We toured in March of 2007, beginning with a concert in New York's Carnegie Hall.

Postscript to the session: After a celebratory dinner in an Italian restaurant outside of Stuttgart, we met back at the hotel where Thomas was doing a little jig or dance, cracking everyone up by his singing and dancing "Oh — I'm — a — little motherfucker, I'm a little motherfucker, I'm a…"

Shortly after this project, Zawinul called me up at home asking for Vince Mendoza's telephone number. As I looked it up on my computer, I told him all about Quasthoff, ending with my little epilogue about the song and dance. Zawinul's last spoken words to me, before thanking me for the info, were, "That's right, he is a little motherfucker."

62. The End

Following a sold-out and triumphant concert in the Philharmonie Hall in Köln with singer Thomas Quasthoff, Annette Hauber, the production coordinator for the WDR Big Band, tells me without warning that "Joe is dying of cancer." I walk back to the hotel in the cold dark of night and terrible news, numb and in pain all at the same time. Not knowing what to do next, I stay up for most of the night listening to one Zawinul composition after another, missing the man while charting my own growth as a musician, which happened to parallel the growth of a new music beginning in the early 1960s and continuing up to the millennium and beyond.

And I think of a poem, sent to me by an unknown female correspondent via postcard when I was an 18-year old drummer with Stan Kenton:

> *There's a drummer,*
> *beating,*
> *amidst all this America.*

> *There's an Annie Green Springs drinker —*
> *drunken over time thinker*
> *underneath this America.*

> *There's a line somewhere, I know,*
> *from all people to all people*
> *from all suffering to peace…*

And the circle, just like the music, keeps going 'round and 'round.

63. Last Letter to Me from Joe

Peter

Thank you so much for your message; you are indeed a good brother -

I will survive my illness, as a matter of fact I am touring all the time and haven't missed a day of work. Unfortunately my beloved wife's situation is much more serious.

She is on Life support, cannot speak, being fed through tubes, very very sad --

but all of us have to live with or overcome obstacles.

Don't cry that it is over, smile that it was ---one wise man said --- I feel blessed to have had the fortune to share 44 years of my life with a wonderful person, the center of my Universe, my Maxine.

much love to you and your family

it is a great pleasure to know you

always your friend

zawinul

photo: Mutsy Erskine

The End

Appendix 1: People

Herein people mentioned in the book but not given enough due verbiage, or folks missing in the narrative altogether. For any sins of omission or indiscretion, my apologies. The names appear in alphabetical order, by first name.

Aaron Serfaty

Aaron is a great drummer from Caracas, Venezuela. I met him when he was drumming for Cuban trumpet virtuoso Arturo Sandoval. He came and paid me for some jazz drumming lessons; I stopped that arrangement pretty quickly and we began to trade information — swing for salsa as it were. He has since become a colleague professor at USC — a favorite among the students! — the most reliable and expert of drum tuners, a favorite at my house, and a dear friend. He's also my first-call sub when I cannot make a gig in town.

Alan Broadbent

Pianist and accompanist par excellence, music devotee nonpareil. We were working together on an album for singer Dianne Schuur that was being co-produced by Barry Manilow and Eddie Arkin. Barry is a big-star entertainer and hit-maker while Eddie is a well-respected film music guy in town, and their synergy seemed to be more or less in sync, though Barry displayed a tendency right off the bat on this project to over direct everything that was going on. Not a great idea when you're dealing with jazz musicians and you're hoping for jazz musician results. Anyway, we're at day number two or three on this thing, and Barry wants us to try a ballad in a sort of Fats Domino/triplets-on-the-piano "On Blueberry Hill" style. We give it a shot, but the results are not impressive and so we call it a day. Well, the next morning Eddie Arkin asks us to play the same song in Bill Evans trio style — out of earshot of Barry, of course — so when we begin the rhythm track take and Barry hears this, he runs into the studio and more or less physically assaults Alan in the form of making body contact while reaching over him from behind and screaming "No! I…want…it…like…THIS!" banging out triplets on the keyboard like a madman until Eddie can catch up to all of this and try to pull Barry off of Alan and away from the piano. Silence. Broadbent looks over at me in the drum booth and I see the face of The Incredible Hulk just before he transforms into his scary self. I could have sworn he was going to slug Barry right in the kisser. Oh, Mandy!

Alan Pasqua

Formerly the head of Jazz Studies at USC's Thornton School of Music. Our Fuzzy Music recording *Standards* earned us a Grammy nomination. Our trio with Dave Carpenter was a dream group. Bassist Darek Oles now plays with us, and our latest recording is *The Interlochen Concert*. Whenever we play together, it's like we're picking up a conversation in a dream and carrying it forward, guided in our starts and stops, silences and notes by an unseen hand. We've been doing it for so long, and it's the most intense in-the-moment thing, and yet we're hardly there at all. I hope that our duties in academia will only serve to bring more playing opportunities our way as time unfolds. Meanwhile, I'm grateful for every chance we get to play, and Alan proved to be really good at the university jazz department stuff. Making music with him is the most effortless process I've experienced. We complete each other's thoughts without saying anything; that's pretty cool.

Alan's a musical genius, no doubt about it. And we both feel blessed to have Darek Oles in the trio.

Alex Acuña

One of the great survivors of the Weather Report experience, Alex went on to become one of Hollywood's busiest studio percussionists while maintaining a musical and personal relationship with Zawinul that lasted until Joe's passing. Alex has always been my first call for percussion, and the drumming gifts he gave us all on *Heavy Weather* still rank as some of the best drumming ever recorded, in my opinion. The quintessential "Reporter," I am proud to call him my musical brother and friend.

Anne Hills

Folk singer, composer, rights advocate, and conscience/awareness raiser, also my first love and girlfriend throughout high school and the beginning of college. We've remained friends over the years and always seem to get back in touch just when one of us is thinking about the other. One of the nicest and smartest people I've ever known. We collaborated on the recording *October Child*, her album of Michael Smith songs, with Vince

Mendoza, Paul McCandless, Jimmy Johnson, Jim Cox, Bob Mann, and the legendary Carlos Vega on drums. Carlos' time was incredible: We didn't use a click track but he used a stopwatch to check the lengths of each measure during playback — never more than a couple hundreds of a second off. I was so knocked out by Vince's writing and the band's playing that I mixed Anne's voice too low, an unforgivable sin for a record producer to commit. I am lucky that Anne is a very forgiving woman. Also glad that my wife has been such a good sport about Anne's and my friendship and of our remaining in touch over the years. It's the lucky man who gets to go back in time by being in the present with the people who matter the most to him.

Bernhard Castiglioni

Bernhard is the man behind drummerworld.com, THE place to go for photos, audio, video clips, and biographical reference materials relating to just about every drummer of note on the planet, past and present. My wife has always commented on how remarkably giving the drum community is, and no one gives more than Bernhard. His creed: "The DRUMMERWORLD project was created 15 years ago by Bernhard Castiglioni in Switzerland — that's me. My intention is to spread the word and show the younger drummers and students the masters at work — from the beginnings to the present. I want to keep DRUMMERWORLD clean, fast, and free for all drummers and friends." Add drummerworld.com to the list of notable Swiss contributions to the world — ahead of cheese and the cuckoo clock, somewhere just behind chocolate.

Bernard "Pretty" Purdie

A hero. The man should be the recipient of a Pulitzer Prize for all of the great work he has done, in my opinion. (Bassist Chuck Rainey would be my other choice.) If an album had Bernard's name on it, I bought it. That was a lot of albums, and he plays great on all of them. In high school I really got into Purdie, who I still think is incredibly underrated. When I play his stuff for my students at USC, they're like, "Holy crap," amazed at the fatness of the groove. We've never collaborated on any project, but we've always enjoyed one another's company and drumming, I'm proud to say. I hope and am pretty sure Bernard knows how much I respect him, I really think the world of his drumming, and I believe that his drumming has made the world a better place.

Bill Platt

One of the great American symphonic percussionists, Bill Platt just retired after being the principal percussionist in the Cincinnati Symphony Orchestra for forty years. The circumstances of our meeting and subsequent friendship point to the dogged determination of destiny to connect the dots: Bill's wife, Kazuko, is the sister of my wife's translation colleague and pottery partner, Sachiko. One day, Sachiko happened to mention to Bill that her friend Mutsuko's husband is a drummer, and Bill politely inquired, "Oh? And what's his name?" Sachiko "cannot remember except it's something like Peter," and Bill said, "Peter? You don't mean Peter Erskine, do you?" Sachiko got excited and exclaimed, "YES! That's his name." Well, a breakfast meeting was set up during Bill and Kazuko's next visit to L.A., and Bill and I became like brothers in an instant. He revived my beat-up vintage Rogers Dyna-Sonic snare drum to its original luster and glory. (He collects and restores Rogers drums; he bought his first Dyna-Sonic on the same day and from the same music store as Steve Gadd when they were classmates at the Eastman School of Music.) Bill plays the snare drum in exactly the manner and way that I wish I could. His are the hands of a great musician. He is also an astute teacher. Now that he's retired, I'm looking forward to our getting together more and more often.

Bob Beals

Bob Beals was many things: an innovator as well as historian, a dreamer who stayed pragmatic, a proud but humble man, impatient with things when they weren't right, yet he always had all of the time in the world for a friend. He generously dispensed advice that was always on the mark. Bob was in the music business long enough to have seen it all, and I have many fond memories of his regaling me with story after story about this company or that person.

Bob's company, Evans Drumheads — which he owned and operated for many years before entrusting it to the dynamic and expert hands of the D'Addario family — pioneered many advancements in drumhead design, improvements that raised the bar for the entire percussion industry. I was fortunate to have met Bob when I was eighteen years old, shortly after my joining the Stan Kenton Orchestra. Since Evans was the drumhead of choice for Stan, it was natural that I would play Evans back then, and our association lasted ever since 1972. I posed for my first music industry ad with Bob behind the camera, holding a drumhead while seated poolside at some Kansas hotel. Before Slingerland or Zildijan, Bob Beals put me on the map.

Bob Beals also put me on the path towards a truly successful music career, a career that necessitates our being able to wear a number of different hats in order to succeed and thrive. Bob came to a college gig where I was working as a guest clinician in order to show me a new thing he was working on (his CAD/CAM system for designing and manufacturing drumheads with computer precision and control). His enthusiasm for things technological as well as musical reminded me very strongly of my father, and I suspect that I invested some surrogate son-to-father affection towards Bob; he was like my father in the drum business. And, like a good father, he provided some excellent advice. Seeing how hard I was working by my having to fly all over the place to work — rehearsing, giving clinics and playing in concert — he said, "Peter, you have to learn to make money while you sleep." He said this with his usual twinkle and bemused smile. And, with total thanks to Bob, I returned home with a determination to focus my future plans on creating a musical legacy where my work would not only remain for others to hear, but to create a library of writings, compositions, even musical products in cooperation with various manufacturers, in order to make money while I slept and ensure a gift to bestow to my children and their children. It had not occurred to me before Bob looked me in the eye in that university parking lot in Wichita and told me. I mention the story only because I think of that moment and of Bob often, always with gratitude and a smile — a bittersweet smile now that he is gone. I'd long hoped that someone would sit down with Bob and record his stories before it was too late; I don't know if that ever happened. I hope so. Bob Beals — watchmaker and repairman, drumhead company owner, inventor, tinkerer, technology explorer, entrepreneur, a man with so many gifts who always stayed humble and liked to keep things that way. Bob was and remains my music industry hero.

Bob James

I was thrilled to get to play with Bob during the Montreux Summit project in the summer of 1977 while I was a sideman on Maynard's band. (Maynard had brought over some of his band to play the theme from *Rocky* with him and, as it turned out, CBS superstar drummer Billy Cobham didn't want to play every number that long evening.) The tune was Wayne Shorter's "Infant Eyes." Bob and I would later cross Weather Report paths of a sort again when we played together in tribute to Jaco's memory on the album titled *Who Loves Ya?* Back in the early '80s Bob kindly invited me to record with him on a couple of occasions, one of them being the album *Foxie* with Will Lee on bass. I initiated an impromptu drum solo during the fade-out section of one tune ("Fireball"), and during the playback Bob remarked, "A drum solo?" and I innocently replied, "Yeah! Why not?" and he kept it in. I was still invested in making my presence known on any tune I recorded back then. I eventually got over that. In any event: Thanks, Bob! And now, during the final revising of this book's text, I am enjoying the pleasure of working with Bob along with clarinetist Eddie Daniels and bassist James Genus. We're all older and wiser now, and there's still excitement to be had when different musical worlds collide and collaborate with one another. He's an inspired musician.

Bob Mintzer

Bob and I have known each other since the fall of 1969 when we were both students at the Interlochen Arts Academy, and our musical association is the longest-lasting one for both of us. As of this writing, Bob is teaching at the USC Thornton School of Music where I'm also teaching. We've made 30 recordings together including several with his big band. The big band albums had state-of-the-art audio quality with a process that employed some pretty old-fashioned techniques, such as moving players' positions around a microphone this way or that way by a few inches until the balance was just right. These recordings were also done direct-to-2-track so there's no fixing; the concentration effort is substantial but the results are worth it.

Once, while tracking, we get this terrific beginning going on a tune, and we're bubbling along when all of a sudden there's a honk from the sax section with arms raised and waving for the rest of us to stop. I missed whatever caused this detour, and I'm isolated from the band to some degree by the booth I'm in and the headphones I'm wearing. And so I keep asking no one in particular, but I'm heard by everyone, "What happened? Why did we stop? Why did we stop, I don't get it, that was feeling really good, what happened?" and so on when an exasperated Lawrence Feldman finally offers, in an effort to get me to shut up, "A MISTAKE WAS MADE, OKAAAYYY?!" Bob's big band writing is great, and his small group writing is, too. He is, simply, an excellent musician.

Chuck Berghofer

Chuck Berghofer is responsible for some of the most swinging bass playing ever, period. Relentless. He's also the man responsible for the descending acoustic bass line on Nancy Sinatra's "These Boots Are Made For Walking" hit single and the electric bass funk groove on the *Barney Miller* TV show theme song. And Chuck will quote one or both of those musical bellwether moments on just about every gig. I cherish our relationship both on and off the bandstand.

Colin Schofield

An ardent fan of music in general and Weather Report in particular, Colin was responsible for shepherding the Left Side Ride into reality during his tenure at Zildjian. He was also responsible for introducing me to more delicious curry dishes than I can count whilst performing his artist relations duties. He's been a good and stalwart friend.

Dave Weckl

Guitarist Steve Khan invited me to join him at the Breckers' club Seventh Avenue South to hear a band of young players who were based in Connecticut. The band (Nite Sprite) was okay, but the drummer (Dave Weckl) was great. Shortly afterwards, I was asked to do some more gigs with the band French Toast, which included French hornist Peter Gordon, pianist Michel Camilo, and bassist Anthony Jackson; I had worked one night with them in the club Mikell's. But my schedule was such that I recommended a sub, and that was this young drummer who I'd heard only once but instinctively knew would be great. The rest is history, as Dave and Anthony hooked up immediately and went on to other big gigs, one after the other for Dave. By a lucky combination of his earliest influences — including the rigors of trying to play like Buddy Rich, i.e., technical discipline combined with the latest innovations coming from Steve Gadd, et al, along with his attention to detail (the man brought his own drum PA/sound system with him to the most casual of gigs in Manhattan) — and then being put in the pressure cooker of the high profile Chick Corea Akoustic and Elektric bands (I always hated that "k" spelling, by the way), Dave pushed the boundaries of what was thought possible on the drumset. He enjoyed great popularity, and he suffered an unwarranted amount of criticism due to jealousy in the drum community. There, I said it. I always felt that Dave was a lightning rod of sorts. He survived the insane popularity as well as jealousy to grow into a terrific guy and tremendous musician.

David Benoit

I played on his *Waiting For Spring* album, part of a series of GRP albums in the late 1980s and early '90s that provided a lot of work for me and helped send the kids to a good school. I was and I remain grateful for those sessions that weren't always up to the highest standards of Weather Report or ECM but represented a doorway to jazz for some — not that everybody dug it. Once while in New York I was walking down 7th Avenue minding my own business when I was recognized by some younger jazz musicians with saxophone gig bags strapped around their shoulders, etc. "Peter Erskine?" they inquired, and I smiled and said, "Yeah, hi ya fellas," and was immediately accosted by one of them with a, "What the FUCK are you doin' playing on a David Benoit record?" Shock. Smile. "Just payin' the bills, boys," and they were gone. That was a musical mugging of sorts.

A writer asked me, "What do you attribute your chameleonic drumming abilities to?" I replied, "If anything, a sincere appreciation for most forms of music and the craft of making music. I admire diversity and believe that one experience informs the next." THAT'S what I am doing on a David Benoit album.

David is a nice man and popular musician. *Waiting For Spring* featured the late Emily Remler on guitar. John Patitucci and I also recorded with David, and I later did an album with David along with Mike Brecker and Christian McBride, produced by Tommy LiPuma. Former student Jamey Tate has been playing the drums for him the past few years. (Meanwhile, please see chapter "Whither Jazz Goest.")

Dave Black

Dave is the co-author (with the late Sandy Feldstein) of the most successful drum book in print, *Alfred's Drum Method*. He is now a vice president and editor-in-chief at Alfred Music, which happens to be my publishing home. His enthusiasm for all things musical is matched by his unerring sense of what most effectively teaches and what sells when it comes to instructional products. He's been a dear friend for many years.

David Carpenter
(November 4, 1959 – June 24, 2008)
The sum of a man's life is difficult to measure and nearly impossible to describe in several hundred words. When a comrade-in-arms falls, one is summoned to characterize this person in part to help assuage the grief as well as to help make certain that his or her accomplishments will not fall 'tween the cracks and be forgotten. Dave left us so suddenly that we're all still scrambling for words, not to mention how to fill the gaps in our musical worlds. Dave Carpenter was not the best-known bassist on the scene, 'though his name was always at the top of any musician list I would compile during the 10 years we worked together. And he left us music galore to remember him by.

Dave left his home town of Dayton, Ohio in 1983 to tour with the Buddy Rich band, and then worked with artists including Maynard Ferguson, Woody Herman, Mike Stern, Allan Holdsworth, Sadao Watanabe, Herbie Hancock, Al Jarreau, David Sanborn, Celine Dion, Michel Legrand, Barry Manilow, Toots Thielemans, Ringo Starr, Harvey Mason, Chick Corea, Brian Wilson, Boz Skaggs, Lalo Schifrin, Michael McDonald, Hubert Laws, and Clare Fischer. Dave and I first played together on a recording session for Venezuelan pianist Otmaro Ruiz. My immediate impression was of how comfortable everything felt. Dave knew any standard that would be mentioned as a possible song candidate at any gig, and he owned any style or genre of music or direction where a piece of music might go. He became an indispensable part of recording projects that I produced, and of two bands in particular: the piano trio that Alan Pasqua, Dave, and I shared, and the Lounge Art Ensemble, a horn trio with Bob Sheppard. While there were plenty of saxophone-bass-drum trios around, none of them enjoyed the luxury of the incredible 6-string electric bass chord comping that Dave could provide while at the same time taking care of business in the walking department.

He played 4/4 like the best bass players, comped like a terrific keyboard or guitar player, and soloed like the hippest horn player. He was a one-in-a-million musician. Having worked so closely with another singularly gifted bassist for several years, I can say with total certainty that Jaco would have loved Dave Carpenter.

Dave always WATCHED the drummer, something he learned to do while playing with Buddy Rich. It proved to be a wonderful way of playing in the rhythm section, especially in the piano trio when we would tackle really slow tempos. We could "open" up a bar by playing the next bar's downbeat on the "phat" or late side, and Dave would always be right there.

Dave was simply one of those bass players who made the drummer sound better, and made the whole band feel better. Dave Carpenter understood what it was to be a bass player. I penned a few words for a memorial tribute that was held in Dave's memory; a "Who's Who" of the L.A. jazz scene was there. "Dave Carpenter played with a lot of musicians. If you're reading this, the chances are pretty good that he played with you. It's safe to say that everyone in this room today felt that they could claim Dave as their own — a musical best friend. More than any other musician I've ever known, Dave had the knack and the ability to COMPLETE a band. He was a bassist's bassist, a drummer's most trusted ally, a singer or horn player's dream, and a piano player's best accomplice. The man knew more songs than anyone, it seemed, and he always chose the perfect note to play. His accomplishments on the acoustic and electric bass were of a singular nature. Dave Carpenter was truly great. Dave was also one of the sweetest human beings the world has known. Even when he got surly, losing patience at the idiocy of some dopey situation, his humor got the best of us. You could only love Dave Carpenter, and that's why we're all here today. Dave — we'll always miss you."

Diana Krall
Diana is one of the hardest-working people I've known in the business. While she's enjoyed a tremendous amount of success, I can say from first-hand experience there's no laziness or complacency on her part. She works hard. I get the impression that success has been a double-edged

sword for her: success can bring fame and wealth, but it imposes a lot of limitations along the way. She tried to break away from her audience's expectations by following her muse on the album *The Girl in the Other Room*, many of the songs co-composed with her husband, Elvis Costello. That's where I figured in (I was not as resistant to playing straight eighth-note grooves as Jeff Hamilton was), and I enjoyed the touring up to a point; her hard-work ethic had us touring for longer than I cared for, and so I tendered my resignation, just around the time she started slipping back into her Oscar Peterson/Ray Brown trio-inspired roots. I admire that music but soon feel at a loss when playing it. And, as odd as this may sound, I began to hate staying in such fancy, high-priced hotels. This was before the great crash of 2008, but I could already sense that there was something mighty wrong with the economic state of things — people should not be able to afford staying in such high-priced digs, and despite the generous paycheck, I could not afford the extra charges for WiFi, bottled water, and room service in those places. When you make more money, you spend more money. I returned home from one leg of the Diana tour with an expensive case of wine, and my wife asked me, "What were you thinking?" Guess I wasn't.

Don Alias
Don Alias had the baddest beat on the conga drums, period. Listen to the way he played with Elvin — and Jaco. Genius! One of the funnier and finer gentlemen of music anyone could know. Don is sorely missed by all who knew him.

Don Grolnick
The master of understatement, musically and otherwise. Don came to visit me in a New York hotel while I was still playing with Weather Report; I met him in the lobby, and he asked to come up to my room so he could use the phone. As we rode up, the elevator stopped at a floor, the doors opened, and Jaco came bursting into the elevator car, not acknowledging Don's presence but merely demanding of me, "Have you been to Zawinul's room yet? CHECK IT OUT!" Jaco punched his own chest for emphasis and ran back out of the elevator car, with Don able to chime in "Uh …nice talking to you" before the doors closed. Don did a great Jack Benny. His wonderfully expressive eyebrows also conveyed more musical information, pleasure, or displeasure than any conductor's hands I've ever worked under. Don kept this drummer's musical motives

pure, and the man was worth his weight in gold on any project we ever did together. I really miss him.

Ed Shaughnessy

From a book blurb I recently penned for Ed: "Ed Shaughnessy represents more than just being the man behind the drums on Johnny Carson's *Tonight Show* for years and years. He's also the man responsible for the drumming on some of the best jazz recordings to have come out of New York in the 1950s and '60s. I grew up listening to Ed almost daily, and this was BEFORE I started to stay up late enough to watch the *Tonight Show*. Ed went on to become one of the pioneering drumset educators for Ludwig Drums, and he continues to dispense expert advice to drummers young and old — I learn something new from the man every time I hear him speak. Finally, Ed is the only drummer other than Louie Bellson to go toe-to-toe with Buddy RIch — on numerous occasions —and come out of the experience looking and sounding good! Additionally, Ed is a gracious man with an appetite to keep on learning and drumming, and we're all the better for his being. On top of all of this: I'm a fan." His playing on the Oliver Nelson albums from the '60s is nothing less than brilliant and totally swinging. Ed was the first person in the music biz to send a baby gift to Mutsy and me when our daughter Maya was born.

I recently received the following Blackberry message from Ed: "Peter...back after another great listening of you + Norrbotten Band...I am even more thrilled. I realize U have done many fine things...but WOW...that project has to be up there. Finest collaboration of drummer + big band in jazz history.....+ I know my stuff !! Thanks for kicks + inspiration , Ed Shaughnessy"

And this from his just-released book, *Lucky Drummer*, an inscription: "To Peter — Not only a world-class artist — but a world-class person who brightens my life." Ed's book is terrific (Rebeats Publications). Very sorry to write that we lost Ed in 2013 shortly after his book was published.

Fred Adams Erskine, Jr

Known as "Adam" to his friends, Freddie and I share the same birthdate, seven years apart. We're not in such close touch these days, much to my regret. I'm afraid he always resented the undue attention I got from Dad, due to my interest in jazz drumming. Dad had been a bass player in

college, and jazz was his biggest passion in life. My brother Fred took up
the accordion when he was a kid, and suffered the very bad fortune of
being told by his teacher that he "would never make it." That's a terrible
thing to say to anyone. Still, brother Fred showed a lot of support to me
during my own formative years, and I'll always be grateful for that.

George Cables (Debbie Sabusawa)

It was because of George that I got to work to work with Freddie
Hubbard and make several recordings on the Contemporary label,
including my first solo album. I also met my first real living-with-someone
girlfriend as an adult, Deborah Sabusawa, who happened to be
waitressing at the Lighthouse Jazz Club in Hermosa Beach on the night I
played with George's trio there. We flirted, she said goodnight, and as I
watched her from the sidewalk in front of the club she turned around
with an ebullient smile and blew me a kiss. Cupid's arrow doth pierc'd my
heart! I got her telephone number from the club manager, but when I
called her the next day, a male voice answered, and when I asked if
Debbie was there, he said, "No, she isn't." When I inquired if I could
leave a message, this guy went, "Well, ya can try." I thought that was it,
but he just turned out to be her roommate's wise-guy boyfriend. Anyway,
I wooed and won her with a morning bouquet of fresh-squeezed orange
juice, champagne, and some cashews and flowers — blame it on the
Trader Joe's. So, thanks to George, I met Debbie. And I got to play with
one of the great jazz piano players. Zawinul always spoke highly of
Cables, one of the few keyboard players he actually seemed to like.

Gregory Itzin

Famed actor, university friend of Jeff Ernstoff, and theatre colleague of
mine as a result of Jack Fletcher and Andrew Robinson-directed plays
over the years. Even though I've lived in Hollywood, figuratively
speaking, for a number of years, I don't know that many actors outside of
the theatre community there. However, some of the most-engaged actors
and actresses constantly return to the stage, and so I've been fortunate to
work and get to know some wonderful artists. Greg is always at the top of
that list. I love listening to actors talk about their work process; it's very
informative as it can apply to music. Interestingly, most good actors I
know really like jazz. A good number of the cast members from the hit
television show *24* are Weather Report fans.

Gordon Johnson

Gordon is the primary reason I left college a 2nd time to go on the road: his bass playing was that good! We were best buddies on Maynard's band, and getting to play with him night after night was the best preparation for playing with Jaco (who was a big fan of Gordon as well as his brother Jimmy). Gordon now lives and plays in Minneapolis.

Jack DeJohnette

One of the nicest living legends you'll ever meet. Jack has been killing it on the drums ever since he first hit the scene as part of Charles Lloyd's band or with Miles, and of course with Keith Jarrett's trio. Jack is one of those endlessly creative drummers. Not always the most supportive, but in his assertiveness is always the invitation for the other musicians to step up to the plate.

He is also a good guy. During the first day of recording John Scofield's Blue Note album debut *Time On My Hands* (I produced those sessions), the Dolby noise reduction system went haywire. It was a Sunday, and we were basically looking at several lost hours. We were just about to pack it in for the entire day, but Jack kept everyone so enthralled and entertained by telling stories and keeping positive — and at one point giving everyone a master class on the history of jazz drumming styles — that by the time we got things working the band was in a really good mood to make some music — all thanks to Jack. The man has a lot of spirit, and it shows in his music.

Jack Fletcher

Life-long friend and theatre music mentor, our collaborations brought the gift of composing my way. Jack has turned out to be my compositional muse, and he is one of my biggest cheerleaders. Jack and his wife, Ellen, live in San Francisco, but we try to get together as often as the miles will allow. My favorite sentiment of his: "The universe is right on schedule."

Jeff Ernstoff

It's nice when the guy you think you dislike most in the world winds up becoming one of your closest friends. Thanks to the trusted word of Vince and Pamela Mendoza, I gave Jeff a second chance after our "Clash of the Titans" work experience when he was my Radio City

Music Hall-producing boss for a 1994 World Cup Final Game Opening Ceremony gig. Vince and I were hired to put together a "Salute to the Drum" or "America Welcomes the World Through the International Language of the Drum!" extravaganza as part of the final game opening ceremony, and while Jeff saw it as his duty to put on a good show, I saw my duty as being to protect the integrity of whatever drumming culture was being represented on the pitch (playing field) of the Rose Bowl.

The idea was to have each of the world's continents represented by an appropriate percussive ensemble, so America = drumset, Latin America = congas and timbales, Asia = a Japanese taiko group, Europe = classical percussion, and Africa = well, Africa became an interesting case in point. I reached out to Alfred Ladzekpo, the co-director of the African Music and Dance Program at the California Institute of the Arts; he also chaired the World Music Program at Columbia University, where he taught drum and song seminars in African music and dance for three years, and is considered a Ghanian master drummer. Alfred put together a wonderful bit of music for the pre-record (Radio City saw fit to have Disney *Lion King* parade cast members do the on-field lip-synch or drum-mime performance).

Vince and I spent an evening and a good part of our budget recording this wonderful musical contribution by Alfred and his ensemble, only to be told by Jeff (after his initial "That's it?" response the next morning) that it "wasn't African-sounding enough," to which I replied, "Hey, if you watched too many Tarzan movies as a kid, that's YOUR problem," after which the entire project descended into a sort of musical mud wrestling marathon. There are plenty of funny stories that go with this whole venture; suffice to say that Jeff and I made contact a few years afterwards and got to know each other outside of the boss/client paradigm, and I was able to discover how brilliantly funny, if acerbic, the man can be. Sound familiar?

We now collaborate frequently at innovation conferences where I play the drums (and straight man) to his highly entertaining presentations.

Jim Beard

Fellow Hoosier (Indiana University alum) from a later decade, Jim is a tremendously talented pianist, synth player, composer, and producer. We worked together on the *Skunk Funk* project that won a Grammy a few years back, and more recently on the Metropole Orchestra's tribute to Joe Zawinul. Jim also played on my *Motion Poet* album and took care of the myriad programming duties that recording required. In 1986 he was touring as part of John McLaughlin's band that was opening a series of concerts with Joe Zawinul's short-lived Weather Update. Jim had apparently been drinking after their show and during our set, so much so that when he came onto the Weather Update tour bus looking for Joe to compliment him, it came out as follows: "Joe Zawinul, FUCK YOU!" to which Joe smiled and responded, "Now let's not get carried away." His playing on the Zawinul tribute concerts is anything but an FU.

Jimmy Cobb

While I am interviewing Jimmy on drumchannel.com, I am astounded when he answers my question about what it feels like to be on the recording that's included on every desert island album list — Miles Davis' *Kind of Blue* — and he replies that he's only recently realized that he's "the only one left… I put that album on and I listen to it, and I really miss those guys." The next time I got to ask him a question was in the lobby of the hotel in Cape Town, South Africa when I queried about the sights he had seen since arriving there. He answered, "I haven't been outside my fucking hotel room the entire time I've been here." Most recently I worked alongside him at the Hollywood Bowl for a phenomenal recasting of the Gil Evans/Miles Davis collaborations with Vince Mendoza conducting, Christian McBride on bass, Terence Blanchard and Nicholas Payton on trumpets, with Miles Evans and an all-star L.A. big band. When Jimmy played that cross-stick of his on beat "4" of "It Ain't Necessarily So," I started smiling so much that it almost hurt. One of the greatest concerts I've ever taken part in.

Joe Farrell

Funny cat and terrific player, a hard-boppin' presence on the West Coast. I was a huge fan of his from the trio albums he made with Elvin Jones in the '60s. We were playing a gig at Donte's jazz club one night with a table of three loud and talkative patrons seated right in front of the bandstand: two men and a woman, all from Thailand, I think. These people are annoying us all night, but they become unbearable during a solo flute cadenza that Joe attempts to play at the end of a ballad. He's finally had enough, so he just stops and stares at the three offenders; everyone else in the club is staring, too. Eventually the table realizes that the music has stopped and that everyone in the club is staring at them. In a moment of apparent panic, one of the men yells, "My Cherie Amour!" to the bandstand, followed by the woman chiming in with an almost frantic, "Earth, Wind and Fire!" plea. Silence. Joe speaks on mic, "This shit is driving me crazy." The Thai people stand up, throw some money down on the table and leave. We finish the ballad.

Joe Henderson

I'll resist the shorthand moniker "Joe Hen" that I often hear folks use. Joe Henderson was a remarkable musician and gentle man, though he always seemed to have a volcanic anger buried somewhere far below the surface. I got to work with Joe a few times: once on his album *Relaxin' at Camarillo* (I was not relaxin' playing that album, especially after Chick Corea asked me if he could sit down and try my drums upon our first meeting and he proceeded to play them much better than I knew I would be able to that day!); an all-star jazz festival in Japan (Aurex Jazz, 1980, a band lineup that consisted of Joe Henderson, Joe Farrell, Freddie Hubbard, Michael Brecker, Randy Brecker, George Duke, Robben Ford, Alphonso Johnson, and me); and the George Gruntz Concert Jazz Band.

Joe uttered two highly memorable lines behind the East German "Iron Curtain" while on tour with the Gruntz aggregation: (1) I overheard Joe say this at a bar to a woman after our final concert in East Germany, "Why don't you come up to my room so I can show you how the West was REALLY won?" and (2) the next day, after his failing to woo that woman upstairs, and now entering an East German border police trailer in the middle of the no-man's-land barbed-wire maze that existed between East Berlin and Checkpoint Charlie, where all of us in the band had to turn over our passports to yet another East German soldier: "WOULD SOMEBODY TELL THESE MOTHERFUCKERS THAT WE AIN'T EAST GERMANS FOR SURE?"

Joe Morello

Most of us first met Joe Morello by way of Dave Brubeck's "Take Five." His effortless swing in the-then-unheard-of jazz time-signature of 5/4 was mesmerizing, and his melodic drum solo on the tune — a solo that owed much to traditions old and new but stood on its own as THE way to play musical drums — taught us all a thing or two about music and what was possible on the drumset. His overwhelming technique never overwhelmed the music. Brubeck's album *Time Out* pointed the way to a future where music ruled the spheres, art was king, and jazz was hip. Swing was cool. Joe was the thinking man's drummer, but he made the thinking man's band swing. It's simply impossible to imagine our world without his musical contributions. Thank you, Joe. I'll think of that silver-sparkle Ludwig kit of yours every time I look up at the stars.

Joe Porcaro

Father of the amazingly talented and sorely missed Jeff Porcaro, his other boys incredibly gifted as well, Joe was a mainstay on the Los Angeles studio scene for years. During my first soundstage film scoring date, which was for Pat Williams and the movie *Used Cars*, Joe was the first person to come over to where the drums were set up and welcome me to the scene. He would often look over with an approving and reassuring glance during this and any other film date we happened to work on together. I haven't done that many film dates to be sure, especially in comparison to some of my L.A. Musicians Local 47 colleagues, but I treasure all of the work memories, and none more so than Joe's beatific smiling face.

Joe Testa

Formerly associated with Yamaha and now with Vic Firth, Joe has been a steadfast supporter and dear friend for years. Joe knows how to think big and is helping to bring the drum business into the future with his advocacy and use of new media. He pioneered the legendary Yamaha "Groove Night" events, and he is now completing a series on videos documenting how Vic Firth Inc. makes sticks, which involved inviting a bunch of us to the factory up in Maine where we were filmed during a tour of the stick-making assembly line. I never realized how much love and care can go into the making of a drumstick. Now I know. It was painful to say goodbye to Joe when I left Yamaha; I'm glad that we're back together on the same team at Vic Firth, Inc.

John Abercrombie

Probably the most interesting and compelling musician I've played with, and one of the funniest, too. Early morning departures were always more bearable when John would offer an observation like: "You know, there's nothing like a good cup of coffee in the morning — and this is nothing like a good cup of coffee." "Manfred" Eicher became "My Man, Fred." "I'll be right back" became "I'll be white black." And so on. But his music making was totally serious and uncompromising. One time, when the trio finished its first set of a week-long stint at Joe Segal's Jazz Showcase in Chicago, and after some bewilderingly modern-sounding stuff, Joe Segal got up to announce the coming attractions, punctuated with a "Be sure to come back next week to hear some REAL music" admonishment to the audience. I was talking to some friends when I heard this, reacting by saying, "Hey Joe, come on!" and Joe replied, "Don't you 'come on' me; we're going to have a talk about this as soon as I'm done announcing up here," which was followed by a challenge issued from Marc Johnson: "Why don't we have an open discussion about it right here and now?" The audience started to get in on the act, cat-calling and the like. John really had it out with Joe after that in the lobby. All was made well when we agreed to include at least one Charlie Parker tune during each set.

John DeChristopher

Lennie DiMuzio's heir apparent at Zildjian (Lennie is now working for Bob Zildjian at Sabian), Johnny D displays even more energy than the redoubtable Mr. DiMuzio did, due in great part to his running regimen. Anyone who wants to know how an artist relations person should act need go no further than John and his team at Zildjian. He's a class act and a dear friend. He is married to Kelly Firth (one of Vic's two lovely daughters, Tracy being the other). John retired early in 2013; we will all miss him.

John Scofield

Easily the hippest guitarist in the land, John is one of the few musicians of the "baby boomer" generation to have created such a distinctive musical voice. One note and you're pretty sure it's Sco; two notes and you're certain. Great guy, and his wife Susan is one of the smartest people I know. They just became grandparents; congratulations, Susan and John!

John Taylor and Palle Danielsson

Geniuses and stalwart touring partners for many a European trip, we made four recordings for ECM before inner-group tensions gave way to…well, separate ways. It was a great trio, and I miss playing with both of these guys, even though I get to, on occasion, play with one or the other. Singular, singing, and strong, thank you John and Palle for some of the finest musical experiences I've known.

Kenny Werner

My hero. His book *Effortless Mastery* is a masterpiece, and so is everything the man plays.

Larry Goldings

One of the newer of my keyboard acquaintances, Larry and I first worked together on an Al Jarreau album in 2004 and have done several recordings in L.A. since his move out west. An incredible Hammond B3 organist as well as piano player, some of our collaborations include a trio album with Bob Mintzer, another trio album with bassist Chris Minh Doky, plus an orchestra album arranged by Vince Mendoza and Vince's newest solo album, *Nights On Earth*. Larry is not only a terrific musician but also a very funny guy with lots of humorous videos posted on the Internet. He does a hilarious Chico Hamilton impersonation, every bit as good as John Abercrombie's. In general, jazz musicians do some of the best impersonations outside of professional comedians and actors. It must have something to do with the ear.

Lennie DiMuzio

A "Zildjian" by any other name, Lennie was as much a brother to Armand — and to every drummer who ever played Zildjian — as possible. Lennie is soulful, irreverent, funny, brilliant, supportive, and remains an indispensible part of cymbal lore. Co-founder of the "Junior Executives With-Out Power" (JEWOPs) threesome — along with Jim Coffin (formerly of Yamaha) and Lloyd McCausland (Remo) — Lennie liked to tweak the nose of the music industry while defining the role of artist relations like no other. Lennie was tireless on behalf of "his" drummers, and we all have a lot to thank him for.

Lois Erskine

My oldest sibling. One of the most brilliant people I've ever known. Whatever awareness I have of politics and the world can be credited to her. While I've stayed "left," I think she's turned more "right" with age (she watches Fox News!). That said, Lois is a tremendous writer and observer of life. If nothing else, I hope that this book will inspire her to finally sit down and compile her writings from over the years; I gave her my precious bundle of letters that I've saved from her over the years for that very purpose. Now married to an Italian radiologist named Roberto, her children, Tarik and Tonia, have both grown into wonderful adults, married to great spouses. Lois deserves several chapters alone. Next book.

Manfred Eicher

The man with the vision and the sound. Uncompromising producer and record company executive, agent provocateur for the best of musical purposes but not the easiest of rides. A hands-on producer who knows what he likes as well as what he's talking about. Manfred Eicher is responsible for some of the most beautiful-sounding recorded music in history.

Mary Chapin Carpenter

Mary Chapin is my newest musical friend. I worked with her and producer Matt Rollings and Vince Mendoza in London at AIR Studios — the same studio and orchestra (more or less) that were part of the Joni Mitchell *Both Sides Now* sessions. I love her songs and her voice, and I love her sensibility and being. One of the finest musical experiences I've ever enjoyed.

Maya Erskine

Every father loves his girl the most, and my daughter knows this, so she is suspicious sometimes of anything nice I say to or about her. But here goes: Maya is the most soulful person I know, and she possesses greater insight to the human condition than she can possibly be aware of at this point in her life. And while she exhibits a natural impatience at the long, slow, and drawn-out process of becoming a working actress, I know in my heart, brain, and artistic soul that she's the most talented Erskine to come off the assembly line yet, and I'm looking forward to her discovering that when the time is right. She's also completely hilarious. Maya was just signed as a series regular on amazon.com's new comedy show *Betas*. She is very funny in this as well as in her own on-line series *MANA*.

Michael Brecker

I first heard the tenor saxophone playing of Michael Brecker on an LP titled *Score* that his older brother, Randy, put out in 1969. Randy was featured on the cover wearing corduroy bell-bottomed pants with boots and a fringe jacket, a style I emulated that approaching sophomore year in high school (I was 15 at the time). Michael must have been a mere 18 years old at the time of the recording, a former art student turned tenor titan-to-be, exploring the outer reaches of the horn amidst the stylistic confluence of Coltrane meeting Sly & the Family Stone and King Curtis. I don't mind saying that I immediately recognized Michael's voice as being one that would accompany me throughout the remainder of my life. A few months later, a group of us were standing around a stereo record player in awe as we listened to the playing of Mike Brecker and drummer Billy Cobham duking it out in the band Dreams. Here was Elvin and Coltrane for our generation! Two explorers on the edge of possibility.

I've never known a more dedicated musician than Michael Brecker. Mike never stopped practicing, never stopped trying to improve himself, whether on the horn or composing or in simply and complexly being human. Mike always looked for the better and best way, and he always did so in a state of complete humility. And it didn't stop with the music. Mike dedicated the last half of his life helping addicts to overcome their dependence, and even transformed the last years of his life into an effort to raise the consciousness about the need for more comprehensive bone-marrow donor testing in our society to help persons suffering from leukemia-related diseases. Mike never complained once about his lot in life: following a two-and-a-half-year battle with MDS (myelodysplastic syndrome) and then leukemia, Michael passed away. American society elevated baseball player Lou Gehrig to the highest plane of respect because of his bravery and selflessness regarding the affliction that was ultimately named for him; I nominate Mike Brecker to the same level of international stature.

So, I became a huge Brecker fan at the age of 14 or 15, By the time I was 24, I was in the recording studio, playing drums on a Michel Colombier album that would house a couple of Mike Brecker tenor solos atop my drum tracks! I was already in Weather Report, we had just finished recording both the *Mr. Gone* and *8:30* albums, and yet this was the proudest and most exciting moment in my drumming life: I was on a track with MIKE BRECKER! I remember telling every available friend about this at the time. Mike Brecker was FUNKY and Mike Brecker was hipper than hip. He was MIKE BRECKER. We wound up appearing on some 40 albums together and literally played hundreds of sessions and gigs.

Mike's playing always contained the elements of life and death. It was, in a sense, death defying. Mike believed in a solo attaining the "5th gear" in terms of emotional intensity. Mike always pushed the envelope. This is a guy who practiced the saxophone inside of a garbage can so as to obtain reverb. He also jammed with drummer Eric Gravatt during his formative years in Philadelphia. He was the leading post-Coltrane improviser, who managed to define a new standard of musical excellence, excitement, and fun for several generations of music lovers. Mike gave. Not to mention the countless hours he spent helping others in leaving their addictions behind.

May any and all of us attain one tenth of the selflessness that Michael Brecker achieved in his short life. To quote an email from John Scofield's wife, Susan, immediately upon Mike's passing: "I've been thinking about what Michael said to me this summer — he said he's had an amazing life — so much more than a lot of people get and for that he was really grateful. He said he didn't have the right to complain. (I disagreed.) He was quiet and hopeful and not one bit self-pitying. Michael was a really good man and a huge talent. At least he's leaving behind a tremendous legacy — and I don't just mean all the musicianship, recordings, accolades, and the humongous talent. He helped change a lot of lives in a number of arenas."

Michael Brecker may prove to be one of the most universally loved musician ever. Certainly, he was the defining musical stylist of our time. How lucky we all are to have been in his company.

Michel Colombier

His eponymous album has some of Jaco's best playing, many of those tracks with Gadd. Jaco was really excited and proud of this album after he had worked on it with Steve. Jaco and Michel really "got" each other.

Mitch Forman

His album *Train of Thought* featured some of the more audacious drumming of my early career, mainly in "Wonderama," which we recorded late at night during a no-holds-barred session with Marc Johnson on bass. The song inspired us to totally go for it in a fusion sort of way. The tune "Milton" fared better in the playing discretion department. Mea culpa; all of that being said, it remains an impressive recording. Mitch and I also worked on the Gary Burton/Pat Metheny *Reunion* album and did the subsequent tour. Mitch would play an energetic solo during the basic tracking on *Reunion* and then overdub a more lyrical solo to replace what he had done; meanwhile Will Lee and I were responding to his original playing, and this happened more than a couple of times, so I turned his keyboards way down in my headphone monitor mix. I didn't want to be distracted by a solo that was going to be replaced anyway, but it still hurt his feelings when he came into the drum booth and looked at the headphone mixer console only to see that his keys were turned off. Sorry, Mitch!

Mom

A beautiful woman who put up with a lot of less-than-beautiful behavior from her family (she could respond in kind, too). So many memories, none stronger than her loving smile. Mom took me to Broadway musicals when I was a kid, and this heightened my awareness of melody, drama, and spectacle. My first Broadway show was *Subways are for Sleeping*, a failed production that had some great tunes. She supported me in all of my musical wants but allowed me to hide behind her skirt when I was too scared to get up onstage and play. She kept me home from school to watch a rocket launch on television or to witness the Civil Rights marchers in Selma, Alabama. She wanted me to know what was going on. I inherited her mercurial temper with the ability to go from unbelievably nice to completely ballistic anger without the in-between ramp-up that most people display. She died of a heart attack in my father's arms. I will always love and miss her.

Nancy Erskine

Five years older than me and closest in age, her boyfriends taught me as much about jazz as anyone by bringing over albums and introducing me to Elvin Jones, Tony Williams, Jack DeJohnette, et al. Nancy married Kenton bassist John Worster shortly after I joined the band, and their son Damian is now tearing up the music scene (and playing in my New Trio). When I first went to college, she shared her rented farmhouse with me in Bloomington, Indiana. Nancy went on to earn a Ph.D and enjoyed a successful career as a psychologist. Now retired, she is married to a terrific guy named Bill.

Patrick Williams

I've been a fan of Pat's writing ever since I was a freshman in high school. His music is always fun, swinging, and majestic at the same time. I first worked with Pat on the film score for *Used Cars* in 1980, and I drummed on his *Sinatraland* and *Aurora* albums. At a recent special screening of *Used Cars*, an audience member asked Pat afterwards what was his "best inspiration to write music." His answer: "A deadline." (Pat wrote the entire score in less than three weeks.) He's not only fast, but gracious: When I went up to him following a recent concert where everything had gone wonderfully well, except for one really huge mistake I made — a mistake that was obvious to everyone in the room, especially the guy standing right in front of the band — he merely said, "I don't know what you're talking about." Classy guy. Here's a note I got from Pat afterwards:

"Peter...please permit me an indulgence. I have always felt, from the time I started to listen to big bands at about age 3, that the drums were the engine, and often dictated the musical personality of a particular band. But more importantly, it was the almost unconscious connection between the leader (writer, arranger) and the drums. Think of the great records and how you can't imagine a different drummer. Whether it was Mel and Thad, Tiny and Woody, Louis B. and Duke, Jo Jones or Sonny Payne with Basie, Joe Morello and the Brubeck quartet, and on and on. There is a remarkable musical connection that sometimes defies intellectual description. I think I feel that with you.

Thanks, P"

Like I said: a classy guy.

Peter Donald

My best musician friend in L.A., he and his wife, Darlene Chan, have been like family to Mutsy and me ever since we moved to Santa Monica. In fact, they ensured that we would move to Santa Monica by getting us in touch with their real estate agent when we began looking for a home in southern California. I knew Peter and Darlene back in the Weather Report days: Darlene was producing all sorts of festival gigs including the Aurex Festivals in Japan and the Playboy Festival at the Hollywood Bowl. I was getting a lot of compliments intended for Peter Donald when I first moved to L.A., as our names are similar and we looked alike. I would always smile and thank the person for telling me that I was one of their favorite drummers, only for my smile to dull and wane a bit when they would continue, "So what's it like to work with Toshiko Akiyoshi?" I think that maybe Peter got a few of my compliments, too. At any rate, he has been like a big brother to me for all of the years we've been in L.A. He is also the world's greatest Sonny Payne fills fan and expert extant. And he cooks a mean barbecue. He co-led a group with Tom Ranier and Abe Laboreil Sr. called "3prime." Peter Donald has retired from playing, but in his own prime, he was one of the finest drummers I've ever heard.

Rick Mattingly

Rick got me into the book-writing game way back when I was living in Manhattan. We spent many an enjoyable hour sharing barbecue and drum stories, all of which resulted in a number of *Modern Drummer* and *Percussive Notes* magazine cover stories and drum books. He has an unerring eye when it comes to text, and he has been unwavering in his support all of these years. Thanks, Rick.

Rita Marcotulli

Italian pianist and composer, I first met Rita while she was playing with Billy Cobham's band. We later worked together as part of her trio and a collaborative trio with bassist Palle Danielsson. Rita's a lovely woman but is also one of the boys; she can tell the worst jokes with the best of them, each one followed by "Ees terrible!" from her. Her father was the recording engineer for many Ennio Morricone soundtracks recorded in Rome, and she attended many of those same sessions as a child. Some of my most memorable musical experiences in Italy have been with her.

One memorable but not purely musical experience occurred in Salerno when a video cameraman got carried away with his handheld camera and began walking all over the stage during our first tune of the concert, ostentatiously positioning the camera in full view of the audience, or worse, getting extremely tight with the camera lens right in Rita's face as the poor woman is trying to concentrate. I see this guy but decide to wait until the end of the song — "Be professional, Peter; wait until the song is finished" — but this guy has already ruined it for everyone. Still, I manage to hold off getting up from the drums until song's end, whereupon I set upon him with a "Turn that fucking thing off and get the fuck off the stage NOW… Turn off the fucking camera… HEY, GET THIS MOTHERFUCKER OFF THE STAGE," and I realize two things: one, his camera's red light is on, indicating that he is recording everything I'm saying, and two, the audience can hear all of this very clearly. While he is hustled off stage, I turn to the audience and raise my arms in "mea culpa" with a hearty "Excusi," which is greeted by appreciative applause. Rita, Palle, and I finish the concert. I then look for and find the promoter as soon as we leave the stage and ask for a private word with her, to know what in the world was going on with that cameraman, and THERE HE IS backstage in this promoter's office, leaning against the doorframe and vibing me big-time. I walk right over to him and fashion my two hands into a make-believe camera lens and get right in his face with a Joe Pesci-inspired "Do you like that? Do you like that, huh? Hey, do you LIKE that? Hey, well guess what, genius: THAT'S why they invented the ZOOM LENS!" I walk several feet away, turn quickly and add, "If I ever see any of this on YouTube, I will personally come back here and kick your ass."

Tough guy. I watch too many movies. Like Rita would say: "Ees terrible!"

Sadao Watanabe

On the other end of the behavioral spectrum is Japanese saxophonist and media star Sadao Watanabe. Suffice to say that Sadao is one lovely human being, with the closest sound to Charlie Mariano's Boston-days alto sax I ever heard. People the world over love Sadao. His message, whether musical or personal, is always the same, and that's one of harmony and love. *Domo arigato*, Sadao-san, for all of the enjoyable opportunities to work with you.

Scott Goodman

The man who introduced me to Zoom digital recording devices while head of Samson Technologies, Scott and I met when he hired me to put a band together for a NAMM party. Terrific guy, he saw how uptight I was getting by one of the musicians being late for the gig. He told me that his uncle Benny (Goodman) once remarked about Buddy Rich: "That guy could make a cup of coffee nervous." Scott knows how to enjoy life and I appreciate his frequent reminders for me to smell the flowers (if not the coffee!).

Seth MacFarlane

If I didn't know anything else about the man, I'd say that Seth MacFarlane is a great singer. On top of that, of course, he's a hilarious writer and voice actor, director, and incredibly successful film and TV producer, plus an amazingly well-read fellow on physics. Probably one of the coolest people I've had the pleasure to know. His *Music Is Better Than Words* album, arranged and produced by Joel McNeely, is one of the better recordings I've been on. I recently worked with him at Ronnie Scott's jazz club in London, where he announced between tunes, "And we have Peter Erskine playing the drums. How fucking cool is THAT?" We followed that by recording his Christmas album in Abbey Road studio #2 (aka the Beatles room), and then flew back to L.A. on his private jet. How fucking cool is THAT?

Steve Gadd

On a rare night off while on tour, Zawinul, Jaco, and I decide to go to Ronnie Scott's in London to catch Louie Bellson's band, and as we're walking towards the club we see Steve Gadd and some bandmates from the Paul Simon tour he's doing approach the club from the other direction. Hey, it's a party! Somehow we're all seated together in the crowded club, except Jaco, who is standing in the aisle but not minding apparently, telling a long joke to Gadd. The rest of us are seated there when the Bellson band begins its second show. Jaco is blocking the view of a gentleman seated behind us who impatiently (and with good reason) tells Jaco to sit down and get out of the way. Jaco barely glances back at the guy, ignoring him so he can continue with his joke. This goes on for a while, with the elderly patron becoming more and more agitated. I forget what transpires next, but we listen to the band and are drinking beers and yapping away. I finally decide I've had enough, and so I grab my room key and stand up from the table, probably teetering a bit at this point, and I'm on my way.

At about 7 A.M. the next morning, Saturday November 8, 1980, the phone in my darkened hotel room rings. "Hello?" I barely mumble. "Hey Pete! It's Steve! Steve Gadd!" Wow. "Uh, hey Steve!" I say, sitting up in bed and fumbling to turn on the bedside lamp. "How're ya doin'?" "I'm FINE," Steve says, "the question is: how are YOU doing?" Huh? "Well," I reply, "aside from a hangover, not too bad. Um… WHY?" "Somebody said that you pulled a knife on some guy last night, so I just wanted to check in on you," Steve says. "A knife? Me? Waittaminute…," and I wonder what possibly could have started this rumor. Then I realize and start to laugh: "Steve, the room key for this hotel is brass and kind of long, and I did grab that and stagger away from the table when I left. Somebody must have mistaken the room key for a knife —maybe that guy that got into the scene with Jaco." Steve realizes the case of mistaken circumstance, we share a laugh, sort of, I thank him for checking in on me, and he signs off. Nice guy.

When I tell Zawinul the knife story later in the day, his reaction is, "Don't deny it; it'll be good for your image."

Steve Khan
I talk about Steve quite a bit in the book, but thought the following would prove of interest. As the first edition of the book became available for iPad, I received this bit of an email (apparently sent in error) from Steve responding to a guitarist from the Netherlands regarding his being "in the book" or not:

Steve wrote: "Honestly, I don't know, whether or not I'm mentioned in Peter's book. If it's a recollection of his entire life, it's possible that I might be in there. But, it's hard to say. If it's just a remembrance of the *"Weather Report"* years, then it's possible that I might not have been mentioned at all. I believe that Peter moved to New York after Weather Report. I first met him when we recorded together with **Maynard Ferguson** in 1977, for an album entitled **"NEW VINTAGE."** Then, we spent some great time together during the rehearsals and performances for CBS Records' **"MONTREUX SUMMIT,"** and there's a great story of how I helped, emotionally speaking, Peter recover from a terrible encounter/rejection with/by Dexter Gordon and Woody Shaw. But, I don't know that he would want to tell that particular story. During a part of the early '80s, Peter had sublet **Warren Bernhardt**'s apartment, which was directly adjacent to mine, and so, Peter and I were neighbors for a number of years. We saw one another almost every day, and spoke about virtually everything. Then, he moved to Los Angeles, and we saw one another much less. So, it's hard to say if I appear in his book!!! Eventually, someone will tell me if I'm there or not. I'm going to write to Pete and congratulate him on the publication!!!" ...

Steve then wrote the following to me: "Dear Peter: I never meant to send that e-mail to you!!! Oh fuck!!! Well, it's full of love for you pal!!! Pierre Larroque wrote me from the Netherlands about your book, and asked if I was in it!!! You saw my response.....It's probably good that the *Montreux* story isn't in there - but, I remember the two of us sitting in a bar some hours later, and I told you - "One day, you will have the last laugh, the best laugh at those two assholes!!!" And look what happened - not too long afterwards, you had become one of the most important drummers in Jazz!!! So, the best revenge is living well!!! Love you man. **Wishing you every possible success with the book**!!! You are, as always, ahead of the technological curve!!! Love to the family!!! S " Steve enjoys using exclamation points as much as I do. Oh well...now the *Montreux* story is in the book. Thanks, Steve!!!

Steve Smith

I first met Steve at one of the Kenton summer camps that I was teaching at, and we hooked up as friends right away due to our similar age and appearance (we both had long hair back in 1973). Steve graciously acknowledges some of the information and influence I was able to pass along, in much the same way I was fortunate enough to receive summer drumming counsel from Alan Dawson and Ed Soph, et al. Steve has gone on to become one of the most authentically versatile drummers, having played with big bands, fusion groups, the rock band Journey, and my old band Steps Ahead. We taught together at a drum fantasy camp, and I really enjoyed the two-drummer jams with him: The guy has a beat that's easy and fun to play with. Drummers reading this, listen up! Maybe that's why he stays so busy...

Taichi Erskine

I am the proud father of Taichi, son and best friend, Final Cut Pro and all-things-video and Mac expert. Taichi was a much-loved teacher on the campus of the Los Angeles County High School for the Arts. He founded the school's annual Moondance Film Festival, and exhibited the same patience and talent for tutoring that his grandfather Fred showed him when they first met back in 1986. When the best of a previous generation is passed along and made manifest in the following generation, one like me in that middle generation can only say "thanks" to the gods. Taichi is now working as a free-lance editor, and shares a production company named Olde Payphone with his two friends and colleagues Miles Grey and Hunter Mossman. Be on the lookout for some funny stuff from these guys.

Thomas Moss

Another life-long friend, also from my freshman year at Interlochen Arts Academy (like Jack Fletcher and Anne Hills). A tremendous supporter as well as confidante, Tom and I have shared everything from illicit midnight walks after curfew at Interlochen to hiking adventures in the Rockies and emails in cyberspace. He is a golf pro and instructor now, but played the French horn in school. He writes about this book: "Ultimately, with each chapter, this reader will be looking for the answer to the question: What was it, exactly, that I heard from those first 32 bars of your drumming at age 14 with the IAA studio orchestra at its first rehearsal that caused me to be awestruck?" Methinks you heard some distilled Mel Lewis, but thanks as always for the support, Tom.

Tommy Igoe

Insanely accomplished drummer, son of the late Sonny Igoe, Tommy held the musical director chair for *The Lion King* on Broadway for many years. Recently relocated to San Francisco, he continues to lead his Birdland Big Band in New York while fronting a big band on the West Coast as well. Tommy and the band played host to a Buddy Rich tribute in New York a few years back, and I was asked at the last moment to sit in for one tune. While everyone else had their own kits and drum techs, I simply sat down at Tommy's drumset for the one-pass rehearsal, and when I declined his kind offers to adjust this or change that, he turned to a student of his in attendance and said, "You see that? THAT'S a fucking professional!" As sardonic as he is talented, Tommy inspires all of us to play better.

Toots Thielemans

One happy memory from Jaco's Word of Mouth Big Band Japan tour debacle was the moment when Toots Thielemans gave an impromptu improvisation class during a short flight between cities there. One of the musicians in the band had asked Toots a question about blowing, and Toots responded by playing and demonstrating with great enthusiasm — non-stop enthusiasm that attracted a crowd of nearly all the band members standing around Toots' seat. After an announcement was made for everyone to fasten their seatbelts for landing, Toots kept right on playing and laughing and talking, and everyone stayed where they were, transfixed by his magic. It took a bevy of JAL stewardesses to corral all of them back into their seats, just in time for the plane to touch down. Toots was still playing his harmonica when the wheels hit the runway.

Vardan Ovsepian

The newest member of my trio, now called the New Trio, he lived and worked in Boston before moving to L.A. Armenian-born, talented and unique, harmonically gifted, and a lovely person.

Vic Firth

Vic is an artist and a successful businessman, probably the only person I can think of who has excelled in both realms so completely. For years he was the timpanist of the Boston Symphony Orchestra. Founder of Vic Firth, Inc., the finest and most successful stick, mallet, and brush making company in the world, he is also an incredibly important teacher, innovator, composer, and industry guiding light. A multiple-hat wearing gentleman examplar. Also one of the funniest men I know. And smartest.

I was once asked to give Vic a ride from the Anaheim trade show to a hotel located at Los Angeles International Airport so he could catch his early flight back to Boston in the morning without too much trouble. "No problem," I replied. So my wife and I meet Vic and get him and his bag loaded into the car. Vic sits in the front passenger seat and my wife sits in the back seat, and all of a sudden Vic is on his really good behavior because my wife is in the car, and I'm on my really good behavior because he is on his really good behavior, and besides he's starting to remind me of my being with my professor. We're not music industry buddies gossiping or cursing the night away in some restaurant or bar, and it's like the most awkward one-hour drive ever. Sorry, Vic. I got kind of awed in your presence all of a sudden.

Note to Vic: You have always been incredibly kind to me, ever since we first met at Henry Adler's drum shop in New York when you showed up to show him some of your timpani mallets, and I was in high school visiting Manhattan and my dad and I dropped into Henry Adler's shop — all of us there unannounced and enjoying Henry's full attention, which is more than I can say for the poor kid who was stuck on the practice pad in the back room for what seemed to be the longest time. THANK YOU, VIC.

Warren Bernhardt

One of my heroes from all of the work he did with Gary McFarland back in the 1960s, Warren was a Bill Evans disciple and friend (Bill left many of his personal manuscripts with Warren; I believe that they were Manhattan roommates at one point). I also loved the solo recordings he made in the late 1970s, and so I was very pleased to be able to make a number of albums with him beginning with the trio recording on dmp with Eddie Gomez in 1983. Warren's rendering of Bill Evan's "My Bells" still moves me every time I hear it. The man has a gorgeous touch and sensibility. He was also a terrific pianist for Steely Dan's touring band(s), and I enjoyed working with him in that setting during 1993 and 1994. He continued to make audiophile recordings for Tom and Jean Jung's dmp label into the millennial years. Warren is a legendary fixture on the New York recording scene and has been an essential part of many bands over the years.

Will Lee

Will is the bass player who makes everything sound and feel better, and his presence can light up a room more than a thousand-watt bulb. Plenty of times we'd record something and Will would quietly ask, "Let me do another pass, okay?" We'd all be watching him as he played, and there'd always be that moment when he would stand up from the folding chair in the studio and really begin to rock and totally take the track home. And he would, somehow, always remember where the drums might have pushed or laid back, and he would always play the right thing to make any bit of drumming feel good.

As far as "live" tracking goes, when we were recording *Motion Poet* and were at the end of a long, long day with just enough time to get one and only one take on a complicated Vince Mendoza piece ("A New Regalia"), and we're all counting silently during the count-off and tacet measures, which will eventually be festooned with a brass chorale overdub, and the tension builds before we make our entrance, Will jumps out of his chair and yells to the room, "AWRIGHT, LET'S EAT THIS PIECE OF SHIT!" just one second before I begin the drum fill to mark the rhythm section entrance. This loosened everyone up; I was smiling and laughing throughout most of the take, which we "got," so everyone could go home by 1:00 in the morning. Will Lee just makes everyone and everything feel better.

Appendix 2: Music

From a discography of almost 600 albums, I've selected fifty or so that merit discussion outside of the main body of the book's text for one reason or another; many of the recordings I've done are discussed at length within the primary content of the book. If a picture is worth a thousand words, then an album must be worth at least one or two hundred. These are listed in order of appearance.

1. **Fire, Fury and Fun** (Stan Kenton, 1974) — My fifth and final album with Stan, we recorded it as we had done the other studio albums: daytime sessions sandwiched between nightly gigs on the road, this time in Chicago without playing the music we're recording until that night AFTER we've struggled with the new charts in the studio. In other words, Stan seemed to treat the album session as a rehearsal for the gig. Hank Levy penned a drum feature for me in 7/2 and 7/4 time titled "Pete is a Four Letter Word." I remember being disappointed by my performance — not the first or last time that's happened. When I listen to it now, it's not that bad.

2. **Montreux Summit, Vol. 1** (CBS All Stars, 1977) — Having been brought to Montreux, Switzerland to accompany Maynard Ferguson on his hit feature "Gonna Fly Now" (the theme from *Rocky*; Maynard was popular enough to demand and get this accommodation from CBS), bass player Gordon Johnson and myself wound up playing on a couple of other tunes during the marathon concert, including Wayne Shorter's "Infant Eyes." Not particularly fun to play brushes on Billy Cobham's gargantuan clear plastic Fibes drumset, but I do my best to play pretty. It's a beautiful song, and Stan Getz and Bob James both play wonderfully on the tune. Afterwards, Stan sees me backstage with a young woman seated on my lap and he says, "You're not fooling anyone; you're a fag." As my brother had just come out of the closet, I wasn't sure whether to panic because I might be gay or because I played brushes for the entire tune and, damn it, I should have switched over to sticks! I confessed/ratted this story to Stan's daughter, Beverly, when she was touring as a vocalist with Buddy Rich's band, and we were conversing at some gig. Bev later told me she confronted her father with this, chastising him for saying that to me, and he replied, "Hey, tell him I only talk that way to people I like!"

3. **New Vintage** (Maynard Ferguson, 1977) — I invited a woman to New York to attend some of the tracking sessions for this album. The two of us were seated on the floor in the drum isolation booth during someone's overdub, and she flashed her boobs at me in the studio. This is one of my fondest memories of Mediasound in New York. The other was nailing Maynard's remake of "Maria" in one take, unheard of for us as we had so little recording experience. Guitarist Steve Khan was a tremendous help during these sessions and we became life-long friends as a result of our working together on this album. Despite the presence of "Airegin" (recorded at Columbia's 30th Street Studio), the album received pretty bad reviews. I guess people didn't appreciate the disco arrangement of the theme from *Star Wars*.

4. **Raise!** (Earth, Wind & Fire, 1980) — Jaco and I go to The Complex studio in West L.A. to visit with Weather Report management, and we run into Maurice White, who invites us to the EW&F session taking place in another part of the building. Then he asks us to join the band for a handclap overdub on the tune "You're a Winner." You can hear Jaco yell near the end of the handclaps/breakdown section of the tune. I think you can hear me clapping ahead of the beat on about half of the handclaps. But Jaco and I had fun. Meanwhile, Zawinul always regarded Maurice White as one of the most talented and clever musicians he knew. The other pop musician (and band) who caught Joe's eye and ear? Peter Gabriel.

5. **Word of Mouth** (Jaco Pastorius, 1980) — So many stories about this one. Jaco stayed at my rented house in Silver Lake, an intended stay of a week or two that became several months. The burden of genius coupled with an excess of budget and expectation. The music is Jaco, but he was very much not himself as I had known him up to that point. It seemed like he had begun to fight everything that was being made available to help him. Jaco brought Michael Gibbs to L.A. in order to conduct the orchestra for the overdubs, but then refused to allow Mike into the studio that day. It took three different string sections to finally get one that could play Jaco's music in the right spirit as well as in tune. Jaco's proudest moment of the entire process, as far as I witnessed, would have to have been when Burt Bacharach was brought to one of the mixing rooms at A&M Studios where Jaco was working on something, and Jaco played

"Three Views of a Secret" for Burt. Jaco could not stop looking over at the rest of us, beaming and smiling from ear-to-ear as Burt listened and nodded approvingly. The album's birthing process wore the people at Warner Brothers out, and they failed to realize what a masterpiece they had on their hands, if you ask me.

6. **Weather Report** (Weather Report, 1981) — The final album that Jaco, Bobby Thomas, Jr., and I played on together, the final day's session was an extended jam that resulted in the two tunes "Dara Factor 1" and "Dara Factor 2." An extra-large reel of two-inch tape is prepared for us to jam and record onto, and an expectant crowd gathers in the studio lounge at Power Station with speakers being run into the lounge for the benefit of techs, assistants, and visitors to listen to. It was an event, a *coup d'grace* of the album; no tunes now, just a fabled WR improvised jam. I'm not even sure if the tunes are that good, but I believe that we all felt we had to create something out of the jam to justify its existence. With some clever editing and mixing, we wind up with a pretty cool couple of tunes in any event. Like many "free" tunes on albums, this process reveals that such tunes don't always begin or end like the listener might think they do.

Before I played the drum intro that starts one of the jam tunes (a groove that Christian McBride never fails to sing to me whenever we work together), I was attempting to convince Joe that a less-convoluted and less-original drum beat might be more "fun" for us to work with as a starting point, and Joe said, "Okay, let me hear it." So I played a real straight up-and-down simple beat — it must not have been very funky, to be honest — and Joe demands, "What's so fun about that? I don't hear nuthin' fun in that. Forget it!" Ladies and gentlemen: "Dara Factors 1 and 2." At least Joe shared the writing credits for the composition with the other improvising musicians. When we recorded "Brown Street" in his living room a couple of years prior — a tune that came to being because I started playing the "Brown Street" beat (which got its inspiration from a Dom Um Romao drumbeat; there's that circle again), and we jam and it winds up on *8:30* — I ask Joe about sharing some small portion of a composing credit. He retorts, "Oh yeah? Sing me one melody you wrote on that. Sing me one. Can't? You're not getting any composing credit." Okay: the earlier story in this section can reside in the Genius category, but this last story could be filed under "N" for Not Nice.

7. **Steps Ahead** (Steps Ahead, 1983) — Don Grolnick's "Pools" is the star of this album and proved to be the band's enduring opener. It was the perfect tune for that band and a wonderful vehicle for all of the soloists. Even though Don had left by the time we made the *Steps Ahead* album, the man's whimsy permeates the group sound and Eliane Elias does a wonderful job — at such a tender age — of making the piano chair her own. Eddie Gomez and I loved playing the baião with her, and Mike Mainieri's "Islands" is the result; Mainieri is a genius at the art of the catchy tune. Mike Brecker's "Both Sides of the Coin" was a result of his composition studies at the time, and my song "Northern Cross" is a typical drummer's tune — key of C, no chord changes, just open blowing for the band!

8. **Hearts and Numbers** (Don Grolnick, 1984) — One of the great albums of all time.

9. **Na Pali Coast** (Peter Sprague, 1985) — I was flown from New York to Los Angeles to work on this album — against Concord Records founder Carl Jefferson's wishes, I found out. While setting up the borrowed drumset (in Chick Corea's Mad Hatter Studios), I met Carl and shook his hand, thanking him for all of the great music he had produced, being polite as well as political, and he replied, "Well, you know… I've heard some of your music, and I can't say that I've enjoyed that much of it." To which I could only reply, "Hmm…well…some eighth notes are straighter than others, I suppose…." Which wasn't much of a reply, but I guess it beat some of the things I could have said. Peter Sprague is a wonderful guitarist and musical soul. I always find his music refreshing.

10. **Short Stories** (Bob Berg, 1987) — The scene of another Erskine compositional crime, this time by penning a tune with a melody that sounds suspiciously like the country hit "Behind Closed Doors." While Bob was overdubbing the head to replace the melody once we heard indeed how similar it was, he protested to producer Don Grolnick, "Yeah, but I like the other melody better!" to which Don replied, "You like the other melody better, I like the other melody better, and Charlie Rich's lawyers unbelievably like the other melody better. Please play the new

melody. Thank you." Bob Berg is another musical giant who we lost way too soon (April 7, 1951 – December 5, 2002).

11. **John Patitucci** (1987) — Eponymous album featuring John on electric and acoustic basses in various rhythm-section settings. I was very fortunate to be included on the cut with Chick Corea on piano and Mike Brecker (overdubbed later in New York) on tenor. We cut this at Chick's Mad Hatter Studios; I'm playing on Peter Donald's Yamaha drumset as I had just moved to L.A. and didn't have a bebop kit handy yet. Longtime Chick engineer Bernie Kirsch got a great sound on this tune as well as the entire album. To be honest, I've really only paid attention to that one tune. Surprising how many people have heard it and still comment on it. Hip song ("Searching, Finding"). Patitucci can play anything; he's really an incredible musician. John, you are the Sal Mineo of the bass. Tag, you're it.

12. **Second Sight** (Marc Johnson's Bass Desires, 1987) — Marc was my musical brother for many a tour, many a mile, and quite a few years. We worked at the music we played, and I think we proved to be a good yin to each other's yang. Remarkable bassist and musical force, Marc created the Bass Desires band because he heard that sound in his head — two guitars, bass and drums — and John Scofield and Bill Frisell are brilliant in their roles. This is some of the most fun I ever had playing. The ECM sound works perfectly, and this was also some of the most jazzed I ever saw Manfred get during a project. Heavy band.

13. **John Abercrombie, Marc Johnson, Peter Erskine** (1988) — The trio of John, Marc, and myself recorded an entire tour's worth of concerts on my grey-market DAT machine, which I purchased pretty much ahead of the curve (originally for the purpose of using in the Westwood Theatre production of *A Midsummer Night's Dream*). Longtime Maynard FOH engineer Tony Romano, who also worked with Steps Ahead and then Michael Brecker and Diana Krall, made this live recording in Boston on April 21, 1988.

When I returned to my hotel room after that long day (two shows), I was surprised to find my room door locked with a chain from the inside. Voice inside: "What do you want?" "I want to get inside my room."

"Well this is my room now." The hotel had packed up my bags, set them behind the front desk, and checked someone else into my room while I was at the club, and of course they were now sold out for the night and it's after 2:00 in the morning by the time I stumble upon the mess. I never found out why the hotel did this, but when I think of this great album, that's what I remember.

I also remember how beautiful John and Marc sound on "Haunted Heart." Manfred and longtime ECM engineer Jan Erik Kongshaug added reverb to the live mix and did some mastering EQ, but you can get a very good idea of how that trio sounded in concert. Nice band! By the way: I've consistently had bad luck with hotels in Boston: thefts, noisy rooms next door (I'm talking tailgate party, a dozen people in the room with beer kegs noisy) and being unceremoniously checked out without provocation or cause. Nice city, otherwise.

14. **Don't Try This At Home** (Michael Brecker, 1988) — I play on one tune, Don Grolnick's brilliant "Talking to Myself." This was a result of a trade: I agreed to play on Mike's new Impulse album as well as provide studio time from my Denon album project *Motion Poet* if he would play on one tune of my album (Vince Mendoza's "Hero With a Thousand Faces"). I always considered that I got the better end of the bargain, for Mike's playing on *Motion Poet* is nothing short of astounding. As I recall, Don's tune was a first take, as was Brecker's solo on my album. Bing! Bam! Boom! We liked to work quick.

15. **Motion Poet** (Peter Erskine, 1988) — For all of the recordings I've done under my own name, this one remains a favorite. The band is stellar, Vince Mendoza's writing is top-notch, the sound by James Farber is pristine yet soulful, and Don Grolnick's production was as much fun as it was focused and helpful. One of the French horn players stopped me in the hallway of the studio during the brass overdub tracking day and told me, "This is noble, what you're doing; this is very noble." Not sure if he meant the sound, the writing, the concept, or merely the fact that I was using my budget to employ so many musicians. But the results are indeed noble thanks to the incredible playing by all involved. Vince's arrangement of Weather Report's "Dream Clock" pays honor to fallen comrade Jaco Pastorius by doing a tuba flyover at the end with the bass

being absent in the flight formation. As I recount earlier in this book, Zawinul's only stated reaction to me when I proudly played this for him at his home: "It's too slow. Come on, let's have a drink!" I like the French horn player's take on the album more, so, THANK YOU Jerry Peel.

16. **Reunion** (Gary Burton/Pat Metheny, 1989) — Any time I find myself making music with Gary Burton, I have to stop and pinch myself to remind me that this is real and, yes, I am playing with the greatest vibraphonist ever. It might just be a percussionist thing, but Gary is beyond legendary. Always great when combined with Pat Metheny, the *Reunion* album proved to be an excellent combination all the way around; I was proud to have brought Will Lee into the mix, for purely selfish reasons, if nothing else because Will always makes me sound better, plus he's so much fun to work with. When we toured this album (Marc Johnson on bass instead of Will), Gary came out of the closet and told us he was gay during our first group dinner together after the first day's rehearsal. It got real quiet all of a sudden and no one said anything. I broke the silence with a "Far out." I probably then asked someone to pass the ketchup.

17. **Flying Cowboys** (Rickie Lee Jones, 1989) — This was the first time I got to work with Walter Becker. He's a terrific producer as well as Steely Dan-ist. Rickie Lee and I hit it off really well, in part because she knew that I was a friend of one of her former back-up singers who had told her nice things about me (i.e., I wasn't a creep, I guess). This album, along with my *Big Theatre* compilation, is one of the rare places where you can find Vince Mendoza playing trumpet. I tracked one of the tunes on a Yamaha electronic drumset. Walter wound up calling me for some more album work — until I told him I would be leaving a session at the scheduled end-of-day so I could go listen to the Korngold Violin Concerto being performed in concert with the L.A. Phil. He seemed stunned by my plans. First things first. I thought that would be it for our work relationship, but he surprised me by calling me for the Steely Dan tour in 1993. I would work again with Rickie Lee on her 2000 album *It's Like This*.

18. **Start Here** (Vince Mendoza, 1989) — The opener for this album, "Babe of the Day," has become legendary for its complicated rhythmic

structure and bravura performance by the band. Friend Jack Fletcher came up with the title of the album. During a break after the recording of the hauntingly beautiful "Her Corner," I found a weeping Jerry Peel standing outside the studio — not copiously weeping, but gently so — and when I asked him if he was okay, he replied, "This is why I became a musician." Vince is one of those 100-percent pure musicians whose loyalty to music always brings things back into proper artistic perspective. Listening to it as I type this: GODDAMN! It's good. Special mention to Laurence Feldman, Fred Sherry, and Bob Mintzer. And Gary Peacock, Marc Copland, Will Lee, Ralph Towner, John Scofield and ensemble. My book *The Drum Perspective* (Hal Leonard) has the original "Babe of the Day" track on the included CD, and another version of the tune can be found on the recently released *Caribbean Night* album of the WDR Big Band with Andy Narell, Luis Conte, Michel Alibo, and myself.

19. **Music for Large & Small Ensembles** (Kenny Wheeler, 1990) — Any album with Dave Holland on it is going to be good. Add John Taylor and John Abercrombie to the rhythm section, along with Kenny Wheeler's playing and writing, Norma Winstone's voice, and the best big band in the United Kingdom, plus Jan Erik Kongshaug engineering with Manfred producing = wow. We recorded the big band tracks in London's CTS studios, where many of the James Bond film soundtracks were recorded. Kenny's writing is out of this world. The double album also contains some small group tracks culled from the *Widow in the Window* album sessions in Oslo.

20. **Sweet Soul** (Peter Erskine, 1990) — *Sweet Soul* was done in two days' time, with a short rehearsal the afternoon before. The first tune to be recorded was "Touch Her Soft Lips and Part," a William Walton composition written as part of the soundtrack for Laurence Olivier's *Henry V* film. It's a gorgeously tender tune, and Joe Lovano, with the splendid accompaniment of Kenny Werner and Marc Johnson, rendered the loveliest performance of it imaginable. What a way to start an album! We listened to the playback, and I offered to the band, "Well, it's beautiful, and we got it. Does anyone want to play it again just for fun?" Engineer James Farber, who was tracking the album direct-to-stereo, mentioned that he'd like another pass at the song now that he was getting the sound better dialed in, and so everyone agreeably agreed.

Now, this is not a decision I take lightly, as I see the arc of a session as a vital part of the entire creative process and end result. In other words, I believe in capturing the musicians' energies and their creative sparks as they arc upwards, not on the way down after something is played too often or to death. Walter Becker and I stand at odds on this philosophy, by the way. He sells more records than I do, too. But I stand by my way.

In any event, it was with great dismay that we heard one of the Japanese executive producers say, "Okay, Joe, but this time, please try to play more lyrical." My mental image: children's birthday party going perfectly well, then a hand grenade is tossed into the middle of it. The look on Lovano's face propelled me into emergency mode: I grabbed him as quick as I could and pulled him outside of the control room. "Jesus, Joe! I am so sorry for what he just said. Are you okay? Need a minute? Talk to me, Joe…" Joe avowed he was cool, although years later he confessed to me that he almost walked out of the session altogether after that heedless and needless comment. The poor Japanese producer had no idea how badly he had just insulted Joe Lovano, who had just played one of the most lyrical solos extant, EVER. And so, once I got the band back into the studio, I went into the control room and told this guy: "LISTEN, if you want to run the stopwatch and keep track of song timings, then that's good, and if you want to order lunch and let us know when the food gets here, then that would be very helpful, too, but DO NOT SAY ANOTHER WORD TO ANY OF MY MUSICIANS!"

He remained quiet after that, and we finished the album in good time.

Meanwhile, my favorite memory of that album is watching Kenny Werner do the one overdub on the album, adding a "string pad" to Vince's "Ambivalence." We're going DAT-to-DAT with no room for error or fixing; Kenny is playing a synth in a remote booth, unaware that I'm watching him play; he conducts himself as he improvises his chordal arrangement. He's in ecstasy, and so are we.

21. **Free Play** (Eddie Del Barrio, 1991) — A brilliant musical experiment, a horrible experience when a "talk back" microphone's channel is left on, "hot" in my headphones as well as in the control room. After successfully recording the first movement of this Prokofiev-meets-

jazz piano concerto (first take, prompting a one-man standing ovation from album producer Herb Alpert), I am asked to begin the third movement with a loud cymbal crash. The cymbal, of course, is situated next to the talk mic; the count-off click starts in my headphones, I follow the count and hit the cymbal, and OH MY GOD! A rush of pain and nausea overwhelms me as I throw off the headset and try to imagine what to do next. Which is more powerful, the sudden pain or the mounting anger? When I finally look up and into the booth where the errant engineer must be sitting, I realize that everyone in that enclosed space got it nearly as bad as me through the loudspeakers. Needless to say, this stopped the session cold for an hour or so. Despite the accident (which resulted in further hearing loss and exacerbation of my tinnitus), the project was a laudable one. Herb Alpert is truly committed to art, and I respect the man for that. His wife, Lani Hall, has been one of my favorite singers ever since I was a kid listening to Sergio Mendes & Brazil '66.

22. **StAR** (Miroslav Vitous, Jan Garbarek, Peter Erskine, 1991) — I flew to Oslo from Los Angeles on January 15, 1991, the same day that was designated as the deadline for Iraqi troops to pull out of Kuwait. I arrive on the 16th, and after washing up in the hotel, go to Rainbow Studio ostensibly to set up the house Sonor kit (my ECM recording ritual, which means replacing the heads with a fresh set of Evans heads and tuning the drums to my liking; this was a gorgeous rosewood kit that belonged to Jack DeJohnette). I lose track of the date and time and am concentrating on the drums. Meanwhile, Miroslav and Jan start running down some of the tunes, and Manfred decides to record what we're doing. We wind up recording about half of the album that way/that day. I'm exhausted by the end of the long day and head straight back to my hotel room. I wake up with a start at around 2 A.M. Oslo time and get a sinking feeling right away as I wonder, "Hey, whatever happened to that deadline in Kuwait?" I turn on the TV just in time to hear CNN intone, "Bombs are falling on Baghdad…," and I said, "Oh, shit …" out loud to my empty room.

I brought the tune "Anthem" in as a peace anthem that next morning, and otherwise existed in a relative news vacuum for the duration of the album. That changed when I flew to Cologne a few days later for my first project with the WDR Big Band (with Kenny Wheeler). Shades of anti-American sentiment everywhere you looked, not seen since the Vietnam

War. How different Cologne would be on 9/11/2001, and how much the same again a short while later.

Anyways: Garbarek and Vitous are both master musicians. Manfred did a terrific job on this album, as well and as usual.

23. **Benny Rides Again** (Gary Burton, Eddie Daniels, 1992) — I wish that I had studied or been more hip to the drumming of Gene Krupa before this session. I had the chance recently to listen to some Gene, and then play some of the Fletcher Henderson charts from the Benny Goodman book (with Ken Peplowski on clarinet); great stuff! The older I get, the more I dig the older stuff. Meanwhile, Eddie and Gary are both real virtuosos on their instruments.

24. **Fantasia** (Eliane Elias, 1992) — Another first take, the Milton Nascimento medley arrangement by Eliane is a fantastic piece of music, played so well by her and Marc Johnson, with Café on percussion and Randy and Eliane's daughter Amanda singing the hauntingly beautiful melody of "Ponta de Areia." This happens to be one of my favorite pieces of drumming I've ever done. Obrigado, Eliane.

25. **Jazzpaña** (Vince Mendoza, et al, 1992) — At the point of recording *Jazzpaña*, I'm two-and-a-half years into my relationship with the WDR Big Band, and Vince Mendoza is now in the fold. Music legend Arif Mardin has penned one of the compositions for the album, and Vince has put together an ambitious suite of original music plus arrangements of authentic tango meets jazz — an oxymoron of sorts. This hybrid is the calling card of the new breed of Spanish jazzers who are brought to Köln for the project by producers Wolfgang Hirschmann and Sigge Loch. As usual, the drums are the bridge between the various musical worlds being explored. One day that exploration takes the form of the percussionists, who up to this point have been playing *palmas* (hand clapping), all being given shakers to shake because one of them complained that they didn't have enough to do, and so… This development is unbeknownst to me when we start a take of one of the tunes, and all I can hear in my headphones is a whole lotta shakin' going on. I tear off my phones and march rather suddenly into the main room of the studio and yell up to the control room, "Hey! It feels like I'm

playing in a bag full of fucking rattlesnakes! Somebody tell me what's going on!" "Rattlesnakes" became the code word for "funny" over the next couple of years whenever I would work at the WDR. A great album, by the way.

26. **Alive in America** (Steely Dan, 1993) — The tracks from the 1993 touring band are added almost as an afterthought to the album, but I'm glad that the band with Drew Zingg and myself is represented on this album. "Third World Man" is a standout. "Green Earrings" is me trying to sound like Bernard Purdie, and Walter Becker's "Book of Liars" is me trying to sound like me, I guess. My kids got a huge kick out of my doing the Steely Dan tour. I was conflicted for much of the trip, due to missing my jazz trio work, but it was fun to get the gig.

27. **Michel Plays Legrand** (Michel Legrand, 1993) — Flying back to L.A. from Cleveland following the final show of the Steely Dan 1993 tour, Bob Sheppard and I catch a ride on Walter Becker's private jet. We stop for refueling somewhere in Colorado and get home before dawn. That afternoon I'm in Entourage Studio in North Hollywood to play on a Michel Legrand album with acoustic bass, acoustic guitar, acoustic piano, the drums, and flutes all in the same room. From stadium slammin' rock to *un petit Francais au jazz*, sticks please, but not too loud. This confirmed my realization that some of the best drumming moments in music are those that the audience is never aware of.

My favorite Michel Legrand recording is his magnificent *20 Songs of the Century*. If you can find it, reward yourself with a listen; it's stunningly good. Grady Tate on drums, and you can easily hear how great he plays on this recording.

28. **Simple Things** (Chuck Loeb, 1994) — Nice album. Most memorable aspect for me was my being able to get out of New York just ahead of a second approaching ice storm thanks to Chuck rearranging the recording schedule to accommodate my request, thus arriving home just scant hours before the Northridge Earthquake hit. Thank you, Chuck! I am so glad that I could be home with my family for this terrible event. The house got damaged, but there were no serious injuries, and Daddy was there. Some Band-Aids came in handy: during Chuck's

session, I noticed that Will Lee had some bandages on his hand, and when I asked him what had happened, he merely replied, "Hey, these glow in the dark; give some to your kids!" and he handed me a bunch of glow-in-the-dark Band-Aids. After the earthquake's first big seismic event subsided, and Mutsy and I had the kids gathered in one safe spot, I remembered having these Band-Aids and thought they might help in the now-completely-darkened house with no electricity in the dead of night. I reached into my carry-on bag, pulled out the Band-Aids, charged each one for a few seconds with my flashlight, and adhered them to Taichi and Maya's foreheads. This proved to have a terrific calming effect. Thank you, Will! When the shaking finally settled down, we got the kids back to sleep and Mutsy and I made some coffee on the gas range, which was still working, made some toast in a frying pan, and began cleaning up the ungodly mess.

It's funny what a musician remembers from an album, while most people just think of the music and remember where they were when they first heard a particular song.

29. **American Diary** (Mike Mainieri, 1994) — A marvelously complex yet folky album, this was the gist musically of the touring band that Mike would take on the road with George Garzone and Mike Formanek (who played on the second album; this particular CD was done with Joe Lovano and Eddie Gomez). Mainieri did a great job with the arrangements, the "Vivace" movement from Aaron Copland's "Piano Sonata" being noteworthy (literally). I use a 10-inch drum on this recording, a mounted tom that I liked to tune up a bit more tightly than the way most drummers would use that drum. (Steve Gadd popularized the use of the low-tuned 10-inch tom as part of his kit's setup.) Engineer James Farber and I referred to this drum as "the Beaner." I don't know why we called it that, but the name stuck. "The Beaner" sounds mighty good on this album, and so do the other instruments as played by the other musicians!

30. **The History of the DRUM** (Peter Erskine, 1995) — I got a telephone call in my hotel room in Birmingham, England while I was on tour, advising me that I was to meet with an arts council rep in 45 minutes' time to pitch my writing a dance piece for an African ballet

corps that was based in the U.K. This was all news to me at that moment. Wash my face. Grab a tea. What to pitch? A "history of the drum" is something that no arts council can resist or refuse. Bingo. From a review by Hal Howland in *Modern Drummer*: "Africans dance in New Orleans, balaphons find their way to Jamaica, claves color the streets of Calcutta, and the sampled voices of Papa Jo Jones and Louis Armstrong mingle with drum machines, synthesizers, and acoustic polyrhythms, all unified by Peter's familiar and accessible triadic themes and harmonies." He forgot to mention the key of C. I actually still like parts of this album, as improvised as it all turned out to be. Two of the pieces have successfully found their way into the world of percussion ensemble literature: "Calypso" and "Exit Up Right," published by drop6 Media, Inc.

31. **Justin Morell** (1996) — I came home one day and my wife (reminder: she's Japanese) told me that I had "a phone call from Judd Sommelier." Hmmm. Interesting name, but I do know another Judd (Miller), so I dial the number, and when the phone is answered I say, "Hi, this is Peter Erskine, and I'm returning the call of a Judd so-mah-lee-ay" and the voice on the other end answers "Uh…this is Justin Morell." Badda-bing! Love those R's and L's. It is always memorable to work in the studio with Jimmy Johnson on bass. I toured with his brother, Gordon, on Maynard's band for nearly two years.

32. **Lava Jazz** (The Lounge Art Ensemble, 1997) — The conceit of this band became the habit of taking existing song structures and adding new melodies on top of the established harmonies, but the title also had to be clever for the song to be eligible to be considered. Thus, Dave Carpenter reworked "I Hear a Rhapsody" into "I Hear a Rap CD," Bob Sheppard took "It Had To Be You" and changed it to "Did It Have To Be You?" and so on. We made two albums on Fuzzy Music; this was the first. I played the entire album on a stand-up cocktail kit. Why? Just for the challenge, and I liked the sound. Our second album, *Music For Moderns*, features some great writing and playing by Bob Sheppard and Dave Carpenter. Carp was one of the very few people who could swing on the electric bass, and he knew how to sing on it, too. That pretty much put him and Jaco in the same club as far as I'm concerned.

33. **Sinatraland** (Patrick Williams, 1997) — I've been a fan of Pat Williams' writing since high school; his Verve albums from the late '60s and early '70s sparkled with wit and sonic sophistication (thanks to Phil Ramone's engineering and the rhythm section work of Chuck Rainey and Bill LaVorgna, et al. Great New York brass sections, too). I was thrilled to get the call to work with Pat on the film score for *Used Cars* when I was first living in L.A., and the one disappointment I felt leaving L.A. for New York was the thought that I wouldn't be able to work for Pat again. He and contractor Joe Soldo righted that situation by calling me for *Sinatraland* some nine years or so after I moved back to town. The album was an all-instrumental opus to Sinatra featuring different soloists on various hit tunes that Sinatra had recorded. This was my first opportunity to work with bass player Chuck Berghofer, but thankfully not the last. The charts are models of big band writing perfection. Among the great soloists, Phil Woods came in and nailed the first of his two tunes in one take. During playback when Pat asked Phil, "Phil, it sounds great; do you want to do it again?" Phil simply replied, "No!" Like Babe Ruth, Phil Woods hits it out of the park when he wants.

Pat's newest album, *Aurora*, is a look-back tribute to his own *Threshold* LP from the '70s as well as a look-forward to big band writing. L.A.'s finest were on the date, and I was honored to be part of the team.

34. **Stormy Weather** (Sheryl Crow, et al, presented by Don Henley, 1988) — This project might have been the genesis for the Joni Mitchell *Both Sides Now* orchestral album, as Larry Kline was involved with the production, and Joni was one of several songstresses to sing on the charity concert — and I know she loved the setting. Some of the vocalists had scant enough experience singing with an orchestra, let alone navigating through Vince Mendoza's uncompromising charts. In addition to Joni, another vocalist who did not exhibit the deer-in-the-headlights syndrome of panic detectable in many of the singers was Sheryl Crow, who was equally at ease singing with the band or looking at the score. When she was being introduced to the band at the first orchestra rehearsal, she interrupted with, "PETER ERSKINE! My parents took me to see you play with Weather Report when I was thirteen years old," to which I could only reply, "Oh, hey Sheryl! Yeah! That must have

been…uh, when I was, like…FIFTEEN years old." This album is hard to find.

35. **Yes I Know My Way** (Pino Daniele, 1988) — Playing drums on Pino's hit tune "Amore Senza Fine" on this album has gotten me excellent service in Italian restaurants, better seats on Italian airplanes, and if nothing else has been a good ice-breaker whenever I meet an Italian who doesn't know what I do. This became the new signing of the word "drums" after my name in Italy [smile]. The session: I received a forwarded fax message in Vienna just hours before me, Mutsy, and the kids were going to go to the train station to ride the overnight train down to Roma, where we were going to visit my sister Lois for the Christmas holidays, and this fax was asking me if I might want to come to Italy to record with Pino. I telephoned the number on the fax and told them, "Yes, in fact I'll be in Rome tomorrow!" So a session was hurriedly put together for the day after Christmas. Terrific song, and Pino is a terrific guy. Wound up doing several albums with him, including one entire CD with the trio of Alan Pasqua and Dave Carpenter (*Passi D'Autore*, 2004). A lot of first takes on that one. Do I like these first takes because I am lazy? No. I like them because I believe the listener will discover the tune at the same time and in the same way that we do. Needless to say, the band needs to be good to be able to do this. And needless to say, that band with Alan and Dave was really good.

36. **The Hudson Project** (Mintzer, Abercrombie, Patitucci, Erskine, 1999) — Another good band; of course, look at the lineup! Created for the D'Addario Company as a touring band of endorsing musicians. D'Addario is the world's most successful string-making company; Abercrombie and Patitucci use their strings, and D'Addario distributes Rico Reeds (Minter) and manufactures Evans drumheads (me). We introduced the band at a NAMM convention gig and then took the show on the road, presenting product as well as educational clinic/ workshops while playing in concert, most of the time in a music store-turned-jazz club for the event. The New York City setting sounded great (Manhattan Place ballroom), even though the audience seemed far away, especially in comparison to the cramped quarters we had been touring and playing to for the two weeks leading up to this DVD and CD recording. Sometimes what looks good on paper sounds good in real life,

too. Yay! You can check it out on YouTube.com, but the album is actually worth getting.

37. **Short Cuts** – The Jazzpar Combo (John Scofield, Hans Ulrik, 1999) — Another band-on-paper that sounded as good as it looked. Hans Ulrik is a leading jazz musician on the Copenhagen scene, and Swedish bassist Lars Danielsson joined Americans Scofield and me as we celebrated the 1999 Jazzpar prizewinners — Europe's Pulitzer (or Nobel) for jazz. We were the international entertainment (not prize recipients), but man, did we have fun. Did my second-line tune "The Music of my People," and Sco's funk playing is beyond belief for me. He's a genius.

38. **Green Chimneys** (Andy Summers, 2000) — This looked like a fun project. Bassist Dave Carpenter brought me on board, and we rehearsed all of the Monk tunes (almost thirty of them, as I recall) in Andy's Venice rehearsal space. I brought a nice 5-piece kit with an 18-inch jazz bass drum to the rehearsal, Andy seemed to dig it, and so everything seemed all set. I get to the recording studio and set up the same kit, and Andy comes into the room with the engineer all worried-looking and finally asks me, "Is that it?" I reply, "Is that it, what?" and they both point to the drumset as if there's something obviously wrong with it. I say, "What?" and they finally blurt out, "It's so small!" I'm not sure what they were expecting, but I thought Andy wanted to make an album of Monk tunes, so I stuck to my guns and we tracked a boatload of Monk. I heard later that Andy was prepared to jettison most of what I had done, but Sting came to the rescue, going on and on about how great the drumming was on "Round Midnight," and so Andy got embarrassed, I think, into keeping the tracks with my drumming. That didn't prevent the engineer from doing all sorts of digital cutting and pasting of my playing. Some people have an odd idea of what jazz is.

39. **Both Sides Now** (Joni Mitchell, 2000) — This album gets it right in every department, every aspect, every nuance, and every moment. One of the finest recordings ever made, in my opinion. Vince Mendoza outdid himself on this one, and so did Joni, whose performances on the CD are, for the most part, from her first takes in the studio WITH THE ORCHESTRA. Herbie played live, Wayne was overdubbed, everything else is pretty much "what you see is what you get." A security guard came

up to me at one point during the recording at George Martin's AIR Studios in London and said, "I don't know what you folks are doing in there, but I've never seen musicians act like this during a session — all serious and respectful like, and concentrating and all." I knew what he meant. Playbacks in the large room result in tears streaming down players' faces. All of us are looking around knowing that this is something really important and really great. My friend the British composer Mark-Anthony Turnage is sitting with me in the drum booth as we begin to run down Vince's arrangement of "Answer Me, My Love" with its incredible six French horn intro, and as I'm counting the open measures and listening to this for the first time along with Mark, he grabs at my shirt sleeve and I turn, still trying to keep track of where I am in the music so I won't miss my entrance, and he says "D'ya hear that? It's like Brahms, only BET-TAH!" I can only smile and agree.

Joni's really done her homework; she is singing great. Larry Kline is proving to be an insightful and extremely effective producer, and Chuck Berghofer is holding the whole thing together beautifully.

A film crew was there to document one day of the recording, and so a makeup artist was flown in from California; he was effeminate and his name was something like Juan or Miguel. Anyways, he's there waiting for something to do because Joni is in work mode, and we all crowd into the control room for another playback, only this time there's someone sitting in Joni's usual chair. So she stands and meets this guy, lights up her American Spirit cigarette, and begins to listen to the playback without the benefit or comfort of being seated. I see this and I'm about to go up and ask or tell the guy to move, but the producer isn't saying anything and Joni isn't saying anything, so maybe he's a friend of Larry's or he's somebody important from the record label. But I'm still bothered by this, and so I go hunting for a chair for Joni. I find a metal folding chair, pick it up, and gingerly work my way through the crowded control room towards Joni. All of sudden Juan, or Miguel, or whatever the fuck his name is, grabs the chair right out of my unsuspecting hands and grandly proclaims "a - Joni? a - CHAIR?" She seems so grateful for his thoughtfulness, and meanwhile I want to wring this fucker's neck.

Joni and I share a very pleasant talk in the studio canteen during an orchestral break, chatting away like two lost friends, until I make mention of the fact that my father is a psychiatrist. Note to self: You might want to omit that information if you ever get the chance to have a first talk with Joni again. Not sure what's up with that, but I do hear later from a drummer who accosted Joni in Brentwood at a coffee shop she frequents, getting her autograph, that she made the following comment when my name was introduced into the conversation: "Oh, Peter Erskine; he's a nice man despite the fact that his father's a psychiatrist." Despite her misgivings, we enjoyed a terrific tour together playing this music with orchestras from one end of the country to another. Vince's writing has spoiled me. Just like Jaco on *Hejira*: if Jaco wasn't on a tune, it was no fault of the other bass players, but they were the enemy as far as I was concerned. Same thing when I hear another writer for the most part. If it's not Vince, I'm usually not too interested.

40. **Seven Pieces** (Lennart Åberg, 2001) — One writer and musician I will tolerate and look forward to working with every time is Sweden's Lennart Åberg. He's the only guy I've heard who can sound like Wayne, in great part because he doesn't try to sound like Wayne (that might be the secret, at least when it comes to Wayne). Another first-take wonder (the first tune, "Spiraltrappan" or "The Spiral Staircase"), the album sparkles with European sensibility and dazzling sound; it won the Swedish Grammy equivalent. The studio was the same place where ABBA recorded their hit song "Dancing Queen." The drum booth was small and sweaty, and Lennart likes to talk a lot between takes. Right before one of the takes, and just after he had been speaking in Swedish for about 15 or 20 minutes, he turned to me and said through the glass walls, "Oh, Peter, I am sorry, would you like me to translate what I have been saying?" I cried, "Please, NO, let's just play the goddamn piece already." From where and whence did I get my profane-laced language, anyway?

41. **The London Concert** (Don Grolnick Band, 2001) — Recorded by the BBC during Don's jazz tour of the U.K. in 1994, this concert in the Queen Elizabeth Hall at London's Southbank Centre was memorable for several reasons: (1) the band played great, (2) the BBC recorded it, and (3) for me, great fun because Steve Gadd was there. It's funny — when you

hear the music you forget about the travel logistics of getting from wherever we were that morning to London, the problems we had getting checked into our hotel rooms, the interviews we were asked to do for some British TV jazz program, the setting up, soundchecking, and looking for a suitable dinner before the concert, and so on. But you hear the music and you forget everything and remember only how great all the musicians were and how much we all loved playing Don's music, being on tour with him, and getting to know each other. The combination of players was brilliant. I'm so glad that I got a DAT tape from the BBC producer and eventually received the blessings of everyone involved to release the recording of the first set. The proceeds from the sales of the album go towards the research for finding a cure for lymphoma.

42. **Christmas Memories** (Barbra Streisand, 2001) — Memorable because Barbra Streisand shows up and begins to sing, and she absolutely nails it the first two times around, both takes equally fresh and vibrant and great. I now know what all of the fuss was about when she was young and new to the recording scene. This woman has chops! But then, of course, one person after another in the cavernous yet crowded control room in SONY (formerly known as the MGM Soundstage, now bearing Ms. Streisand's name) chime in with their five cents' worth, to the point of engineer Al Schmidt coming into the drum booth, which is about a football field's distance from the mixing board, on the pretense of adjusting a microphone, but when I ask him if everything is okay drum mic-wise he says, "Oh yeah, this is all fine. It's like a fucking Marx Brothers movie in the control room, though. Everybody's got a fucking opinion." And so a three-hour session with orchestra becomes an eight-hour session. The orchestra brass players are getting worn out, and this thing is going to drag on forever for me until Dave Carpenter and I both have to leave for a trio gig in Hollywood. It turns out that Barbra goes with the first or second take anyway. And like most Christmas albums, this is recorded in July.

I know she's not at all interested in my opinion, but here it is: She has the chops, so she should just learn to trust herself and the music a bit more. That will be five cents, please, thank you very much.

43. **Badlands** (Peter Erskine, Alan Pasqua, Dave Carpenter, 2001) —
We recorded this album in my backyard studio. We played the room, the
dynamics and vibe, and all. Something magical could always happen
when the three of us got together; this album seemed really special.
During post-production, 9/11 hits. For all of the other fears and
concerns and questions that everyone is wrestling with, we're wondering,
"Does it matter that we even put this out? And if we do, what's
appropriate?" I had originally planned an Americana theme before 9/11,
but once that catastrophe occurred, I felt that any "Americana" hint
visually or otherwise would be exploitative at best, so we killed a really
nice album cover design that had fit the music perfectly. My mistake.
Other albums came along and, somewhat shamelessly, I thought, used
"Americana" imagery as a rallying cry of sorts. I was still in mourning
not only for our country but also for the world. At any rate, we came
across a bit of text that seemed to justify or fit the music and why we
wanted to release the album, and so with Brandt Reiter's kind permission
I included it on the back cover of the CD. Big mistake to include
something written by an astute listener that appears to suggest how this
music should be listened to or appreciated; critics do not like that, and I
think the album's reviews suffered as a result. *DownBeat* gave us a really
shitty review (as in lukewarm), so much so that DB's publisher expressed
shock to us. I also expressed shock because (1) I know a good album when
I make one, and (2) we had just spent a lot of money (for us) advertising
the album in the magazine. Thanks but no thanks. I still regard this as
one of our finer titles, and the lady doth *not* protest too much.

44. **Fractured Lines** (BBC Symphony Orch., Leonard Slatkin, Evelyn
Glennie) — Speaking of ladies, I am joined by the delightful Evelyn
Glennie on this double concerto for percussion composed by Mark-
Anthony Turnage, based on a theme of mine (the song "Bass Desires").
Mark and I formulated much of the structure of the piece on a large
piece of paper in a fish-and-chips restaurant during the week I was in
London doing Joni's album. We tried recording the concerto with the
battery of percussion set up in front of the orchestra, but this made some
of the rhythmic coordination with the band difficult, so we moved
everything to the back of the orchestra and this seemed to work. Hard to
hear them, but they could hear us, and so that was good; also, the string
players were relieved to have the percussion soloists so far away. Evelyn

and I each play on a Yamaha Club Jordan cocktail kit, and then she concentrates on marimba and metallic percussion while I play the drumset as well as hands-and-sticks-on-skins things (bongos, djembe, congas, timbales, etc.). Leonard Slatkin conducts the excellent BBC Symphony Orchestra. People often assume classical records are recorded in beautiful-looking concert halls. This was done in what looked like a beat-up school auditorium or community center in a pretty dumpy part of London. Go figure.

45. **North and Il Sogno** (Elvis Costello, 2003, w/London Symphony Orch., 2004) — Two albums by one man, Elvis Costello. Elvis discovered me on a BBC documentary about my work with Mark-Anthony Turnage. He told me he liked how the orchestra responded to the live (and jazz) drums, and so he was inspired to have me play on his orchestral piece "Il Sogno" (*Midsummer Night's Dream*) that was going to be recorded by the London Symphony Orchestra. We met in my Santa Monica studio (on the morning of the day he would meet his future wife, Diana Krall; small world) and I prepared a demo for him of what the drums might sound like on this piece, overdubbing onto a live recording he had of the ballet orchestra in Bologna doing the piece. When it came time to do the recording in London, I begged Elvis to reconsider his plans and allow me to track the drums as an overdub in L.A. so we could really control the sound and get the exact drum performance he might be looking for. But he was proving to be more adventurous than me on this one, and so he insisted on flying me to London IN FIRST CLASS for a one-day session at Abbey Road with the LSO. Michael Tilson-Thomas is conducting, and there's a lot of music to get recorded during this afternoon session. We have just enough time to run everything once and then record it — one take, maybe two at most — and Elvis wants me to take chances with this stuff. I do my best. I had also done my homework, and that paid off — so much so that a very pleased Elvis said to me in front of the entire orchestra on his way out to a gig (pointing to me): "Fearless!" I liked that. I also enjoyed getting to work with Neil Percy, principal percussionist of the LSO as well as the head of percussion studies at the Royal Academy of Music.

North was a last-minute session, as Elvis decided he wanted to record a love-song album of ballads, inspired by his wife-to-be, and his excellent band is not a jazz ballad-playing band. So I got the call, and I recommended Mike Formanek to play bass, and this proved to be a terrific combination. I really like the way Elvis writes and sings, and the man has a tremendous work ethic. I contributed by suggesting that his pianist (the excellent Steve Nieve) not worry about trying to play like a jazz musician, but rather play the way he was most comfortable playing, in this case going back to his childhood classical music roots. It seemed to work to good effect. It kind of brings it all back to that Cannonball Adderley intro when Joe Zawinul was in the band and they're recording at the Village Vanguard in New York: "You get a lot of people that are supposed to be hip, and they act like they're supposed to be hip, which makes a big difference." He continued: "Hipness is not a state of mind, it's a fact of life. You don't decide to be hip, it just happens that way." And there you go.

46. **Aerial** (Kate Bush, 2005) — Kate Bush saw the same BBC documentary that Elvis Costello did — the power of television, even with hip people! — and she personally dialed our home phone and spoke with my wife for a while, who then handed the phone to me. I realized halfway through the call that this was the woman who sang on the Peter Gabriel tune "Don't Give Up." I'm not yet aware of the cult following that has dogged Kate for years, but I find out soon enough when I'm given specific directions of what to say to whom and what not to say as regards where I'll be working, and this complicates getting a drumset to her home studio, but we eventually get everything worked out and I truly enjoyed the experience of being around this person. Kate Bush is a highly creative artist and a lovely woman. She and her production and musicians are all taken aback somewhat by my apparent need for speed during the recording process. I want to get as much done as possible for her in the limited amount of time we have, but everyone else seems content to let the tunes and the days unfold as they will. Maybe I know that I don't want to spend endless hours at night doing something that could be gotten in the afternoon if everyone simply concentrates a bit and acts, like, professional. I'm not saying anyone acted unprofessionally, it's just a different pace. For example, bassist John Giblin — a really excellent British rock bassist — runs through a tune, and I enter the control room as he starts. It's all sounding REALLY great, and he's inspired and responding to the music like a skier having a great run down a steep but beautiful slope. When he's finished the engineer says, "Okay, you want to record that now?" which is like the oldest dumb-engineer

joke in the book, only HE'S NOT JOKING and John is not in the least bit upset. Yes, he IS now ready to record, thank you very much. Meanwhile, I'm flabbergasted and saying to the engineer, "You mean you didn't record any of that? What the fuck were you doing? All you have to do is press one little fucking red button; it doesn't cost a thing to do that." Del Palmer just kind of smiled and wished that I would go away, and so I did. The live band tracking was the most fun with Kate playing piano and singing. We tried a lot of tunes in a lot of ways.

Kate would often fetch tea for the boys, who would always say, "Aarghh, Kate, yor a fine woman!" like a pirate or something. The Brits really like that kind of stuff. As for Kate, she really liked the Yamaha David Garibaldi signature snare drum I had brought to the studio as part of the arsenal of drums to choose from. "Peter? Could you please get that lovely little BLUE drum out again?"

Aarghh, Kate, yor a fine woman!

47. **Some Skunk Funk** (R. Brecker, M. Brecker, Will Lee, WDR Big Band, et al, 2005) — The sweetest prize, the bitterest pill to swallow. Michael passed away before the Grammy award for this album was announced. I felt privileged to say a few words on his behalf and in honor of him, essentially reminding everyone at the Grammy event that every solo Mike ever played was worthy of a Grammy award (his solo on "Skunk Funk" had just been announced before the album's prize). Thanks to the record company and especially Randy Brecker for agreeing to include our names on the front cover, we could all share in a Grammy, including the WDR Big Band, Vince Mendoza, Will Lee, Jim Beard, percussionist Marcio Doctor, myself, and Mike and Randy.

Meanwhile, Grammys aside, the DVD of the concert and the audio recording of the music are mighty impressive. I would like to hear some of the studio takes we tracked leading up to the concert.

I was playing the final tune of the concert and album, Mike Brecker's "Song for Barry," for a student of mine at USC, and the emotional power of the performance really struck him. He asked in innocence and with sincerity, "How do you get so much emotion into a performance?" It was and remains palpable. I replied, also with sincerity but not so much innocence, "The only answer I can give you is that you really have to give a shit." Poor choice of words, but the sentiment remains: you really need to care.

I submit that's why a Mike Brecker performance is so searing even after all of these years: the man really cared, and it shows.

48. **Standards** (Alan Pasqua, Dave Carpenter, Peter Erskine, 2008) — This album was rightfully nominated for a Grammy, and sour grapes aside it should have won. The audio quality is stunningly "you are there," recorded with a pair of stereo microphones in an acoustically rich hall where we set up the piano, bass, and drums very close to one another and used our ears to guide how loud and how much we played. WHAT A NOVEL CONCEPT! No headphones, no mixing, no editing, no overdubbing. And no rehearsing!

Alan Pasqua came up with all of the arrangements. The music played itself, and we all had a good time listening to it as it all unfolded. You can't beat great tunes. *Standards 2, Movie Music* is just being released as I write this book. It's our collective homage to film music, and the stars of this recording are Bob Mintzer, Darek Oles, Alan, and myself. I used to think of myself as being the Claude Rains of drumming, but my friend director Jack Fletcher thinks I'm more the Spencer Tracy type.

49. **The Avatar Sessions** (Tim Hagans, Norrbotten Big Band w/ guests, 2010) — On the fourth and final day of recording in Manhattan's Avatar Studio C, I returned to the apartment my wife and I were renting for the week and she commented, "I've never seen you so excited about anything you've recorded before. I am so happy for you; this must be something really special." Indeed. After the success of the live recording of the Norrbotten Big Band in concert with Hagans and me at the helm (*Worth the Wait*), we decide to get really ambitious and record the band in the best studio in the world — that would be Avatar (formerly Power Station, where the Steps Ahead, Burton/Metheny, first Bass Desires, Diana Krall *Look of Love*, and so many other albums have been recorded) — with the band's "A" list of soloists. Joe Lovano can't make it, but he is ably replaced by George Garzone, and Randy Brecker, Vic Juris, Dave

Liebman, and Rufus Reid all join in for the fun. Hagans' writing is better than ever, and so is his playing. I'm feeling invincible and at the top of my game.

Can musicians keep getting older and do their best work as their hair turns grey? Or do we only believe that that's what we're doing, but in reality our best years are behind us?

To be honest, I have to believe that it is possible to keep getting "better," and for one's work to improve in quality as well as relevance. To think otherwise, perhaps, is to admit defeat. For whatever reason — and as much as I enjoy a lot of these older recordings (more for the memories than the music a lot of the time), I truly think my latest work is my best.

Four newer albums of note:

Standards 2, Movie Music, with Alan Pasqua, Darek Oles and Bob Mintzer (Fuzzy Music). Using the same state-of-the-art stereo microphones developed by KMF, the quartet records once again in the acoustically rich concert and lecture hall in La Jolla where we made the Grammy-nominated *Standards* album. Everyone chips in with arrangements, and we have a ball playing music from the movies. The band also doubles as the USC Faculty Jazz Quartet, and part of our mission is to redefine what West Coast jazz means nowadays. I like to think that Webster's Dictionary as well as Shorty Rogers would approve.

Also on Fuzzy, my New Trio's debut album *Joy Luck*, featuring Vardan Ovsepian and Damian Erskine. The title track ("Joy Luck Club") marks my marimba-playing debut on one of my own albums. This might prove to be one of our most popular CDs to date.

Last but not least, I had the pleasure of playing in a remarkable big band with strings for multi-talented Seth MacFarlane, the creator and voice for "Family Guy" and other shows, who happens to be a really great singer. *Music Is Better Than Words* is the album's name. Joel McNeely did the arranging and producing, and the album was recorded onto analog tape with no punching in or digital fixing. The "A" and "B" rooms at Capitol Studios served as the playing venue, and I used an old Gretsch kit with calf heads, recorded with a single ribbon overhead microphone. There's no sound like all of the musicians playing in the same room at the same time: the ultimate in concentration and commitment. Plus, with Chuck Berghofer and Alan Broadbent in the rhythm section, and Wayne Bergeron playing lead trumpet, you know this music swung!

Honorable mention as well to Vince Mendoza's latest opus, *Nights On Earth*. Beautiful, and enlightening. Wow!

I can only look forward to completing another list that highlights 50+ more albums out of *x* many in the future.

Afterword

Thanks to my wife, Mutsy, for providing the time, space, and place necessary for me to write this book. My deepest appreciation to photographer Shigeru Uchiyama for making his library of Weather Report tour photos available to me. Shigeru quickly became the most-trusted and favorite photographer of the band, as evidenced by the extraordinary number and quality of photos taken on and off stage. And a huge tip of the hat to: Stanford University's Jon Krosnick for insisting I undertake this writing endeavor (and for reading through the early drafts), with thanks to Jerry McBride and his team at the Music Library and Archive of Recorded Sound at Stanford University for digitizing my audio and videotape collection. Thanks to Mitch Haupers of the Berklee College of Music for his generous Foreword and advice. Thank you, Bill Bruford and Neil Peart. Biggest thanks go to all the others whose names are mentioned in the book; the story could not be told without you. I trust that my memory will prove both accurate and adequate; for what it's worth, I kept notes during most of my years of touring — and I am grateful for all of the experiences and music shared. And thanks to you, the reader.

BE SURE TO CHECK OUT www.petererskine.com for additional media resources: videos, audio files, more photos, and an ongoing blogsite to keep this book a living document.

photo: Shigeru Uchiyama

photo: Shigeru Uchiyama

photo: Peter Erskine

photo: Peter Erskine

photo: Peter Erskine

PETER ERSKINE   ELIANE ELIAS   MICHAEL BRECKER

EDDIE GOMEZ   MIKE MAINIERI

STEPS AHEAD

PHOTO CREDIT: CAROL FRIEDMAN/1983

JOHN ABERCROMBIE   PETER ERSKINE   MARC JOHNSON   ECM RECORDS

photo: Rick Laird

MARC JOHNSON
WITH PETER ERSKINE, JOHN SCOFIELD AND BILL FRISELL (FROM LEFT TO RIGHT)

ECM RECORDS
PHOTO CREDIT: PETER SCHAAF

with Vic Firth and Louie Bellson, 1983 PASIC convention

American Drummers Achievement Awards dinner, 1998, Boston

photo: Mutsy Erskine

photo: Mutsy Erskine

The "Sweet Soul" band: Randy Brecker, Kenny Werner, Marc Johnson, Peter Erskine, Bob Mintzer, John Scofield and Joe Lovano…wow!

The "ECM Trio" with Palle Danielsson and John Taylor

Presented by Newly Designed KIRIN LAGER
An Evening With
STEELY DAN
FEATURING
Walter Becker and Donald Fagen
MUSICIANS
TOM BARNEY················(BASS)
CORNELIUS BUMPUS(TENOR SAX)
DIANE GARISTO·······(CHORUS)
CATHERINE RUSSELL··(CHORUS)
BILL WARE·······(VIBES, PERC)
DREW ZINGG············(GUITAR)
WARREN BERNHARDT··(PIANO)
PETER ERSKINE·······(DRUMS)
CHRIS POTTER················(SAX)
BOB SHEPPARD···(TENOR SAX)
BRENDA WHITE-KING(CHORUS)
OFFICIAL AIRLINE JAL
スティーリー・ダン JAPAN TOUR '94 公演日程
4/19[TUE]·20[WED]·21[THU]
東京:代々木第一体育館
OPEN 6:00PM/START 7:00PM
S:¥7,500/A:¥6,500(税込)
[問]H.I.R :03-3475-9999
主催:TBS / J-WAVE
4/15[FRI]
大阪:大阪城ホール
OPEN 6:00PM/START 7:00PM
S:¥7,500/A:¥6,500(税込)
[問]キョードーチケットセンター:06-345-2500
主催:毎日放送 / FM802
4/16[SAT]
名古屋:市民会館大ホール
OPEN 6:00PM/START 6:30PM
S:¥7,500/A:¥6,500(税込)
[問]キョードー名古屋:052-962-0511
主催:東海テレビ放送/ZIP-FM
4/23[SAT]·24[SUN]
福岡:市民会館
OPEN 6:00PM/START 6:30PM
(4/24はOPEN5:30PM/START6:00PM)
S:¥7,500/A:¥6,500(税込)
[問]くすミュージック:092-791-0999
主催:TVQ/FM九州
■協賛:キリンビール株式会社
■協力:日本航空 / WEA JAPAN / MCAビクター
■招聘 制作:H.I.R

with Alan Pasqua and Dave Carpenter

photo: Jean Radel

photo: Karen Miller